SOCIAL
RESPONSIBILITY
AND STRIKES

SOCIAL
RESPONSIBILITY
AND STRIKES

Neil W. Chamberlain

ASSISTANT DIRECTOR, THE LABOR AND MANAGEMENT CENTER,
AND ASSOCIATE PROFESSOR, DEPARTMENT OF ECONOMICS,
YALE UNIVERSITY

Assisted by Jane Metzger Schilling

Harper & Brothers . Publishers . New York

SOCIAL RESPONSIBILITY AND STRIKES
Copyright, 1953, by Harper & Brothers
Printed in the United States of America

All rights in this book are reserved.
No part of the book may be used or reproduced
in any manner whatsoever without written per-
mission except in the case of brief quotations
embodied in critical articles and reviews. For
information address Harper & Brothers
49 East 33rd Street, New York 16, N. Y.

FIRST EDITION
I-C

Library of Congress catalog card number: 53-8535

CONTENTS

CONTENTS

INTRODUCTION

THE LITERATURE of industrial relations provides frequent examples of the following type of solution to some difficult problem, such as strikes in public utilities, or management's defense of what it conceives to be its exclusive prerogatives, or labor parties in politics: "What is needed is more social responsibility. When our managers and unions come to appreciate their social responsibilities, problems like these will become manageable." Sometimes the word "maturity" replaces social responsibility, but the purport of the argument remains the same.

The extent of the reliance which is placed on the development of social responsibility to eliminate the "devilish" problem is discouraging. The phrase is used almost like a modern incantation to exorcise whatever evil spirits cannot be touched by explicit program or policy. It amounts to a confession of impotence or resignation: a danger to the integrity or continuity of society as presently conceived exists, but we don't see what can be done to avoid it—unless the parties posing the threat perceive the consequence of their actions and, restraining their own immediate selfish interests, conform their behavior to the requirements of an orderly society. If they fail to exercise such "social responsibility," however, the outlook is hopeless.

At other times the trusted formula appears to cover analytical inadequacies. Examination reveals a problem without apparent solution, a social dilemma without resolution. The analyst who has qualms about leaving his readers in so uncomfortable a position, however, can always fall back on the escape clause: social responsibility on the part of someone or other is the answer. I, like others, have used this formula. Yet retrospection frequently reveals that the dilemma was a false one, the result of inadequate analysis. A large measure of skepticism concerning its soundness may well attach to any economic study which concludes with "social responsibility" as the means to some end.

Examples of the prevalence of this escape device are not hard to come by. Public officials have frequently reminded unions and managements of the power of their respective organizations and have exhorted them to use that power with a restraint based on regard for community welfare. A new school of labor leaders, of whom Walter Reuther is usually cited as representative, has taken as part of its credo that unions can only advance with society and not at its expense. "Those who possess union cards must accept the fact that with greater advancement of the worker also comes greater responsibility of the worker," as an editorial in the *Railroad Workers Journal* asserted.[1]

Perhaps even more strikingly, American business leaders in large corporations in the last two decades have vied with each other in announcing their assumption of "social responsibilities," even to the extent of denying the legal fiction which binds them in single interest with their stockholder-owners. "The financial and managerial components of our Free Enterprise System must prove, by deeds as well as by words, their full comprehension of their social responsibilities. . . ."[2] "The concept of the responsibility to society is gaining ground."[3]

The professional economists, when turning from deductive analyses to wrestle with policy problems, have at times apparently found these problems insolvable except by an injection of social responsibility. William Beveridge and Alvin Hansen, concerned with the bargaining power of unions in a full-employment society, fall back upon that comfortable cushion. "When society as a whole, through the government, undertakes responsibility for full employment and social welfare, labor may be expected, on past experience, to respond by living up to its social responsibilities."[4]

Professor J. M. Clark embroiders this undefined term, "responsibility," into an economic principle. "To repeat what seems to be the most

[1] September, 1946. The *Journal* is published by the Railroad Yardmasters of North America.

[2] Charles E. Wilson, as president of the General Electric Co., speaking before the American Institute of Electrical Engineers, January, 1941, reproduced in Edwin G. Nourse, *Price Making in a Democracy* (Washington: Brookings Institution, 1944), p. 142. Nourse provides other statements of a similar nature. More recent professions are cited in Chamberlain, *Union Challenge to Management Control* (New York: Harper & Brothers, 1948), Chs. 1 and 9.

[3] Arthur T. Davenport, as general manager of Sweet-Orr and Co., before a 1939 meeting of the Society for the Advancement of Management, New York City. Davenport, who was a member of a panel discussing "The Social Responsibility of Management," went on to say that the old theory that the proprietor's business was his to dispense regardless of the responsibility to society for the success of the venture was unsound. *The New York Times*, October 7, 1939.

[4] A. H. Hansen, *Economic Policy and Full Employment* (New York: McGraw-Hill Book Co., 1947), p. 246. Beveridge's comments are to be found in *Full Employment in a Free Society* (New York: W. W. Norton and Co., 1945), pp. 194-207.

crucial of economic principles for the age we face, the amount of liberty that can survive is dependent on, and measured by, the degree of responsibility with which economic power is exercised."[5] I might likewise cite sections from my own book, *The Union Challenge to Management Control*, which run in the same vein.

Even though questioning such reliance on social responsibility, however, I would not deny that social responsibility (in some sense) is an effective tool to force the solution of vexing problems. My question really concerns the current usage of the term—undefined or ill-defined as it has been despite the vast purposes which it has been made to serve, relying on some intrinsic meaning which is not there. One purpose of this book is to attempt to provide the term with an operational significance useful for policy purposes.

A principal concern will be to reorient the concept of social responsibility from the ethical or moral connotations with which it has been surcharged. At times it appears to be used to foist on some class or group a course of action which is opposed to its own interest but which the particular writer thinks would be good for "society's interests." The term thus provides a euphemistic way of enjoining some party to behave decently toward other people because the result will be to make the world a pleasanter place. Social responsibility thus used connotes self-restraint, self-denial, altruism, enlightened attitudes toward the importance of social relationships, a belief in ethical ideals. An appeal to one's sense of social responsibility is an appeal to one's better nature, as the term is now widely employed. There is, of course, no harm in such appeals, but relating them to social responsibility confuses a process with attitudes.

At times this widespread usage of the term lends itself to partisan purposes. Special interests—sometimes with academic or governmental cloak—urge other special interests to forego some course of action as a matter of social responsibility, when in fact their concern is with their own welfare. Social responsibility thus degenerates into whatever the spokesman chooses to read into the term. To some employers, social responsibility requires unions to forego the strike weapon. To some consumers, unions should restrain their wage demands and businessmen their price increases in the name of social responsibility. To some unions, employers should concede improved pension plans and shorten

[5] J. M. Clark, *Guideposts in Time of Change* (New York: Harper & Brothers, 1949), p. 200.

the work day as demonstrations of their social responsibility. To some academic economists, large corporations and labor unions, to maximize the welfare of society as a whole, should behave according to the theoretical models which have been devised for small-scale enterprise without labor unions.

One intent of this study is, then, to establish a conception of social responsibility which is free of this kind of morality. It is not because of any rejection of the moral element that I have been drawn toward this objective, but because morality is so subjective a guide that it can scarcely provide that basis for public policy which "social responsibility" is supposed to offer. In the conception which will be developed here, no more merit attaches to the performance of one's social responsibilities than of his legal responsibilities. Morality inheres in the term only to this degree, that to the extent we maintain that one *ought* to obey the law we may maintain that one *ought* to recognize his social responsibilities, and that failure to meet the obligation will normally invoke sanctions. But this is removed from conceiving of social responsibility as a matter of conscience, involving sacrifices that others can hope for without expecting.

Social responsibility, as here conceived, is enforceable by social sanctions without respect to personal ethics; social responsibility as generally encountered in the literature carries no sanction except the person's own conscience. It is perhaps worth repeating that the distinction made in these pages is due to no disregard for the guide of conscience or to a belief that conscience has no place in public life. Personal morality is so important an ingredient of any society that one cannot do without it if he would. It is, however, an insufficient basis for achieving satisfactory union-management relations, as insufficient as it would be as a substitute for the criminal code.

This point may be restated because of its importance. Obviously, there is a moral substructure to legal codes and enforceable sanctions. The criminal code has grown out of a consensus of people's feeling about certain actions which have been categorized as unethical or immoral. But once so established such laws do not depend on individuals who hopefully exhort others to abide by them, or on the conscience of the individual citizen. Though rooted in morality, they do not depend on personal conviction or persuasion for their effectiveness. They are enforceable, even against some individual's denial of their relevance to him. Social responsibility is here similarly conceived: even though having its origin in ethical conceptions, it is not dependent on the individual's conscience for its effectiveness.

Chapters 1 and 2 develop in detail the concept of social responsibility. What follows is more specific and directly pertinent to the present American industrial relations scene. Readers not theoretically minded may prefer to start with Chapter 3. The foundation for the study is laid in the two preliminary chapters, however. What follows not only does so in presentation but did so in analytical development. The rest of the study was (and without the slightest predetermination) purely a derivative of the initial concept.

A volume related to this study is appearing under the title, *The Impact of Strikes* (Harper & Brothers). Both studies are complete in themselves, but in that volume will be found the basis for some of the materials which are presented as conclusions in this book.

Jane Metzger Schilling participated in virtually all phases of this investigation and is largely responsible for Chapter 13. My wife, Mariam K. Chamberlain, aided in the collection of data on which Chapter 12 is based. In the preparation of the manuscript credit is due to Pat Larrowe, Elizabeth Keith, Dorothy Loucks, and Grace Waite.

SOCIAL RESPONSIBILITY AND STRIKES

CHAPTER ONE

The Meaning of Social Responsibility

IN ARRIVING at a meaningful and useful conception of *social* responsibility, it will be necessary to explore certain attributes of a society, since obviously it is only out of social relationships that responsibilities arise. It is only through the development of an adequate theoretical framework for analysis that the specific question may be answered. We are interested in identifying those characteristics of a society which place a compulsion on its members to behave in a manner which we call responsible. This is not an exercise in pure theory. We shall discover that the pressing labor problems of our day can be more sharply defined if we approach them from an adequate theoretical background.

The Existence of Cultural Patterns

Any group of people living together must carry on many activities in cooperation in order to satisfy the goals and objectives which individually they pursue. Business, family life, religious worship, political organization, games, warfare, and so on are activities necessitating relationships between numbers of individuals in the society. Such relationships cannot be avoided. They arise through the inescapable fact of interdependence.

Interdependence takes familiar forms like the relation between husband and wife, or production by division of labor, or the pooling of resources when joint action is necessary to some result, such as the common effort of two men to raise a weight which is beyond the capacity of either individually. It also arises whenever the action of one so influences the behavior of another as to demand that the first consider the reaction of the second before himself acting—a man refrains from striking another because the second would probably retaliate if he did.

In any society, then, the unavoidable necessity is for individuals to

1

learn how to get along with others. This need gives rise in any society to patterns of conduct for the common or important relationships in which individuals find themselves. Those who enter into a given relationship (whether voluntarily or involuntarily) can then be expected to follow the associated pattern of conduct. By following the established pattern, they can count on creating the desired relationship. Failure to conform is likely to mean failure to evoke from others the usual responses of the particular relationship.

This does not mean that a society's culture is a neat set of behavioral patterns which in their totality describe and prescribe conduct for all types of situations for all members in that group. Such a conception is obviously fallacious when we recognize in our own society numerous variations of a particular kind of relationship, some indeed constituting polar extremes. Thus in the employer-employee relationship we find some individuals behaving, as employees, with deference to their employer, while others may treat him with indifference or hostility.

The notion of behavior patterns in a society does not, however, rule out individual variations or departures from the pattern. Recognizing individual uniqueness of personality and circumstance, we can nevertheless maintain that certain situations in a society can be expected— as a matter of statistical probability—to evoke a generalized kind of response from the individuals who become party to the particular relationship involved. For example, if we were to assume any situation— an employer and employee when the latter is asking for a wage increase, a minister and a member of his parish or congregation when the former is soliciting a contribution, a private responding to his sergeant, a college boy meeting the mother of a friend, a doctor and his patient in the conference room, a sandlot baseball player and his teammates on the field, legionnaires at a convention—we could pretty well describe the expected attitudes and behavior of the individuals involved. There are stereotypes or patterns to which we expect that most individuals will conform in a rough sort of way. The degree of conformance is significant enough to retain the concept of a cultural pattern in a given social relationship.

Such patterns are not immutable, nor do they spring from any supra-individual source. We need not think of some personified "society" as presenting individuals with ready-made blueprints for behavior, or codes of etiquette designed to fit any situation. The pattern *derives from* the interactions of individuals pursuing their own objectives. But the nature of their objectives and the methods of pursuing them are not individually improvised; rather, the individual's goals are conditioned by the goals of those around him, both of his own and the predecessor generations, and his methods of gaining them are influenced by the behavior he observes or by ideas which he has had communicated to him.

In this learning process of acquiring goals and methods the individual is contributing to the strengthening or reshaping of cultural patterns. His faithful adherence to patterns of conduct he sees around him, his acceptance of goals which the cultural patterns make feasible, will—in their own small way—strengthen existing codes of relationships. To the extent that an individual seeks to modify existing relationships or to strike out for goals not contemplated by those relationships, he will —in that measure—weaken the current behavioral molds.

Thus the process of building cultural forms is carried on by all the individuals in the society. It is not surprising, then, that some patterns become confused and uncertain, where individual or class interest appears to dictate divergent goals and conflicting methods of reaching them, while other patterns may become rigid, where the interests of the preponderant majority in the group converge.

If we were, then, to identify "a culture" it would be by reference to the whole series of behavioral patterns, with their varying strengths and precisions, covering the principal recurring relationships among a group of people.

The Right of Expectancy of Conduct

The cultural behavior patterns of a society are necessary for its existence as a society. The most significant service of such patterns is that, for each individual in the group, they create a predictability as to how others are likely to behave toward him and how they will expect him to behave toward them. Without this predictability every inter-personal relationship would involve the hazard of an unfavorable or re-taliatory response. Indeed, it is impossible to conceive of a society in which *some* element of predictability of interpersonal conduct is not present. Memory serves to remind us how persons have responded to our actions in given situations, and we repeat the actions which bring satisfactory responses. Other individuals behave similarly toward us, and out of these interpersonal relations are distilled the patterns of behavior in specific situations which most nearly satisfy the wants which involve others. As Professor Ralph Linton has pointed out, from the viewpoint of the individual "socialization" is simply the process of learning how a person should behave to others and how he can expect others to behave toward him in the variety of situations in which he finds himself.[1]

Cultural patterns thus provide individuals with expectancies of conduct. These expectancies held by other people create certain restraints on one's behavior. As the price of integrating one's self with his society, of winning the acceptance of his fellows, he must conform reasonably closely to the patterns of conduct expected of him. Conformance to this kind of constraint ordinarily comes so naturally to us that we are usually not even aware of its pressure. We walk on the right-hand side of the sidewalk because others walking expect us to. We respond to our names. We answer the telephone when it rings. We wear clothes—usually suited to the specific occasion. There are, however, other restraints of which we are more conscious; of some we may be uncertain: to help support ourselves by however menial an employment when no other job is available; to be faithful in marriage; to observe posted speed limits; to rear children with church instruction. Restraints of which we are conscious or uncertainties about the conduct expected of us are usually indicative of changing mores.

In many instances the conduct which others have a reason to expect of us becomes embodied in law. We become subject to legal claims. An immense variety of interpersonal relationships is defined by legislatures and courts, so that individuals can enforce their expectancies of conduct upon others. Those who fail to conform to the restraints imposed by certain cultural patterns may be haled before judges or juries, who may place penalties upon them for their failure.

The variety of interpersonal relationships which can be subjected to the legal code has been suggested by Professor Wesley Newcomb Hohfeld, who introduced a complex terminology to underline distinctions which had previously often been overlooked. Legal relations, he argued, were two-way social relationships between individuals, which could assume four major forms. If we think of such relationships from the point of view of *both* individuals who compose it, then we need terms to describe the generalized sort of conduct which the law expects of each. Professor Hohfeld identified four different types of legal ex-

[1] Ralph Linton, *The Cultural Background of Personality* (New York: D. Appleton-Century Co., 1945), Ch. 1.

pectancies of conduct. We need not be detained here with the examination of each of these, but it is worth observing briefly the nature of the four legal relationships he described. First, one individual may possess a *claim*, which necessarily means that the other party to that relationship owes a *duty* to him. This duty Hohfeld called a correlative of the right, since it was a necessary reciprocal aspect of this particular type of relationship. In other situations a person may have a *privilege*, which imposes no affirmative duty on someone else but involves only his negative obligation not to prevent the other's initiative if he chooses to exercise it; to this negative obligation Hohfeld gave the awkward name of a *"no-right."* If one individual possesses legal *power*, the correlative relationship is one of legal *liability*. If one possesses legal *immunity*, then some other party to the relationship must necessarily face a legal *disability*.[2]

Hohfeld developed this terminology because he believed that jurists were misusing the word "right." Claims, privileges, power, immunities —all were "rights," he argued, setting up enforceable expectancies of particular kinds of responses, the correlative relationships of which he denominated duties, no-rights, liabilities and disabilities. Now just as Hohfeld identified four types of "rights" in legal relationships, we might with equal justification term his four correlatives "obligations." There is the obligation of specific performance, the obligation of nonintervention, the obligation of submission, the obligation of nondeprivation.

In this framework of reciprocal rights and obligations what is the nature of responsibility? In this legal system the possession of a right carries with it an authority, an authority to compel specific performance from another whose specific obligation is the correlative of the right. The latter person has a *responsibility* to comply. In the legal sense, there is no "responsibility" resting on person A toward person B unless person B has "authority" to command or compel some action from person A. And the extent of this "responsible" action is no greater and no less than the action which person B has the "right" to expect and the "authority" to compel. Responsibility is specifically and solely for A the reciprocal of the authority of B.

Yet we must appreciate, from the previous section, that a wide area of expected conduct inheres not so much in the law as in the general cultural behavior patterns. Certain of these patterns are made explicit

[2] W. N. Hohfeld, *Fundamental Legal Conceptions,* edited by Walter Wheeler Cook (New Haven: Yale University Press, 1923).

on the statute books, and stated penalties can be applied to those who fail to conform to the restraints of the pattern. It was these legally described patterns in which Professor Hohfeld was interested. We should be making a serious error, however, if we were to believe that Hohfeld had identified *all* rights in his four categories; for those cultural patterns which have not been translated into specific laws nevertheless carry with them expectancies of conduct, embodying obligations as to and constraints on the behavior of individuals in particular relationships.

Rights may be nonlegal as well as legal, carrying with them their correlative obligations or responsibilities. Legal rights are simply those expectancies of conduct which have been embodied in legal codes—the cultural patterns which have been written into law. Other cultural patterns remain matters of habit or routine or custom or tradition, however. They may be no less strong because unwritten; they may carry with them "rights" (nonlegal to be sure) of expectancies of conduct by others, in particular situations, which are just as real. And just as failure to perform the obligations or responsibilities corresponding to those expectancies of conduct which have been embodied in legal codes may be checked by legal sanctions in the form of court proceedings, so may failure to perform the obligations or responsibilities corresponding to those expectancies of conduct which derive from unwritten cultural patterns become subject to nonlegal but equally strong sanctions, such as social ostracism, contempt—even violence.

In sum, rights for one person are defined by the conduct (obligations) he can expect from others, and authority is defined by the conduct (responsibility) he can command from others. In some instances these rights and obligations, or authorities and responsibilities, are made matters of law. In other cases they remain matters of custom or patterned behavior, but in these latter instances they are none the less real, none the less rights and obligations, authorities and responsibilities. In mid-twentieth century, for example, there is coming to be a recognized expectancy on the part of employees that they shall not be discharged without "adequate cause." This expectancy is not confined to situations where it is protected by a legally enforceable contract, but appears to be spreading in application to the employment relationship wherever found. Violation of this right of expectancy (even if nonlegal) may lead to sanctions against the noncomplying employer: lack of labor supply, slowdown on the job, refusal of full worker cooperation, boycott by consumers, and so on.

In either the legal or the nonlegal setting, such responsibilities arising from rights of expectancy are meaningful only in terms of specific conduct toward another person. A vague notion of someone's owing a general kind of responsibility—by an employer to be "fair" to his workers, by a union official to be "just" to his members—is relatively meaningless. "Fairness" or "justice" as responsibilities take on content only when they are defined as certain identified actions which employers and union officials can be and are expected to take with respect to their followers in given situations—actions which can be and are demanded by their followers as matters of right, whether legal or nonlegal.

The specific patterns of conduct which make up right-obligation or authority-responsibility relationships may be either competitive or cooperative. There may, for example, be employer rights of expectancy of worker conduct (involving obligations as a correlative) in a strike situation, which is a competitive relationship. There may equally be employer rights of expectancy (with their correlative obligations) in the production process itself, a cooperative relationship.

So far we have noted the existence of cultural behavior patterns in a given society, out of which may be distilled rights of expectancy of particular conduct enforceable by one individual against another either by legal or nonlegal sanctions.

The Process of Change of Relationships

Cultural patterns change over time. The employer-employee relationship is not today what it was two hundred years ago. Neither are the parent-child, the pastor-communicant, the teacher-pupil, the husband-wife relationships. With such changing relationships, rights of expectancy change. How different the species of behavior patterns and rights of expectancy in the serf-lord relation, the journeyman-master relation, and the employee-employer relation today! How different from the latter can we reasonably expect the corresponding relationship of the future to be!

In the process of change, the rights and obligations or authorities and responsibilities of relationships may understandably become confused. What conduct can be expected from others is no longer clear. The predictability of others' behavior is uncertain, introducing an uncomfortable insecurity into interpersonal dealings. In such situations emphasis on responsibility is likely to refer to *past* relationships and outdated expectancies, as those who most suffer from the change seek to preserve the benefits of prior patterns of conduct. Even some for whom the change bodes good may hanker for the former system of relationships, which were at least certain and familiar, whereas now one's attitude and conduct toward others is no longer a matter of habit but one requiring thought and conflict.

Conscious attention to changing patterns of relationships and conflict over the refashioning of expectancies, that is, of rights and obligations, in modified situations are inescapable, however. There is no utopia where all relationships are rendered forever harmonious. The responsibilities of today are constantly becoming outmoded; the conduct we feel we now have a right to expect from others we may not expect in the indefinite future. Uncertainty, insecurity, and struggle in the definition of rights and obligations (both legal and nonlegal) are unavoidable.

The Role of Interest Groups

Thus far we have been concerned with the conduct and relations of individuals in society. But many of our gravest problems—certainly in the field of industry—stem from group behavior and relationships, and we shall have to consider how interest groups affect rights of expectancy.

The only factor in the origin of groups which need concern us is the existence among certain individuals of some common interest. The common interest may be one that gives rise to or arises out of relations solely between members of the group—as when a number of amateur writers in a community come together to read and criticize each other's poetry. On the other hand, the common interest may be one that arises out of relations with individuals external to the group. The labor union has for its members a primary common interest in the terms of their relationship with an outsider, namely, the employer. The basis for the union's existence as an interest group is what its members may be able to do collectively to improve their terms of relationship with their employer. To improve the terms of relationship the members must seek some advantageous change in the rights of expectancy which they have with respect to the employer's conduct—rights which, as we have seen, may be both legal or nonlegal.

The existence of some common interest as the basis for the existence of the group does not mean that the relationships among the individuals *in the group itself* are necessarily harmonious. Wherever two or more individuals come together there are likely to be divergent (competitive) individual interests no less than common (cooperative) interests. Disagreements arise over the specific objectives to be adopted in fulfillment of general aims, over the techniques to be used against the common protagonist, and over the division of such gains as may accrue to the group.

In a union, the dispute may wax hot among members as to whether to seek a pension or a straight wage increase (as it did in Local 600 of the United Automobile Workers in the negotiations of 1947). There may be disagreements as to whether to strike (as is often the case); members may fall out over the question of whether the more skilled of their number are entitled to a greater wage increase than the unskilled (as spinners in textile plants have sometimes fought for greater "recognition" than untrained women workers). These efforts to establish a framework of interest relationships *within* the group sometimes are carried to the point of disrupting the group itself. As long as the common interests remain stronger than the divergent ones, the group has a chance to survive. When divergent interests assume greater importance than common interests, the group dissolves. An important phase of group life is the resolution of divisive differences among the members of the association.

Since changes in rights and obligations can be expected in society, as a matter of course, the interest group is forever presented with new problems of relationship affecting the common goals and interests of its members. The employee-employer relationship (the basis for the union organization) is undergoing change in response to new business forms, such as the large corporation with its ownership and control separated, new technologies, changing market structures, product innovations, and so on. The efforts of the union—one interest group on which our attention is primarily focused—must thus be addressed to modifying favorably to it the relationship between employees and employer under the circumstances of externally conditioned changes. Its purpose is advantageous adaptation to such changes.

The Meaning of Social Responsibility

In any society there are cultural behavior patterns from which are derived the obligations and rights of expectancy of individuals in particular relationships. Individuals having a common relationship interest may form a group for the purpose of influencing the expectations, that is, the obligations and responsibilities, to which they are subject. As the relationships among individuals change over time—in consequence of technological, geographical, population, or other developments—rights and obligations likewise change. Individuals and interest groups seek to direct the course of change of rights and obligations to their own advantage.

As we have seen, a responsibility is an obligation—whether legal or nonlegal—owed to someone having authority to compel performance in a given relationship. Every relationship gives rise to certain responsibilities, as the correlative of the authority possessed by the other party or parties to the relationship. These rights of expectancy and resulting obligations, the authorities and corresponding responsibilities, in fact define the nature of the relationship. If we refer to such obligations as private responsibilities, then social responsibility arises from the integration of such private responsibilities into a workable consistency. A given relationship in society is only one among many. It does not exist in a social vacuum.

When we use the term social responsibility—in contrast to private responsibility—we shift from an exclusive concentration on the obligation which one party in a relationship owes to the other party in that relationship, and consider the impact which that obligation (and, inescapably, the correlative right) has on all the other important rights of expectancy and their correlative obligations in the society. It is the compulsion to establish compatibility between the rights and responsibilities in any given relationship and the rights and responsibilities of all other dominant relationships which is the essence of *social* responsibility. For despite the fact that societies are not planned systems but evolve in rather haphazard manner, the major relationships of its individuals (defined by their obligations to and expectancies of each other) must be compatible if the group is to function as a society. People living together are interdependent. If their relationships to each other are in some major respects inconsistent, so that the expectancies and obligations in one relationship interfere with the expectancies and obligations of another relationship, one relationship must be sacrificed to the other. If both relationships are important, however, this sets up a threat to the integrity of the group as a whole. Thus the rights of expectancy of a parent should not impose on an adult son, for example, obligations which are inconsistent with the son's recognized obligation to his wife, to his own children, to duly authorized government officials, and so on.

Every right (legal or nonlegal) is an authority commanding some correlative responsibility. But two rights may sometimes conflict, so that if one right commands its correlative responsibility the other right forfeits its expectation of a responsible performance. The private responsibilities of the two relationships cannot both be met—if one responsibility is commanded, the other is frustrated. That the two private responsibilities are incompatible with each other is thus a product of the incompatibility of the two rights (legal or nonlegal) which create the responsibilities.

We may now set up our basic definition of social responsibility. Social responsibility is the obligation to exercise one's private authority (rights, whether legal or nonlegal) in such a manner that the performance of the correlative obligation does not frustrate important rights of expectancy held by others. As we shall see, however, to meet this social responsibility does not require one simply to abnegate his rights; it does require him to seek an adjustment of his rights and the rights of others.

For purposes of simplicity, this formula may be reduced to the obligation to exercise one's rights so that they do not contravene important rights held by others. On either definition, however, this obligation is not a matter of moral injunction; it is not simply a precept appealing to one's conscience. It is a prerequisite born of the fact of people's reliance on culture patterns to govern conduct in social settings, and of the necessity for some degree of compatibility of major culture patterns to achieve that minimum degree of order without which societies could not function.

In any given situation, then, the *social* responsibility of individuals (singly or in groups) is simply that their command over a *private* responsibility in a *particular* relationship be exercised to render it compatible with the performance of the private responsibilities in other relationships in the society. The rights and obligations of any relationship are sanctioned in the final analysis by their consistency with the rights and obligations of all the other significant relationships in the community. Social responsibility is simply the obligation which must be assumed or enforced if a consistency of relationships is to be maintained.

As a matter of fact, reference to someone's social responsibility commonly arises when there is an *inconsistency* between two or more relationships, so that the exercise of rights by one in a particular relationship violates the rights of another in some other relationship. Charges of social irresponsibility thus mean, most simply, that someone's right of expectancy in a relationship has been rendered meaningless by the person or group whose action is complained of.

This is the concept of social responsibility which will be here adopted, and it will be well, therefore, to elaborate on it.

We have said that responsibility is the correlative of authority.[3] Social responsibility must therefore be, in some sense, a correlative of "social authority." But what can be meant by such a term?

Church officials, vested rulers, and legislators possess one kind of authority which we may refer to as "specific," in the sense that these are formal originators of doctrines having a compulsive power over people's conduct and themselves have varying kinds of power to compel performance. In contrast to such specific authority we may range an authority that is possessed not by any specified individuals or pressure groups but by the members of a society considered as a whole. Their authority is based upon their general acceptance of a set of basic culture patterns embodying rights and obligations, coupled with their power to enforce those patterns—a power to be discussed shortly. Social authority is thus a people's command over the behavior of their component members, requiring conformance to accepted patterns of basic relationships which —because basic—must be kept compatible with each other. It is a nonspecific authority in the sense that it is not enunciated nor enforced by any specified individual or groups but by the community at large. It is nonetheless a genuine authority, as real as the complex of culture patterns which permit relationships to be reasonably predictable.

This concept of social authority reveals more clearly why it is difficult to give specific content to its correlative concept of social responsibility. In order to define that responsibility it is necessary to discover expectancies and obligations in a variety of private relationships which are currently demanded *because of* the present constitution of society. And this is a matter of interpretation, subject to challenge. No individual or agency can stand for society as a whole—not even the government, which is composed of individuals and represents its own specific interests—so that no individual or agency is vouchsafed a special pre-

---

[3] We have already argued that a right of expectancy, even though nonlegal, places authority in its possessor. If it is accepted that a thirsty man is entitled to receive a glass of water when he asks for it, we may reasonably say that a thirsty man possesses an authority to command a glass of water. Those whom he addresses owe a responsibility to provide him with water.

rogative to identify the "nature" of society as a whole and the private relationships which compose it.

There are thus multiple readings of what constitute the rights of expectancy and obligations of individuals in particular relationships at a moment of time. Whether the expectancies and obligations presently inhering in the private relationships between union officials and union members, or between union officials and management members, or between management and stockholders render those particular relationships incompatible with each other or with the complex of relationships in our society, would be a matter of variant opinion on the part of union officials, union members, management, and stockholders, for example.

This vagueness of definition of social responsibility does not, for that reason, mean that the concept is without significance. Despite difficulty of definition the notion is valid. There is a complex of private relationships which must not remain contradictory if there is to be "a society." From this requirement arises the burden of social responsibility resting upon every member in that society—to seek an adjustment of those private relationships in which he is involved so that they are compatible with the other dominant relationships of his society. As will be underscored frequently, however, this is not a burden of conscience but one externally imposed; it is not an ethical sense which must be heightened to secure performance of the social duty, but simply a capacity for judgment.

Social responsibility is thus defined as the arrangement and implementation of rights and obligations (authorities and responsibilities) in a private relationship so that they are compatible with the rights and obligations (authorities and responsibilities) in the whole complex of private relationships in society. Social responsibility can be satisfied only by performance of obligations to particular individuals, and not to "society" as a whole. This point cannot be overstressed. Whenever we argue the need for someone—a union leader or a high management official—to assume greater responsibility, we can only mean that in our opinion certain relationships between him and others should be modified because those relationships are proving injurious to the performance of other important relationships in our society. Indeed, a person cannot owe obligations to an "organization" or a "group" or a "government" or "society" *except* by owing an obligation to another individual. All obligations refer only to relationships with other persons, and unless they can be defined in terms of conduct toward others they are empty and meaningless.

This important point may be illustrated by reference to one of the most troubling problems of industrial relations, where we frequently encounter the charge of social irresponsibility—a major strike involving the health or safety of the community. Suppose that the supply of electric power to a city is cut off by a walkout, so that city streets and homes cannot be lighted, and power cannot be generated to turn the motors of home or factory. At once the cry is raised that the union is displaying a lack of social responsibility. In our analysis, this must amount to a charge that the rights of expectancy and obligations of this union-management relationship violate the rights of expectancy and obligations of other relationships. What are these rights which are presumed to have been violated?

We might say that the obligations of the electricians' union toward their employer did *not* involve continuous service. On the contrary, the union possessed a right to strike (a privilege, in the Hohfeldian terminology), imposing an obligation on the management of the company not to prevent their carrying out this design if they so chose. The employer's right of expectancy did not include a no-strike pledge from his employees. The employee-employer relationship, then, did not preclude the former from striking (let us say, at the time of contract renewal) to secure a wage increase which the latter had no obligation to grant. So far so good. But wherein is this relationship, with its various expectancies and obligations, incompatible with other important relationships in the community?

We might reasonably argue that the right of strike in the employee-employer relationship violates the consumer's expectancy of the continued necessary service. That is to say, one might contend that the employees and employer in the light company are jointly parties to a relationship with the consumer wherein the latter has a right of expectancy of continued service and the former—jointly—an obligation to continue the supply. The consumer's alleged right of expectancy of continued service and the employee-employer obligation to supply that service are not defined in a specific contractual relationship. They are born of the whole complex structure of private relationships in our society. Why and how?

An almost infinite number of economic (employer-employee) relationships have been reared on the implicit assumption that specialized services (like light and power) will be demanded and supplied by particular individuals, who are willing to perform only that service because their needs will in turn be met by a variety of other individuals performing specialized services like carpentry, baking, raising corn, making clothing, and so on. This means that millions of people have entered into certain relations on the assumption that their variety of wants will be met by specialists in other fields, thus rendering it unnecessary for them to minister to all their own needs. The complex structure of division of labor and specialization is thus formed of a multitude of private economic relationships based on a right of expectancy of continuity of service by one specialist vis-à-vis all other specialists. When one group of specialists ceases to perform its service (as when the electricians close down the power plant), the right of expectancy of the others to a continued service is violated. That is to say, there is here an incompatibility of important private relationships and of the expectancies and obligations which define them.

On the one hand, we argue that the employee-employer relationship includes rights of expectancy that permit cessation of operations. On the other hand, the whole fabric of our economic society, with its specialization and division of labor, is reared on the premise of a consumer-supplier relationship which includes rights of expectancy of continued service. That these contradictory relationships obtain is due to the pattern of evolution of our society. We are not here interested in the cause of the inconsistency, however, but only in the fact that it *is* an incompatibility between important private relationships which gives rise to the charge of social irresponsibility.

Changes in Social Responsibility

We have earlier emphasized that private relationships are ceaselessly undergoing change. There is little possibility, however, that the whole complex of private relationships in a society will change harmoniously and simultaneously, thus retaining some original internal consistency. Change does not proceed in so orderly a fashion. One relationship is modified while others are continued within the same framework of rights of expectancy and obligations. New relationships are established which conflict with old. Individuals on the frontiers of experience are constantly opening new spheres of "individualism" (that is, defining their own relationships with others, in certain previously unknown areas) even while society's need for integration is closing off other areas of such "individualistic" behavior.

This fact of change provides the need for a constant redefinition of the rights and obligations of specific relations in order to render them compatible with other important relationships. In other words, since social responsibility is the exercise of private authority in one relationship in such a way as to be consistent with rights and responsibilities in other relationships, a change in specific relationships redefines the requirements for consistency and hence the content of social responsibility. It is only in terms of the specific impact of one relationship on other relationships that redefinition and analysis are possible, however. Talk in vague terms of the need for "more" or "less" responsibility can be misleading. Discussion of the social responsibilities of one relationship without explicit identification of the other affected relationships is meaningless.

Some analysts, for example, have been concerned that industrial management, particularly where it is able to perpetuate itself by control over proxies, has been freed from social obligations and is amenable only to the dictates of private conscience. Other investigators have argued that industrial management has imposed on it too great a burden of "social responsibility"—in such forms as minimum wage laws, collective bargaining obligations, social security, observance of increasingly more severe factory legislation, and so on—to permit the performance of the economic functions which we have expected of them in the past. Such arguments as these are less than convincing, however, since they concentrate upon the rights and obligations of particular relationships without anything more than a wave of the hand toward those other rights of expectancy held in the society with which these particular relations are incompatible or which may have given rise to the changed relationship of which complaint is made.

The fact is that particular relationships—especially of an economic nature—have changed over the years. With their change, former rights of expectancy and obligations have been abandoned or modified, and new ones have taken their place. These changes have in turn brought changes in other relationships to preserve some compatibility among the parts of the whole complex. The former obligations of the master craftsman to his journeymen and apprentices and to his customers have had to be converted, in some instances, into obligations resting upon the managements of gigantic corporations, controlling operations so far-flung that they will never come in contact with most of their employees and customers. In the same process of change, relations between the managers of industry and the owners of businesses have likewise been modified. That those changes should destroy old responsibilities and create new ones is not occasion for surprise or criticism. What is involved is neither "more" nor "less" responsibility but rather *new* responsibilities (and rights of expectancy) to meet new situations. In some instances these new obligations are nonlegal; in other instances they are based on law. It is not on grounds of their legal or nonlegal nature, however, but only of their compatibility with other relationships in the whole social complex that the quality of their social responsibility is to be assessed.

Some inconsistency in the complex of relationships is, of course, scarcely avoidable. Where particular relationships are not dominant or vital in the society, their continuing inconsistency can be tolerated without danger. It is surprising how much incompatibility even among important relationships can be accepted for a time. The ability of our own society to accept occasional dislocations of its economy by strikes in significant industries—such as coal, transportation, public utilities —and to conduct its economic activity in the periodically recurring shadow of such a threat (at each contract expiration) is evidence of the survival power of our culture. Indeed, without this degree of flexibility a society would be reduced to static relationships or would disintegrate, for inconsistency is inevitable when change occurs and the compatibility of relationships must be continuously reestablished after having been lost. Yet such survival power cannot be tested too frequently or for too long without serious consequences. Persisting incompatibility among really vital relationships in a society is not a matter to be shrugged off lightly.

Sanctions in Support of Social Responsibility

Social responsibility—the requirement of an effort to secure or maintain compatibility between one's own and other relationships—must be enforceable to have any significance. An unenforceable responsibility remains a matter for one's private conscience. On the argument being presented here, however, social responsibility is more than a private affair—it is the basis for the successful functioning and continuity of the society. So important a service cannot be left to the willingness or unwillingness of individuals, but is, rather, subject to a compulsion. What is the nature of that compulsion?

It will simplify the analysis if we agree to distinguish legal responsibility from social responsibility. By the former we shall mean all those actions required by law and carrying legal penalties for nonobservance. These are the relationships involving those legal rights and obligations the nature of which Hohfeld so painstakingly elaborated. As we have seen, however, in addition to these legal obligations there are a variety of nonlegal obligations stemming from nonlegal rights of expectancy. It is the complex of relationships based upon these nonlegal rights and obligations in which we are particularly interested. It is not a simple matter, of course, to distinguish rights accruing under law from those deriving from custom or tradition. The common law is built upon custom. Nevertheless, our interest in this analysis lies in those rights which cannot be compelled as a matter of law, where we—in our indignation at actions which appear outrageous yet lie beyond the law's reach—splutter about social irresponsibility.

In this sense, then, social responsibility is compelled by no specific laws carrying legal penalties for their violation. Nevertheless, if we are to denominate it as a meaningful responsibility it must be enforceable by some means. And social responsibility is in fact upheld by nonlegal sanctions such as public opprobrium, nonintercourse, violence, interference with one's normal conduct. We are not asserting, to be sure, that wherever these tactics are employed they are in support of someone's conception of social responsibility. A union and a company's management may become locked in a struggle in which they use blacklists, strike or lockout or boycott, strong-arm methods, and picketing against each other in support of their own partisan interests. These same weapons may, however, be employed by outsiders to the particular union-management relationship who believe their own rights—in other relationships—to have been violated by the parties' conduct. We say that "public opinion" rises against the offender or offenders, by which we mean that numerous individuals have reacted to the conduct of a relationship between other parties *because their own private relationships are affected*. By employing the variety of nonlegal sanctions available to them (including a threat to procure *legal* sanctions for the conduct complained of), those who believe themselves (whether realistically or fancifully) to have been injured or to be susceptible to injury seek to force a modification of the rights of expectancy and obligations inhering in the offending relationship. In this sense one may indeed assert, "Look into the fence corners of all the duty norms and you will find that the ultimate sanction is in furtherance of someone's interests."[4]

Often we are inclined to think of these nonlegal sanctions, supported by what we usually term "public opinion," as being weak and relatively ineffective. We feel that individuals pursuing strong selfish interests are unlikely to be deterred by the mere feeling or sentiments or inattention of others. Yet any social scientist will confirm that regard for the respect of others ranks among the most powerful stimulants of our behavior. "However complete may be the indifference to public opinion, in a cool, intellectual view, of the traditional sage, it has not yet been my fortune to meet with any actual sage who took its hostile manifestations with entire equanimity. Indeed, I doubt if the philosopher lives, or ever has lived, who could know himself to be heartily despised by a street boy without some irritation. And, though one cannot justify Haman for wishing to hang Mordecai on such a very high gibbet, yet, really, the consciousness of the Vizier of Ahasuerus, as he went in and out of the gate, that this obscure Jew had no respect for him, must have been very annoying."[5]

Moreover, as we shall find, the sanctions which may be invoked in support of shared conceptions of social responsibility are more various than at first appear. They operate indirectly as well as directly, and sometimes bring to bear on the offending party the weight of an antipathetic authority, who himself is responding to duties expected of him by a constituency to whom he is responsible. A government official coerces an offending company or labor union into actions conforming to widely conceived and firmly held notions of responsible behavior because the electorate whom he must satisfy expects him to intervene on its behalf to secure such a result.

Identifying Social Responsibility

We have defined social responsibility as the obligation, supported by nonlegal sanctions, to secure and maintain a compatibility between the relationships in which individuals or groups are involved and the dominant relationships (cultural patterns) of their society. It consists in the compulsion on the individual to integrate his rights of expectancy in

[4] A. B. Wolfe, "Functional Economics," in R. G. Tugwell, ed., *The Trend of Economics* (Chicago: University of Chicago Press, 1924), p. 480.

[5] T. H. and Julian Huxley, *Touchstone for Ethics* (New York: Harper & Brothers, 1947), p. 57. The reference is to the Biblical story told in Esther 5:9-13.

particular relationships with those rights (both legal and nonlegal) held by others. There are, however, several problems involved in the identification of social responsibility.

First, how is incompatibility between relationships discerned? We may be sure that the existence of incompatibility will be marked with a complaint. The absence of any criticism of one's conduct suggests that no one's rights of expectancy in other relationships are being violated by one's own behavior. On the other hand, the issuance of a complaint against one's conduct may arise from that tactical effort to alter rights of expectancy to another's advantage which, as we have seen, is inescapable because of the fact of change, and which necessarily breeds conflict. Thus, for example, unions may seek allies to bring charges of the "irresponsibility" of management simply as one phase of the continuing union effort to readjust in its favor the balance of rights and obligations in the union-management relationship. Criticism here need not be accepted as proof that management's rights of expectancy of union conduct or obligations to the union are incompatible with other important social relationships. We may thus say that complaints of one's conduct may be but are not necessarily evidence of a need for re-examining the impact of one's own relationships on other people's rights. Absence of criticism may be taken as compliance with one's social responsibility.

This difficulty of identifying social responsibility—due to the absence of any recognized interpreting authority—is further complicated by the ceaselessness of change in relationships. Nevertheless, the inconclusiveness of such identification offers no easy escape from one's social responsibility as long as we recall that there are effective sanctions in support of it. Confronted with criticism of one's conduct as impinging on legitimate rights of expectancy of others, in other relationships, one cannot sensibly shrug off the complaint without first estimating the consequences. If he is prepared to gamble that the criticism is confined to a small number of individuals whose approval is relatively unimportant to his satisfaction, or that it constitutes only a gambit in a tactical maneuver by the other party to the particular relationship to adjust rights of expectancy in its favor, a person may ignore the issue on the reasonable ground that the sanctions which could be applied against him are relatively harmless. But if he gambles and loses, finding to his discomfort that adverse opinion concerning his conduct is widespread and strong, the sanctions applied against him can be costly indeed, as union officials discovered in 1947, for example, when they chose to ignore criticism of their conduct, only to be brought up short, in consequence, by the Taft-Hartley Act.

We have not exhausted the difficulties of identifying social responsibility, however. Even assuming that the parties to a relationship become convinced that their system of rights and obligations interferes with the rights held by others in other relationships, on whom does the responsibility for effecting consistency lie? To begin with, there are two parties to the relationship in question. Does onus lie upon one party or the other? If strikes in key industries are inconsistent with other dominant relationships in our society, imposing a social responsibility for change in the union-management relationship, should the change affect the rights of management or the rights of the union? It takes two to make a strike—the party initiating the demand and the party refusing it. Must we say that one party had no right to make—or enforce—its demand, or can we equally say that the second party had no cause to refuse the demand as made? Or is it simply that the parties should both modify, in some respect, their conceptions of rights of expected conduct in the relationship?

Nor is that all. If we assume that the union-management relationship is inconsistent with other dominant relationships in our society, this in itself does not require the union and management to conform their relationship to others. It takes two (or more) relationships to be inconsistent, just as it takes two (or more) parties to make any given relationship. Compatibility between relationships may be gained by the remedial actions of one set of parties or the other, or of both. On whom should the responsibility for conformance lie?[6]

Once again, however, the vagueness of the matter does not provide an easy escape route for any individual. As long as one senses an inconsistency between his rights of expectancy in a particular relationship and the rights held by others in other relationships, he ignores his responsibility to secure some adjustment only on pain of possible sanctions. For effective sanctions do exist, as we have seen, their effectiveness dependent on the depth and spread of others' feelings as to the "rightness" of one's conduct. And failure adequately to assess the possible effectiveness of sanctions against oneself (as penalty for in-

[6] A satisfying answer to this question can probably be made only along lines of the economist's conception of general equilibrium—that all relationships must be brought into mutual adjustment simultaneously, thus abstracting from any isolated cause-effect relationships. But such a conception is scarcely helpful in real-life adjustments.

action in the face of pressure for a change of rights and obligations) may mean that one's rights will be changed by others, and in a less advantageous manner than if one had participated actively in the change. Here the role of the group leader becomes important, for it is his function to seek adjustments in relations which conduce to the benefit of his followers. It is his part to compromise, where necessary to preserve advantage, no less than to take the initiative in forcing change on others.

The fact that individuals and groups are thus susceptible to the opinions of others—through the imposition of sanctions by others—leads to interest in "public relations." In our own day offices of public relations have been formalized, and their directors are influential in determinations of policy. Whether formal or informal, however, the function of public relations is to avoid sanctions imposed by "the public," by seeking to mold public opinion as to the reasonableness of one's own conduct.

These considerations should prompt one important conclusion. Although all of us owe a social responsibility, in the sense in which that term has been defined here, an acceptance of that social responsibility resolves no problems of inconsistency. The responsibility is in seeking an adjustment where one's own rights are in conflict with important rights held by others, but that in no way imposes particular solutions. It does not even identify the party whose rights should be modified, but only those parties who must be involved in any modification of rights. Thus, to say that strikes in important industries constitute a problem in social responsibility is not to saddle the unions—alone—with a duty to conform their rights to the rights of others. For the other party to the particular relationship—management—is likewise involved, and its rights must be thrown on the table for inspection. Likewise the rights of those who, in other relationships, feel aggrieved by the conduct of union and management—these, too, must come under scrutiny for possible change. Social responsibility thus involves a willingness to seek an adjustment of one's rights when they are in conflict with the rights of others, but this carries with it no onus for a particular solution by a particular party.

In strike situations the "public" is generally confused by the contradictory charges of the contending parties, each accusing the other of misconduct in order to divert sanctions from itself to the other. The common reaction to such a battle of words, "a plague on both your houses," is a most intelligent one. It refuses to place the responsibility for solution on one party's acceptance of the other's solution. It avoids attachment to terms unilaterally conceived. It recognizes that *both* parties owe a responsibility to seek an adjustment, and condemns both for inadequately meeting that obligation.

Characteristics of Social Responsibility

Several characteristics of social responsibility should be noted. First, it is likely to operate as a conservative force. Its conservative nature is shown by the requirement that changes in relationships must proceed with regard to their compatibility with the whole complex of *existing* relationships. Thus an effort on the part of an individual or group to modify its relations with others (employees seeking to modify their relations with an employer, through a union, for example) may trammel the rights of others in other relationships, setting up a pressure on them to conform to the existing scheme of rights and obligations. That the social system is loose enough to permit some degree of inconsistency is some protection to the innovator; without such flexibility there would be an almost complete lack of opportunity for individuals or groups to effect a change in the existing order. Nevertheless, the degree to which innovation in social relationships will be tolerated is distinctly limited. The emphasis of most people is upon the continuity of relationships with which they are familiar—often even when there is objection to the requirements it imposes.

It might be argued that social responsibility is revolutionary rather than static. If one admits the inescapable nature of *change* in certain relationships, then this requires an accommodating change in other relationships in order to achieve compatibility. If instead of focusing on the resistance to change one posits the inevitability of change, then social responsibility—which places an obligation on those whose rights are affected to seek a consistency in their relationships, at least when vital social functions are involved—calls for change to meet change. In fact, however, existing relationships are likely to be widely respected, rendering suspect those who seek to modify them; and to the extent that change occurs, the conservative tendencies in society are likely to create incompatible relations which will guarantee conflict for a time.

Another characteristic of social responsibility, as here defined, is its nonethical nature. It operates with the force of nonlegal sanctions to secure a consistency in the important social relationships, but in itself provides no basis for judging any relationship either "right" or "wrong." Certain writers, such as Julian Huxley and Erich Fromm, have sought to erect an objective standard for appraising the rightness or wrongness of the relationships themselves. Here we are indeed in the field of ethics, where one may be called upon to choose, conceivably, among alternative systems of relationships. Others contend that no objective standard of ethical judgment is possible and that ethics is a matter of private conscience. It is unnecessary to enter into this controversy here, for we are not concerned with ethical appraisal.

Ethical judgments call for particular solutions as logical deductions from moral principles or standards. Social responsibility, as here defined, involves a personal recognition of the need for seeking adjustment or accommodation with others in one's society, in order to secure a compatibility among the dominant relations which define the culture of that society. Social responsibility is enforced by nonlegal sanctions (which derive their existence from what we call "public opinion"), so that its incidence is inescapable. It neither offers nor compels particular solutions, however. It operates, rather, as a pressure to secure adjustments between individuals and groups in their conflicting relationships. The adjustment or "solution," while not dictated, must be acceptable to the society generally, however, if it requires a change in one of the important cultural behavior patterns. It is proven acceptable or inacceptable by the extent to which the culture pattern is in fact modified.

Other definitions of social responsibility may, of course, be offered. The merit which is claimed for this one is simply that it avoids an unwarranted reliance on some mystical, conscience-like, unenforceable inner response to a guilt feeling to secure the resolution of cultural inconsistencies. It offers instead something as objective as a two-sided coin —heads, social responsibility is the exercise of a right of expectancy in a particular relationship which has been sanctioned by its compatibility with the whole complex of relations in society; tails, social responsibility is the obligation, enforced by sanctions, to remove the incompatibility between one's relationships and other significant relationships when it appears.

Since in the last analysis this conception of social responsibility is dependent for its validity on the existence of a correlative authority supplied with sanctions for eliciting or compelling performance of the responsible action, we must turn now to a fuller examination of the characteristics of the authority which is possessed by the general public.

CHAPTER TWO

The Influence of Public Opinion

Who Is the Public?

PUBLIC opinion is the force which supports sanctions enforcing social responsibility. The belief that given private relationships conflict with other dominant rights gives rise to a widespread pressure to render the incompatible relations harmonious. Moreover, although public opinion is not itself equipped to suggest solutions, as we shall see, it ultimately accepts or rejects from among solutions suggested by others where these have important effects on cultural patterns of conduct.

But who is "the public?"

A public consists of a group of individuals having something in common which significantly associates them under given circumstances. A "public golf course" refers to links which are used by those who are associated by community residence and an interest in this sport. We say that an actress has "her public," by which we mean that a group of individuals consciously react to her appearance and dramatic ability. A politician proclaims that he will take an issue to the public, meaning all those having the right to vote for him. There is thus a large number of publics, as has often been remarked, since people may be associated in an almost infinite number of ways. In our examination of social responsibility in industrial relations, however, we shall adopt a definition of "public" which, while conforming to that given above, narrows the basis for the common tie binding individuals together. For our purposes, a public consists of those who are not parties to a specific relationship but who are conscious of being affected by that relationship. In the field of labor relations, for example, a strike at a local gas company involves a different public than a strike in a local steel fabricating plant, while a shutdown of the coal mines affects a different public than a waterfront strike in San Francisco. Those who conceive themselves to be affected by the particular union-management relationship change in number and composition from one situation to another.

Just how individuals conceive themselves to be affected by some private relationship of which they themselves are not a part varies. In some instances they may regard themselves as being directly affected, as when they are laid off from their own jobs because of a strike elsewhere or when their home supply of electricity fails. In other cases they may be affected only indirectly—it is not they who are laid off but some relative, or the effect may be anticipated rather than present—if the mines do not begin operating soon the two tons in the coal bin may be used before more can be delivered. As society has become more interdependent and specialized, people probably consider themselves to be members of more and more publics.

The existence of a multiplicity of publics, each forming around some private relationship, does not mean that the concept of a "general public" must be abandoned. A general public exists under two sets of circumstances: (1) when so large a number of those in the society or community are affected by a given private relationship that for purposes of simplicity we may refer to them as the public at large (a tugboat strike in New York City has for its public virtually all the inhabitants of that area, so that we may justifiably refer to "the greater New York public" as those thus affected); (2) when we are concerned not with a particular private relationship but with a general type of relationship which is so important in the society as to affect virtually all its members (thus we may think not of the public which is concerned with the relations between the United Automobile Workers and General Motors, but of the public which is concerned with union-management relations). The type relationship here is important enough to involve so many individuals that we can reasonably identify them collectively as "the general public." Yet caution must be exercised, for such a general public is not likely to be interested in *all* aspects of union-management relations but only in those aspects which actually do involve it.

The Functions of Public Opinion

Publics are significant for the study of social responsibility only when they have opinions. It is thus to the meaning and significance of public opinion that we must turn.

Public opinion consists of the opinions held by the numerous individuals who compose a given public concerning the matter which serves as their common bond of association. Thus the "juke-box public" holds opinions concerning some current popular song; the automobile-owning public has views with respect to the way an automobile should perform or traffic be regulated; the farming public has views about the way crops should be marketed. In each case these aggregate reactions constitute public opinion.

Public opinion does not mean some single monolithic viewpoint. Insofar as any public is formed of individuals having various backgrounds and interests, that public is likely to possess a range of opinions. At times, however, some modal opinion appears to form and we may reasonably say that it "represents" public opinion—a kind of majoritarian doctrine in sociological rather than political terms. At other times a view not gaining majority support may nevertheless be held with sufficient intensity of feeling to win recognition as the dominant view.

In the narrower definition of a public which has been adopted here— a group of people who, while not part of a given relationship, are consciously affected by or interested in that relationship—the meaning of public opinion must likewise be somewhat narrowed from the more general significance given it above. In this study we shall mean by public opinion the views held by a group of individuals as to the acceptability of some relationship which jointly affects them. That is to say, a collection of people compose a public in that they are all affected in some manner by some relationship, and these individuals all react favorably or unfavorably as to how they are affected. Again, public opinion consists in the aggregate of such reactions, and at times some dominant view may emerge.

Nevertheless, public opinion in this sense is more than a counting of opinions pro and con. Opinions may be strong or weak. It would be possible for a majority of the members of a public to hold a certain view, but to hold it so weakly that it would not motivate action. Not only numbers but also intensity of feelings are important in ascertaining the strength of any given public opinion. Finally, although public opinion is generated by those who are themselves affected by some private relationship, if the relationship is important enough it will attract the attention of some who have no interests of their own actually involved but who subscribe to the prevailing opinion perhaps out of sympathy or a desire for conformity.

With respect to social responsibility, which places on the individual a felt burden to make his relationships consistent with other important relationships in his society, public opinion performs two functions, which we shall state briefly and then elaborate. First, it identifies the areas of incompatibility between important private relationships. Second, it serves to approve or reject particular solutions which are adopted. Public opinion does not itself *provide* solutions to the problem of inconsistent relationships, however.[1]

When numbers of individuals come to believe that certain rights of expectancy held by them or affecting their interests are violated by some relationship, such as the union-management relation, they constitute a public with an opinion—an opinion that some important relationship is in conflict with other important relationships of which they are a part either directly or indirectly. This opinion spotlights the problem. It focuses attention on the need for a solution which will render compatible the relationships now conflicting. Yet this amorphous group of individuals is incapable of itself providing any solution. It waits for others—perhaps the parties to the conflicting relationship, perhaps "experts"—to suggest or institute changes designed to restore some semblance of harmony. From the amorphous public there then comes, over time, some vaguely "representative" opinion, perhaps taking the form of simple acquiescence, perhaps of actual approval, perhaps of modified acceptance, perhaps of outright rejection. In this sense public opinion is best thought of as wordless, operating at so simple a level that it can be conceived of as expressed in a shake of the head, whether in vigorous objection, lukewarm acceptance, or some other shading of negative or positive attitude. If this conception of public opinion appears extreme, it is used to avoid any suggestion that by "opinion" we refer to fully formed ideas.

Sanctions Supporting Public Opinion

Indeed, it is by abandoning any notion of public opinion as dealing with the formulation of complex ideas and by concentrating upon its elemental *acceptance or rejection* of the behavior of others that we

[1] A note on terminology may here be helpful. By "particular solution" I mean a formula or pattern of conduct for carrying on a general relationship. Thus in the union-management relationship there might be a number of suggestions as to what the general culture pattern of this relationship should be. In my terminology each of these several proposals constitutes a "particular solution." It should not be confused with the terms of agreement between a union and company in a specified bargaining relationship (such as U.S. Steel or Goodrich or Westinghouse or the Midwest truckers). For the latter I use the term "particular settlement."

come to appreciate the nature and power of the sanctions which are brought to enforce it. The significance of public opinion with respect to social responsibility lies *solely* in its ability to provide effective sanctions to secure actions by others designed to restore a balance or harmony between important social relationships that has somehow been lost or endangered by the processes of change. Public opinion without sanctions supporting it is likely to signify that the inconsistency which has been identified is not vital; that whatever harm it does to the expectations held by some is not so great that it is worth troubling about. The very nature of public opinion is such that its impact is recognizably felt only if the opinion is important. If the public holds an opinion so weakly as not to make itself known to the parties whose relationship is the offending one, or so weakly that it promises to do nothing about its opinion, then its opinion is literally of no consequence and can be ignored.

It does not follow, however, that all opinions supported by sanctions will lead to conforming behavior. The sanctions themselves may prove ineffective. Social change may rob once potent controls of their effectiveness and new sanctions must be devised to take their place. Nevertheless, it can be argued that any strongly held views of social responsibility will find their means of enforcement in time. The defiance by intransigeant individuals of their society is not likely to continue unchecked indefinitely. The offender is penalized for his disregard of the rights of others, or prevails upon others to modify their notions of right. A society incapable of exacting a reasonable conformance to relatively common conceptions of the responsibilities inhering in the important relationships is likely to prove incapable of maintaining itself. Individuals may continue to live together but the society disintegrates. There may remain social propinquity, but the bonds of social organization become weak and meaningless. The *mechanics* of applying sanctions and their degree of effectiveness will vary from society to society (will differ in democratic and authoritarian communities, for example), but their role and significance remain the same.

Nevertheless, as already noted, sanctions available to support public opinion are often powerful. The weapons available are such as threat of legal restraint and illegal violence, but above all boycott, nonintercourse, and manifest disapproval. So strong is the human's need for social acceptance that any widespread rejection of him constitutes one of the most potent threats which can be made against his welfare. As one writer has put it: "It is not so much the dread of what an angry public may do that disarms the modern American, as it is sheer inability to stand unmoved in the rush of totally hostile comment, to endure a life perpetually at variance with the conscience and feeling of those about him."[2] And another has written: "The need for eliciting favorable responses from others is an almost constant component of such aggregates. Indeed, it is not too much to say that there is very little organized human behavior which is not directed toward its satisfaction in at least some degree. Although this need for response probably varies in intensity at different times, it lacks the clear-cut cyclical quality of those needs which derive directly from physiological tensions. It can thus operate as a motivation of behavior at almost any time. It is hard to conceive of a situation in which the individual's desire for favorable response from others is so completely satisfied that he has no desire to elicit further favorable responses or to avoid unfavorable ones."[3]

This need by individuals for the acceptance of those around them is also felt by groups such as unions and managements. Disapproval of the actions of an organization is reflected upon the members of that organization, subjecting them to the pressures of ostracism or felt disapproval. "The public be damned" is not only an attitude to which few modern corporations or unions would subscribe; it is equally a braggadocio which in any age could be true only of an abnormal individual or group of individuals.

When we recall that a public's direct sanctions may also be employed in an indirect fashion and sometimes with greater effectiveness, we can appreciate still more the power of a public over its constituent organizations. Representatives of government, the press, other organizations, may be induced to bring pressure on a union or management which violates important rights of expectancy held by others in significant number. The public sanction applies to the intermediary who is persuaded to act for fear of penalty if he does not, and who in turn applies all the power of his position to secure responsible conduct from the offending party.

Public opinion thus serves as a guide to action in only a general way. It identifies the area where action is needed if conflicts of interests are

[2] E. A. Ross, *Social Control* (New York: The Macmillan Co., 1901), p. 105.
[3] Ralph Linton, *The Cultural Background of Personality* (New York, D. Appleton-Century Co., 1945), p. 91.

to be resolved, and it approves (sometimes only by accepting quies-cently) or rejects actions which may be undertaken to overcome the difficulty. Even in this limited sense, moreover, public opinion must be viewed as a guide without any moralistic or ethical connotations. It is not necessarily a *good* guide. It is simply that which we use because the opinions of others are important to us.

The Nature of Opinion Formation

Writers have commented on how the process of opinion formation has been made increasingly difficult for individuals by the growing complexity of society. "The world about which each man is supposed to have opinions has become so complicated as to defy his powers of understanding."[4] There is an undeniable validity to such statements, as applied to individuals, but they are irrelevant to the process of public opinion making, as we have defined it. The first function of pub-lic opinion, as we have seen, is the identification of the areas of incompatible relationships. Here there is no need for that omniscience which so many writers have held to be necessary to citizens in a democracy.[5] To identify the areas of inconsistent relations it is only necessary that individuals have opinions concerning not even how but only whether the behavior of others affects their own rights of ex-pectancy and obligations. Thus we believe that unions and manage-ment, in their relationship, impinge upon our own relationships favorably or unfavorably. The fact that in this function of identifying incompatible relationships individuals are concerned only with sig-nificant influences on their own interests limits materially the range of opinions required. Extensive knowledge or esoteric wisdom is not needed to form convictions as to whether the conduct of others ad-versely or favorably affects us, even if those convictions are not subject to proof. Moreover, the number of opinions required is further lessened by the need to reflect only about those relationships external to us which *adversely* affect us. A satisfactory complex of personal relations— a feeling of being compatible with one's fellows—does not require a conscious expression of opinion. Finally, in this first function of iden-

4 Walter Lippmann, *Liberty and the News* (New York: Harcourt Brace and Howe, 1920), p. 37.

5 ". . . Although public business is my main interest and I give most of my time to watching it, I cannot find time to do what is expected of me in the theory of democracy; that is, to know what is going on and to have an opinion worth expressing on every question which confronts a self-governing community." Walter Lippmann, *The Phantom Public* (New York: Harcourt Brace and Co., 1925), p. 20.

tifying the areas of conflicting rights the only opinions required are (as has already been pointed out) simple approval or disapproval. Despite the complexity of the problems involved in the relationship between the United States and Russia, for example, the first function of public opinion is only to array the answers to the question, "Is this relationship, as it appears to me, compatible with my present rights of expectancy?" and the answers need be couched only in terms of "yes," "no," or uncertainty.

To perform this first function of public opinion, then, no great wealth of knowledge or intelligence is required. All that is needed is a conception of whether one's personal interests are favorably or unfavorably affected by someone else's relationship. Awareness of such effects depends upon knowledge and intelligence, but where there is unawareness there is no function for public opinion to perform and hence no grounds for frustration for not having "an opinion worth expressing" on the subject. The periodic campaigns to clean up city government are instructive in this respect. As long as there is no feeling that the relationships of local politicians impinge upon the citizens' rights of expectancy, there is public indifference to corruption. When muckrakers and reformers expose the magnitude of the evil, we say that public opinion is aroused—by which we mean that enough people have become convinced that their own interests are being unfavorably affected by political relationships to mark this as an area where change is required. It is not a wealth of detailed information which is required, however, but simply the aroused conviction that the relationships of politicians and citizens have come into conflict.

The Particular Solutions

Identification of the problem area by a public adversely affected by some relationship does not automatically lead to problem solving. The public is not a thinking mechanism; it is incapable of social invention. "Although the entire society may be made acutely uncomfortable by some situation for which it is not prepared, the problem of how to meet this situation is left to the minds of the component individuals. The interchange of ideas which language and close contact make possible may hasten the finding of a solution, but no society as a whole ever produced an idea."[6]

The origination of particular solutions is thus nothing which in-

[6] Linton, *The Study of Man*, p. 95.

volves public opinion. But we can go farther and say that even the choice among particular solutions, once originated, is a function of public opinion only in an indirect sense.

Regardless of who devises solutions to particular problems, to secure a hearing they must obtain a champion who commands a following. We refer to such a policy sponsor as an opinionative authority—an individual who by virtue of his relationship to others wins their acceptance of the ideas which he espouses. The following of an opinionative authority may come from political partisanship, from religious faith, from economic interest, from intellectual appreciation. The solution which he proposes may, because of its nature, win new adherents to the opinionative authority, but it is equally possible that members of the public who have looked to him on other matters or for other reasons may accept his solution simply because it is he who offers it, without respect to its content.

The opinionative authorities may be roughly classified into the two categories of partisan and impartial authorities. The former consists of those individuals who are immediately involved in the relationship which appears to conflict with rights of expectancy held by others in the society. Thus a strike on a city's transportation system might be viewed as a union-management relationship which violated the expectations of community residents to be able to ride by bus or streetcar to various points in the city. In this case both the union and the management groups would seek to win a favorable public opinion, fearful that an aroused sentiment might force a settlement on disadvantageous terms. The union and the management would thus become partisan authorities, whose arguments would be couched in a manner designed to convert the public to a particular point of view.

Normally partisans seek to identify their private ends with "public welfare." Since the public is composed of numerous individuals differently situated, it is impossible to phrase an appeal which will win the acceptance of an entire public. But the effort can be made to reduce the partisan's appeal to some denominator common to a majority. The extent to which the partisan source will win acceptance as an authoritative basis for public opinion depends on the extent to which it can identify the public interest with its own private interest. In part such an approach represents camouflage, to be sure—propaganda in the worst sense of that term, confusing or disguising issues where necessary, indulging in outright misrepresentation of the other party or falsification of one's own position. But it is also true that this need to appeal for general support by identifying private with public interest also serves to keep special-interest groups from neglecting too cavalierly the rights of expectancy held by others. Propaganda appeals cannot create opinions at will, but must have some regard for existing beliefs, prejudices, knowledge, and interests. Public opinion, by its very nature, thus exercises some restraining influence over the actions of private pressure groups.

In addition to partisan authorities there are those independent individuals whose private opinions command a following. These are individuals who have earned widespread respect because of their achievements, or who have intensively studied the particular problem, or who command public attention because of their position, or who may have been designated by someone high in governmental office to render an impartial opinion, as in the case of fact-finding commissions. On the occasion of any major conflict in rights or threatened incompatibility of important relationships our newspapers are likely to carry comment by their own editorial writers, by elected officials, by ministers, by university professors in the appropriate subject of specialization, by presidents of large corporations and labor unions, and other individuals whose names carry weight. All of these constitute authority for the opinion of some others, and depending on the nature of the issue they may be free of any special interest of their own, or at least of any *direct* interest.

Impartial authorities in the physical sciences are generally accepted in our day. Their achievements have won for them an almost unquestioning faith, at least concerning issues in their fields. The situation in the social sciences is remarkaby different, however. Although experts in the fields of economics, sociology, anthropology, psychology, and political science seek to employ the scientific method, their subject matter is necessarily that about which every lay individual has some knowledge and experience. Hesitating not to generalize from his own (perhaps untypical) experience, the man on the street is inclined to accept as authoritative only those opinions which coincide with his own limited experience. Moreover, the nature of the subject matter— human nature—has proven less tractable than the nonhuman world. Indeed, there is still some doubt that human nature can ever be scientifically known (which would seem to imply some power to control it—but by whom?—or to predict it under given circumstances, which

would revive in new dress the older doctrine of predestination). Operating in an area where so many variables are now beyond control or pre-
diction, the opinions of the experts differ widely, creating a certain
skepticism about the reliability of such authorities.

Given such disparity of opinion by the impartial authorities on
social issues, their views are generally treated in the same manner as
the views of partisan authorities—selected by members of the public
because they appear to coincide with their own rights and interests
and to reflect their own restricted experience, or chosen because of the
attraction of the man himself without real knowledge of his ideas.

Choice Among Alternatives

The original public which identified the problem area is thus split
into a number of small groups following alternative solutions and
normally a much larger group which has no opinion about the merits
of particular solutions but is satisfied as long as some solution is
adopted. These are joined by the parties to the offending relationship—
the partisan authorities and their followers—who have their own
ideas to contribute. In this contest among particular solutions public
opinion plays a small part indeed. The contest is among the opinionative authorities rather than among the solutions, and the views of one
may predominate not because they command a necessarily larger following of "true believers" but perhaps because he is more unscrupulous, more vocal, has a larger corps of secondary thought-leaders
among his constituents, or for some other reason not associated with
the soundness of his solution. Nor is there any reason to believe that
one solution only will win acceptance. In the field of experimentation
with social relations, different tentative solutions may be attempted
in different areas. Conflicting relationships may be rendered compatible by a variety of expedients. The number of local methods for
resolving strikes having an impact on the public is an example of this
variegated growth. Only over a period of time may one solution emerge
as more common than others, establishing new patterns of expectations.

It is in the final acceptance of some new culture pattern as meeting
the test of consistency with the dominant relationships in the society
that public opinion performs its second function. Whatever solutions
are tried must satisfy the affected public that its rights of expectancy
have been adequately protected. Unsatisfactory solutions will leave a
dissatisfied public, continuing to identify the relationship complained

of as one conflicting with its expectations, remanding the problem to the opinionative authorities—both partisan and impartial—for new solutions.

Since one social sanction is the threat of restrictive legislation, embodying legal sanctions, the above statements are applicable to the process of lawmaking designed to accommodate conflicting rights. Once public opinion has identified the area of inconsistent relationships, the adoption of a particular solution is left to the opinionative authorities, in this case the legislative leaders. In the selection of a course of action public opinion plays only a minuscule role. Political expediency is likely to be more important, in the sense that the views of policy proponents from the opposition party will be condemned, or that compromises may be effected between political factions, or political debts to pressure groups are paid. In the determination of whether the legislation enacted meets the need identified by the public, however, public opinion is decisive. If the public's expectations remain frustrated, the pressure for a solution remains. If the public identifies strikes interrupting the flow of essential goods and services as a frustration of a right of expectancy, for example, and if present legislation is ineffective in meeting the problem, we may expect continuing public pressure for new solutions. Moreover, there is no assurance, in this process of trial and error, that a genuine solution will ever be discovered or adopted.

In summary, then, we have defined a public, for our purposes, as those people who are not party to a particular relationship but who are conscious of being affected by it. This restricted definition emphasizes, first, the importance of the complex of relationships in society, with their attending rights and obligations and the possibility of an inconsistency of relationships; and second, the significance of consciousness of the impact of a relationship upon oneself. Without this consciousness there would be no basis for a public opinion concerning a conflict of rights. By public opinion this study refers to the acceptance (perhaps only tacit) or rejection of a specific relationship as compatible with the total complex of important relationships in society. On this definition, if rejection of a particular relationship as incompatible with other dominant relations is decisive, it brings into play social sanctions to secure change. These social sanctions accompanying a firmly held public opinion enforce upon parties to the particular relationship the social responsibility of seeking to regain a consistency with other vital relationships in the society.

The first function of public opinion is thus to identify the areas of inconsistent relations. No special knowledge is generally required to perform this function, but only a felt inconvenience or a strong anxiety. But public opinion plays a second role in ultimately deciding whether the particular solutions adopted remove the conflicts of rights. Here again no special knowledge is required, but only an opinion as to whether the inconvenience or anxiety has been sufficiently reduced to be ignored.

On this analysis, public opinion is responsible for forcing changes in social relationships, as we have known them, but it is responsible for the *kind* of change which emerges only in the sense of giving it ultimate acceptance. On the assumption that more than one kind of change is possible to satisfy the requirement of consistent private relationships, a number of alternative solutions may be offered by both partisan and impartial authorities. Which solutions will be chosen for experimentation is not likely to be a function of public opinion, but public opinion will determine whether any experimental solution is acceptable as meeting the requirements of social responsibility.

With this theoretical background, we can now proceed to examine the evidence with respect to the influence of public opinion on social responsibility in American industrial relations at the present time.

Public Opinion on Labor-Management Relations

Recapitulation: Relation of Public Opinion to Social Responsibility

WE HAVE defined a public as those who are aware of being affected by some relationship without conceiving of themselves as being actually party to it. For our purposes public opinion consists of the views held by such people about the acceptability of the relationship which jointly concerns them. In many cases the relationship may be sufficiently satisfactory as to elicit no continuing, strong, and widespread antagonism. In such an event the parties to the particular relationship can be satisfied that they are discharging their social responsibilities—their conduct of their set of private relations apparently does not threaten any significant expectations of any substantial group of people. In other cases, however, numbers of individuals may interpret the conduct of the parties in the specified relationship as endangering their enjoyment of rights of expectancy which are important to them.

When widely enough held, this critical or even hostile public opinion places a pressure upon the parties to examine their behavior with a view to modifying it to avoid or ease the apparent threat to the expectations of others, or to seek to convince others that their expectations are not in fact adversely affected, or to sustain some share of a burden of proof that it is the expectations of the public and not the behavior of the parties that should be modified. In any of these alternatives there is, however, a pressure on the parties to make their actions compatible with the generally held expectations of the society. We use the term social responsibility to refer to the obligation of the parties to a relationship to seek to maintain a consistency between the rights and obligations of their relationship and those rights which others expect in other significant relationships.

Social responsibility thus rests on public opinion—the attitude of affected individuals toward the parties who affect them. The opinion and the resulting pressure for a conforming relationship can occur in any social setting: a neighborhood, a town, a region, a nation. Not all the individuals in these geographical areas may conceive themselves affected by the given relationship. In the community the group which feels its rights of expectancy threatened by a divorce scandal is likely to be different from the group which sees its "legitimate" expectations affronted by the activities of a union organizer among a shop's workers. On a national scale the pressures for modified behavior are likely to be generated by different individuals where a gambling syndicate is involved, in one case, and a railroad strike, in another instance. The opinion in each case is the opinion of a different public, the one relevant to the circumstances. Each one, no less than any other, creates a compulsion of social responsibility resting upon the particular parties involved.

In this study, however, our attention will be concentrated upon the general public—a public comprising the adult population at large in some defined geographical area, commonly the United States taken as a whole. To affect so substantial a number a relationship must obviously be a vital one, touching other vital rights of expectancy. The views which this public holds about the compatibility or incompatibility of the rights and obligations of particular relationships with its own expectations constitutes general public opinion. Such opinions help to form the framework of social responsibility within which the parties of the given relationships must operate.

This public opinion cannot be regarded as a single monolithic attitude toward the conduct of the parties in some relationship. It is composed of all shades of opinion, ranging from that which finds the parties' behavior completely acceptable to that which views it as completely unacceptable. To say that some one attitude constitutes "public opinion" on the particular issue is therefore patently erroneous. Public opinion is a spectrum of shades of opinions, and it is by a thing of such intangible composition that the social responsibilities of individuals in the particular private relationship are determined. It would be easy to argue that since the parties obviously cannot please those with conflicting viewpoints, however adaptive their behavior, the only feasible plan is to adopt the majority view as "public opinion" on the issue, ignoring less popular opinions. While this may sometimes prove acceptable as practical policy, it remains erroneous to identify public opinion with majority opinion, and can lead to practical difficulties. For a majority opinion may be weakly held, while a minority view may be ardently espoused, so that the parties to whom such views are significant—those whose relationship evokes such views—could more expediently ignore the majority in order to achieve some understanding with the militant minority.

There is thus no escape from the parties' need for assessing the whole spectrum of opinion concerning their conduct in their private relations. For an aroused public, and sometimes a minority of this public, possesses the sanctions—nonlegal though they are—of punishing those whose conduct remains offensive. It is seldom the sanctions which are weak but often the opinions which call them into play. Attitudes indifferently or tentatively held, no matter by how many, are not likely to result in effective sanctions, whereas a determined and resolute minority opinion can release unpleasant consequences for the parties who ignore it. The character of public opinion defines the social responsibilities of any individual, and opinions lacking supporting sanctions cannot be made the basis for anything stronger than appeals to another's conscience or good nature. With the concept of social responsibility here adopted, however, such appeals are unneeded, for it falls to the parties themselves to calculate the concentration and intensity of public opinion in order to avoid sanctions which threaten their acceptance by their own society.

If we are to understand the social responsibilities of unions and managements in their relations with each other in this objective sense, it is necessary, then, to calculate the character of public opinion concerning their behavior. Do particular phases of the general union-management relation frustrate important expectations held by significant numbers in the United States? If so, is there any method of measuring the intensity of opposition? How are sanctions made effective?

Admittedly these are difficult questions to answer, but it is only through an attempt to obtain answers to such questions that we can meaningfully discuss social responsibility in industrial relations. There is no accumulated body of knowledge to which one may readily turn to obtain the needed data. Instead, we can only rely on cautious deductions from fragmentary information. The remainder of this study will consist of such an analysis. The methods employed may prove upsetting to those who ask for laboratory precision. We are faced with the uncomfortable choice, however, of resorting to spotty data and improvised procedures, on the one hand, or abandoning the problem, on the other.

Reliance on Public Opinion Polls

The major source of information on public opinion concerning union-management relations is the public opinion polls which have now been conducted on a systematic basis in the United States for a generation. The most important of the polling agencies are the American Institute of Public Opinion (AIPO) operated by George Gallup, the National Opinion Research Center (NORC), the Office of Public Opinion Research, and Elmo Roper's *Fortune* surveys. From the responses obtained by these agencies to questions concerning union-management relations it is possible to assemble significant conclusions. The nature of this source carries with it its hazards, however. Public opinion polls can be accepted as source material not because of their excellence but because of the unavailability of anything superior.

Precisely because we must rely so heavily on public opinion polls for our data does it become important to recognize the limitations of this source, although we shall here be able to suggest briefly only the major dangers.

In the first place, simply in the nature of the polling technique the public is permitted to express its views only on those topics which the polling agency itself selects. From the polls we cannot arrive at any certain conclusion as to those aspects of union-management relations about which the public is most concerned. We can only determine which of the aspects *about which it was questioned* did the public express greatest concern. This is a serious methodological weakness.

With respect to those polls relevant to our subject, there remains the question of whether the same issue has been presented (in the same form) to the public over a sufficiently long period of time to give us a clue to opinions which may be considered relatively stable. If the public were polled only once on the question of strikes in essential industries, and then during a period when power was being curtailed because of a shutdown in coal or when serious inconvenience was felt because of a railroad strike, the result is likely to reflect little more than reactions under peculiar stress. Repeated questioning over a period of years would, however, elicit something which would have greater claim to be labeled public opinion on this issue.

There are other grounds for questioning the reliability of opinion polls. Agencies obviously cannot contact every member of the general public; they must work from "samples" of the population so drawn as to reflect with a high degree of accuracy the opinion of the whole population. In the designation of the sample, however, there is room for many errors. The size of the sample may be too small, leading to what are known as chance sampling errors. There may also be numerous errors of bias arising out of the fact that the sample chosen does not mirror the whole population in regard to specific attributes which are relevant. Thus, in polling on matters of labor-management relations, it may be essential to include in the sample not only the proper proportions of men and women, of varying age groups, of residents of the important geographical breakdowns, and so on, as are found in the population at large, but the same proportions of members and non-members of unions and of various income groups as are found in the total population. At times, of course, it is difficult to ascertain how such attributes are distributed in the general population. Estimates must be relied on, sometimes of a questionable nature. In arriving at reliable opinions, accurate data on the relevant attributes of the total population are just as essential as a proper representation of those attributes in the sample.

A further possibility for the admission of error into the results is occasioned by the use of the interviewing technique. A number of studies have revealed the extent to which an interviewer may—consciously or unconsciously—influence the response of the interviewee. The response may thus fail to reveal the opinion actually held by the individual questioned. Moreover, the interviewee may incorrectly interpret the question asked by the pollster, or the pollster may misinterpret the reply of the interviewee. In some instances an individual may be led to express an opinion simply because he feels he "ought" to have an opinion, although the idea expressed can scarcely be considered anything but a chance reaction. Even the order in which the questions are asked can influence the result.

Perhaps the most serious limitation is that the polls give no indication of the intensity of opinions held. A substantial number of respondents replying to the same question repeated over a period of years need not be expressing convictions deeply held. Their replies may have the same degree of intensity as an answer to the question, "What is your favorite color in roses?" Nevertheless, though no single question elicits an indication of the intensity of feeling behind the response, we may—

cautiously and with some hazard—infer rough intensities of feeling from a juxtaposition of several questions.

The catalogue of possible deficiencies of the polling technique will not be extended. The cumulative effect of a recital of these weaknesses of public opinion polls may suggest that polls are insufficiently reliable and complete to be made the basis for any investigation into social responsibility. The fact remains, however, that polls constitute our best available source. The alternatives are to rely on one's intuition and personal observation or to make a series of case studies or to attempt systematic observation of some selected group over a period of time or to analyze the content of newspapers and other publications. The greater hazards of these methods scarcely require comment. They give free play to the bias of the observer or invite an unwarranted projection to the larger population of the views of an unrepresentative sample. Used in conjunction with polls, they may provide excellent supplements. They are, however, no adequate substitute. For all its limitations, the opinion polling technique unquestionably brings us closer to valid conclusions concerning public opinion than any alternative.

One further question concerning the use of poll materials is of importance. In a later chapter we shall examine public opinion on wage-price relationships (that is, are union wage pressures on management condemned as contributing to inflationary price rises?). On such a question, one may conceive that *all* union members—indeed, perhaps even all wage earners—are a "party" to the particular relationships, and as such should be excluded as members of the public affected by that relationship. But public opinion polls of course can make no such exclusion without having to omit from their universe a large segment of the American people, which they have not attempted to do. Moreover, even if union members or wage earners were excluded from such polls, the results would be questionable. For when so many in the society fall in the excluded category, the public may be smaller numerically than those party to the relationship, and hence have relatively little effect on it. Public opinion in so restricted a sense would lose much of its power of sanctions.

The point of view here adopted is that on such questions the union member or the wage earner is *both* a party and a member of the public. He is a party in his *particular* relationship (his individual wage relationship or strike relationship, for example), but a member of the public with regard to all other instances of that kind of relationship. Moreover, there appears to be logic in this way of meeting the problem: the union member or wage earner must in fact play these two roles. On issues of wage and strike relationship, he is at times a party and at times a citizen expressing an opinion—an opinion influenced by his ties, to be sure, but not uniquely determined by them.

The Identification of Inconsistencies of Relationships

We are here concerned only with industrial relations in the sense of the two-party dealings between unions and managements and relationships growing out of such dealings. Collective bargaining, strikes, picketing, violence between the parties are examples. Growing out of such dealings there may be issues concerning wage-price relationships, the closed or union shop, the rate of production output, and so on. We are not, however, concerned with issues primarily involving only one party: thus we are not interested in the effects on management attitudes of any separation between ownership and control, or in the operations of the company's personnel program, or in the financial policies which a company unilaterally establishes. Nor are we concerned with the quality of a union's leadership, or the amount of the dues which it charges its membership, or the democratic character of its governmental structure, or the attendance at its monthly meetings. Admittedly, some of these issues have their repercussions upon industrial relations, but we shall draw the line arbitrarily to emphasize the two-party relationship.

We are interested in uncovering those union-management relationships of which the general public is critical, on the premise that they are in some respect inconsistent with other important rights of expectancy enjoyed by the public.

A handful of polls provides us with a direct entrance to this problem.[1]

[1] The chief source of poll data for the period 1935-1946 is *Public Opinion, 1935-1946*, under the editorial direction of Hadley Cantril, prepared by Mildred Strunk (Princeton University Press, 1951). This work will hereafter be cited simply as Cantril and Strunk. For polls subsequent to 1946 the *Public Opinion Quarterly* has been used, hereafter cited as *POQ*.

Questions asked in the four polls referred to were as follows: (1) "What do you think is the chief argument against labor unions?" (AIPO, March 28, 1941, Cantril and Strunk, p. 873). (2) "Generally speaking, what bad things do you feel labor unions do?" (*Fortune*, February, 1942, Cantril and Strunk, p. 875). (3) "What bad things do you feel labor unions do?" (NORC, May 30, 1942, Cantril and Strunk, p. 873). (4) A "Why?" question asked of the 48 percent who replied "less favorable" to "Is your attitude toward labor unions today more favorable or less favorable than it was before the war?" (AIPO, March 20, 1945, Cantril and Strunk, p. 879). It may be objected that the first three of these questions invited negative comments; however, it is in negative comment that we must look for felt inconsistencies of relationships. Similar questions were asked concerning the unions' virtues, which will be considered where appropriate.

On four separate occasions within a span of five years (1941-1945) questions were asked of a sample representative of the general public designed to discover "What bad things do you feel labor unions do?" While the questions were not identically phrased they were sufficiently similar to provide a rough index of opinion critical of union activities, and while they did not confine comment solely to union activities in relationship to management they provide perhaps the best available clue to this subject. The timing of the polls admittedly influenced the responses, since the impact of unions upon preparations for and the conduct of the war was an issue peculiar to the period. Such limitations are typical of the data on which we must rely, and they weaken the reliability of conclusions. As much as possible, however, we will seek supporting data from other sources and from other polls on related issues. Despite the hazards of such reliance, it appears to offer a firmer base for generalizations than is to be found in intuition or speculation.

A number of responses to these four polls can be eliminated. Among such responses are that unions "abuse their power," an opinion which in the four surveys runs from 7 to 14.9 percent of the total replies, a significant showing, but the meaning of which is obscure. Union power may be abused in relationship to members, nonmember workers, the government, the public, or employers. A criticism of unions as "racketeering" suffers from the same defect. It appears that a substantial number of the public take this view (at least from 5 to 12 percent in the four polls),[2] but there is no way of telling whether they are concerned about union racketeering in the sense of mulcting employers, in which case we are interested, or in the sense of preying on workers for dues and initiation fees or in making deals with politicians, in which case we are not interested. One might reasonably suppose that many who gave this answer may have *intended* to lump all such activities together, feeling that racketeering relationships of whatever kind affected them by posing a threat to traditional moral standards which

[2] In the 1942 *Fortune* poll, 24.2 percent of the replies were to the effect that unions "have bad leaders, racketeers and radicals, incompetents." Here we have exhibited one of the worst defects of polls as data for generalization—the composition of replies. For our purposes we are not interested in radical or incompetent union leadership; we would be interested, however, in any beliefs that unions are headed by racketeers in the sense of those who prey upon businesses.

A fifth poll may be cited. To the question, asked of a national cross section of workers of all classes, including unemployed workers, "How many unions—all, most, about half, some, or none—would you say are headed by racketeers who are out for all they can get for themselves?" 40 percent replied that half or more fell in that category. (*Fortune*, June, 1940, Cantril and Strunk, p. 874.)

they strongly supported, thus presenting the same kind of an inconsistency with other relationships that is true of organized gambling or
civic corruption. Our decision not to analyze this type of response
further is not due to any view that the issue is not important, but only
that it falls outside the scope of union-management relationships.

A belief that unions interfered with war production was expressed
by from 4 to 6 percent in the four polls. This issue we do not consider
because its significance was for the most part peculiar to the period
during which these polls were taken.

Two percent of the respondents in the 1941 poll criticized unions
primarily for hurting private enterprise or harming small business; in
the same poll 3 percent were most concerned about the violence and
lawbreaking in which they believed unions indulged. The figures suggest no substantial public concern with these issues, and there are no
related poll questions which might shed further light on the degree of
public concern. To those who may challenge a conclusion that the
public is unconcerned with the union's impact on private enterprise,
two comments may be made: first, it is not asserted that the public is
actually unconcerned, but only that such data as are obtainable from
public opinion polls do not reveal such concern; and second, it is
possible that issues deemed important by some are not so regarded
by many.

In connection with this possibility it is instructive to note that in
none of the four polls referred to is there recorded any criticism of
"featherbedding" tactics—that is, the union's insistence on the employment of more men for a particular operation than the employer would
voluntarily hire, or the union's insistence on the performance of work
which an employer would not himself choose to have performed. Nevertheless, it appears from other polls that a majority of those expressing
an opinion believe that unions engage in such practices, and that a
majority of the entire sample would support legislation outlawing
such practices.[3] One might reasonably conclude that here is an example
of feelings which, while carrying a degree of intensity sufficient to
support legislation of the sort proposed, are lacking in an intensity

[3] To an AIPO question of March 7, 1945, "Do you think that some unions require employers to hire more persons than are actually needed to do the work?" 47 per cent replied
Yes, 19 percent No, 34 percent Don't know (Cantril and Strunk, p. 879). Four other AIPO
polls taken between June 2, 1943, and March 20, 1946, reveal from 60 to 77 percent expressing themselves favorably disposed to prohibitive legislation (Cantril and Strunk,
p. 878).

strong enough to initiate sanctions. Opposition is expressed to a particular relationship, on "general principles," but there is insufficient
consciousness of being affected to create an attitude that the problem
is an important one.

The Issue of Union Security

The issue of union security seems to fall in the same category with
featherbedding, as something to which the public is opposed "in principle" but about which little feeling is shown. By union security we
mean here the closed shop (requiring union membership as a condition
of hiring), the union shop (requiring union membership as a condition
of continuing employment but not as a condition of hiring), and maintenance of membership (requiring present members to maintain their
membership unless they formally resign during a specified "escape"
period at the expiration of the contract).

In the 1941 poll only 2 percent recorded themselves as concerned
about the unions' drive for such security provisions. In the May, 1942,
poll 6 percent may have had this in mind when they declared that the
unions' "hiring policy is unfair." It is somewhat surprising to find such
low totals in view of the fact that it was during this period that the
question of union security was made a national issue by John L. Lewis's
insistence on it as a condition for settling the coal strike in the captive
mines in the fall of 1941, and considerable publicity was being given to
the insistence by some unions that even workers temporarily employed
on defense projects join the union, paying the necessary initiation fee.
Some respondents may have had such practices in mind when they
declared that unions "abuse their power" or that "unions are rackets,"
but there is no way of knowing.

Despite this seeming lack of public concern, polls taken over a ten-
year period have revealed a consistent opposition to any form of compulsory membership in unions.[4] In a dozen polls taken between 1937
and 1947, the percentage opposed to the closed shop never fell below 59
percent and in some instances ran as high as 77 percent. Objections to
the union shop were voiced by from 54 to 61 percent. The proportions
in favor of the closed shop never exceeded 28 percent and in one poll
fell as low as 5. Only from 17 to 36 percent favored the union shop. A
1943 question revealed 48 percent in support of "adding a law to the

4 Results of these polls are presented in detail in Cantril and Strunk, pp. 546-548, except
for a poll of January 18, 1947, the results of which are given in POQ, Summer, 1947,
p. 296.

constitution of this state forbidding the closed shop," with 40 percent opposed; while in 1946, 58 percent would have changed the federal Constitution "so that no worker would have to belong to a union to get or keep a job anywhere," with only 29 percent opposed to such an amendment. Even union members have shown themselves to be far from united in support of union security. In a 1947 inquiry, 41 percent replied that they preferred an open shop, although a majority—52 percent—supported either a closed or union shop.

There can be no doubt here of the apparent consistency of opposition to any requirement of compulsory union membership, despite the apparent lack of concern regarding the issue in the four polls which asked for negative criticism of the unions. There is, of course, nothing contradictory between persistent opposition and low intensity of feeling regarding an issue. Nevertheless, the substantial majorities opposing union-security provisions, on the one hand, and the negligible mention of compulsory union membership among the opinions on undesirable union practices, on the other hand, tantalize one into seeking an explanation. There is no conclusive further evidence, but perhaps a few clues are to be found in three *Fortune* polls not included in the above summary and in some supplementary data.

In January, 1943, the following question was asked of factory labor, miners, and personal-service workers only: "Which one of these places would you rather work in—a place where there is no union and everyone deals directly with his boss or foreman; a place where there is a union only of company employees but no national union; a place where there is a strong national union but non-union men can also work; a place where everyone must belong to a national union?" The results were computed not only for the categories specified but also by union status, that is, whether member or nonmember.

	No Union	Company Union	Open Shop with Nat'l Union	Closed Nat'l Union Shop	Don't Know
Mine workers	18.0	10.7	9.4	54.9	7.0
Factory workers	25.9	16.0	16.3	34.2	7.6
Personal-service workers	42.3	10.2	9.0	21.8	16.7
Union members	7.7	14.9	15.4	58.6	3.4
Nonunion	44.9	12.1	11.9	17.5	13.6

Let us concentrate our attention upon the replies broken down by union status. If we consider that respondents favoring no union, a company union, or an open shop with a national union are essentially expressing themselves as opposed to a union-security shop, we find that some 68.9 percent of nonunion members fall in this category but only 38 percent of the union members. In the polls asked of the general public, between 54 and 77 percent expressed a similar opposition to union-security provisions, the results tending to cluster around 70 percent. Indeed, in the *Fortune* poll of February, 1942, in which a nearly parallel question was asked of the general public, the corresponding categories totalled 69.1—remarkably close to the 68.9 percent of non-union members in the survey under examination. While once again it is impossible to calculate intensity of feeling, it would appear that among the workers themselves—the largest part of the public which one might reasonably assume to be *most* consciously affected by the relationship—opposition to union-security provisions is no more marked on the part of nonunion workers than in the public at large, while in the case of unionized workers only half as many oppose and about twice as many favor union security as in the general public (on a proportional basis). If we remember, moreover, that the number of union members runs to approximately one half the total number of factory workers and nearly one third the total number of nonfarm workers, a very tentative hypothesis may be put forward. Among the largest group which is most consciously affected, the workers themselves, an important segment is favorably disposed toward union security, while those opposed are no more so than are the members of the public who are less consciously affected. The net effect apparently is to relegate union security to a relatively minor status as a public issue.

Some warrant for the conclusion that nonunion workers—even though more consciously affected than the general public—are no more strongly opposed than the public is to be found in the so-called "union authorization elections" conducted by the National Labor Relations Board under the terms of the Taft-Hartley Act until its amendment in 1951. As originally written the act required that before a certified union could even bargain with the employer concerning a union shop, it must be authorized to negotiate for a union shop by a majority of the workers in the bargaining unit (not simply a majority of members in the union). One principal reason for abandoning this provision after a four-year trial was that with few exceptions the unions consistently polled extremely high majorities. Of more than 1⅓ million votes cast in such elections in the one-year period ending June 30, 1949, 93.9 percent

supported union-shop conditions. Of not quite a million votes cast in
the succeeding year, 89.4 percent voted in favor of union-shop conditions.[5] While we have no record of the number of union members in
these voting groups, it seems a safe presumption that nonunion workers
were represented in some unknown proportion which at least in some
few instances was greater than the negative vote recorded.[6] It seems a
still safer presumption that even though a union-security shop had
already been in effect in most companies where elections were held (an
NLRB survey showed that this was the case in 2,025 out of 2,201 cases
in the period May 6 through May 21, 1948), so that most voters were
already union members, such *compulsory* union membership is no
guarantee of a favorable vote. The member who joined under compulsion may be an unwilling member still. Nevertheless, the majorities
rolled up in NLRB-conducted union-shop authorization elections were
impressive enough to convince even the authors of the act of the super-
fluity of the provision.

Thus it may be surmised that among those whom one would most
expect to express opposition—the one half of factory labor and two
thirds of nonfarm labor which are not now members of unions—the
proportion opposed is no greater or not much greater than in the public
at large. It is of course questionable whether the intensity of opposition
is likewise equal. If, however, the group most affected shows no greater
intensity than others much less affected, then perhaps it is easier to
understand why union security through compulsory membership—
which in most cases has come to mean little more than dues payment—
is not regarded as a vital public issue.

[5] The figures as reported by the Board are as follows: "A total of 1,733,922 employees
were eligible to vote in the 15,074 polls conducted by the Board to determine whether the
employees wished to authorize their union to negotiate a union-shop contract requiring
all employees to join the union as a condition of continued employment. Of these eligible
employees, 1,471,092, or approximately 84.8 percent, cast valid ballots, of which 1,381,829,
or 93.9 percent, cast ballots in favor of union-shop conditions. In 14,581 elections, or 96.7
percent of those conducted, the employees authorized the negotiation of union-shop contracts" (*Fourteenth Annual Report of the National Labor Relations Board*, for the fiscal
year ended June 30, 1949, p. 6).

"Negotiation of union-shop contracts was authorized by the employees in 5,377 polls, or
96.2 percent of those conducted. A total of 1,072,917 employees was eligible to vote in these
polls, and units comprising 1,045,162 employees (97 percent of those eligible) authorized the
union shop. Of the 900,866 valid ballots cast, 805,189, or 89.4 percent, voted in favor of the
union shop" (*Fifteenth Annual Report of the National Labor Relations Board*, for the
fiscal year ended June 30, 1950, p. 14).

[6] Even should it be assumed that all favorable votes were cast by union members, the
percentages rolled up in support of union security were vastly greater than those recorded
even for union members in the opinion polls cited.

Finally, there is evidence for the belief that the degree of public opposition expressed is partly due to the wording of the questions. In most instances the respondent was asked whether he believed that workers should be required to belong to a union before they were hired, or after they were hired. No specification was made as to the status of the union itself, in a bargaining relationship, however. This deficiency was remedied in a *Fortune* poll of February, 1944, in which the sample was asked: "Do you think there should or should not be a law passed that requires every worker in a plant to belong to a union *if the majority votes to have a union?*"[7] Almost one third of the respondents (32.1 percent) expressed themselves as favorable to such a law. Opposition was reduced to 55.7 percent. While a majority still opposed such a practice, the split of opinion was by no means as pronounced as in other polls. Only in the case of the Gallup polls of July 12, 1945, and November 27, 1946, was there even an approximation of this manner of wording the question. In those cases the public was asked if it favored requiring union membership "in a company where there is a union." It is interesting to note that although this form still omits the specification that the union exists by majority designation, these two Gallup polls registered higher percentages favorable to the union shop and lower percentages opposed than in all the cases where no specific mention was made of the prior existence of the union.

The condition expressed in the *Fortune* poll—"if the majority votes to have a union"—has indeed been a *necessary* condition for union security, in all except purely local business operations, since the passage of the National Labor Relations Act in 1935. That act prohibited discriminatory hiring practices by employers, making an exception only in the case of union security provisions negotiated by unions winning a majority of votes cast (though not necessarily of eligible votes) in the appropriate bargaining unit. The Taft-Hartley revisions tightened rather than weakened the required qualifying conditions. The *Fortune* question thus expresses not simply one of a number of presently possible alternatives but the *only* circumstance under which union security through compulsory membership can legally be instituted for the vast majority of businesses in the United States.

The significance of the wording is further suggested by an experiment conducted by Paul Studenski at the School of Commerce of New York

[7] Cantril and Strunk, p. 396.

University.[8] Using as his subjects 150 students in a summer session, he first asked this question: "Should every worker be forced to join a union?" The replies broke down as follows: Yes, 9.3 percent; No, 88.9 percent; Don't know, 1.8 percent. A week later the same students were asked about the same issue, but with the question now reworded: "Is it proper for a union to require all wage earners in an industrial enterprise to join the union—

<table>
<tr><td></td><td>Percent in Favor of Each Proposition</td></tr>
<tr><td>—under any circumstances?</td><td>7.4</td></tr>
<tr><td>—when the union controls a minority of the employees?</td><td>2.6</td></tr>
<tr><td>—when the union controls a majority of the employees?</td><td>37.6</td></tr>
<tr><td>—or is it improper under any circumstances?</td><td>45.0</td></tr>
<tr><td>Don't know</td><td>7.4</td></tr>
</table>

Here an original opposition to union security of 88.9 percent was converted by a rewording of the question[9] to a 47.6 percent support of (greater than the 45 percent opposition to) union security under specified circumstances. Even more specifically, the proviso that a union be designated by a majority of the employees is obviously the most important consideration in effecting this change.

On such inadequate evidence, and with confessed misgivings, we tentatively offer the thesis that—even though it may have been a burning issue in the past—union security is not now regarded as an issue of vital public concern. A majority—though probably not a substantial one—remains opposed to compulsory union membership "in principle." Nonunion workers appear to oppose compulsory unionization in no greater degree than does the general public, though our inability to measure intensity of feeling does not permit voicing such a conclusion with assurance. The issue is of greater significance to the parties themselves than to their publics.

Thus a *Fortune* survey of September, 1942, asked a national cross section of business executives: "After the war do you think that labor should or should not be given the closed shop?" The reply of 96.4 percent was that labor should not. Even allowing for the variation in the wording of the question, this total runs higher than the total from any of the many forms in which the question was asked of the general

[8] Reported by Paul Studenski in "How Polls Can Mislead," *Harper's Magazine,* December, 1939, pp. 81-83.

[9] Though other influences may admittedly have been present. The original poll may have stimulated discussion among the students, for example, with discussion leading to an honest change of opinion by the time of the second poll.

public. It appears to be much more important to management than to the public whether provision is made for union security through compulsory union membership, and certainly it is much more important to the union.[10]

[10] It is also interesting to observe the fatalism of the business executives. Although 96.4 percent opposed the closed shop, 50.3 percent believed that labor unions would obtain it in the postwar period. This attitude that "'it is coming" may have been partly responsible for weakening the intensity of the opposition. The *Fortune* poll results are to be found in Cantril and Strunk, p. 548.

Public Judgments on Wage-Price Relationships

OUR interest is next in discovering whether the public regards wage increases as contributing to price advances and if so whether it condemns the unions' program to win additional pay for their members.

The issue is important to economists. In recent years it has been a sharply debated topic. The dominant view appears to be that wage increases outrunning any improvement in productivity in a time of full employment are inflationary. The spread of aggregative economic analysis and the attention paid to full employment programs has led to an examination of the conditions necessary for a stable full-employment economy. The argument has been made repeatedly that in the state where jobs are plentiful—that is, under conditions of a scarcity of labor relative to the demand for it—unions can effectively push for wage increases. The employer must concede the demand or risk losing some portion of his work force, and on the other hand he is in a favorable position to pass along his additional costs in the form of higher prices, thus rendering his concession more palatable. Collective bargaining and inflation are thus likely to go hand in hand, it has been argued. The most pessimistic of the economics profession resign themselves to the inevitability of this result. Even the more optimistic concede the danger but rely on the "social responsibility" of unions to avoid the evil foreseen. On the terms of the argument here presented, however, unless one is willing to regard social responsibility only as an unenforceable appeal to someone's better nature, effective sanctions are required to enforce a responsibility. Such sanctions rely for their effectiveness on a supporting public opinion. We are inquiring, then, whether public opinion supports professional opinion on this issue.

The data available do not permit a conclusive determination of this question, but we can arrive at a tentative judgment.

Only one of the four polls which asked for the identification of unfavorable union practices contains a response category unequivocally related to the wage-price relationship. In the 1941 AIPO poll 2 percent criticized unions on the ground, "Raise cost of living, against common good." Other categories not specifically tagged may well have included this thought, however. Thus on the same 1941 poll 14 percent thought unions "take advantage of their power, never satisfied." It is of course impossible to assess what such respondents had in mind—in what respects does the union abuse its power, with regard to what (power? freedom from management control? income?) are they never satisfied? Similarly, the closest approximation of the wage-price question on the February, 1942, *Fortune* poll was the view expressed by 14.9 percent that unions "have too much power, demand too much, try to run business." It seems apparent that here, as in the previous case, the number who had the effect of union wage demands on prices was something less than the number included in this category. In the NORC poll of May, 1942, 8 percent thought that unions "make unreasonable demands." In the AIPO 1945 poll, 2 percent asserted that their demands were not justified—"wages high enough."

While a contrary case might be made, our conclusion is that such responses do not indicate any substantial public consciousness of unions as the engine of inflation. There is perhaps a greater resentment of the "greediness" of certain unions, a resentment which could as well stem from the fact that the respondent believed he had not fared so well and saw no reason why others should be treated better. But this attitude— if it was a major basis for the opinions expressed—is a far cry from the view that wage increases are themselves harmful because of their economic impact. This tentative conclusion is based upon more than a hunch. There are a number of polls relating directly to the wage and the wage-price issue which suggest this interpretation.

That there is some kind of a relationship between wages and prices appears to be recognized. The fact that wages are a component of costs and that costs are a determinant of prices is apparent to substantial majorities. In four NORC polls conducted between May 22, 1943, and June 23, 1944, between 73 and 78 percent of those responding believed that prices would rise "if there were no limit on wages and salaries." A NORC inquiry of December, 1943, and one by the AIPO in December, 1946, showed 65 and 81 percent respectively believing that pay increases would mean higher prices.[1]

On the basis of this presumed relationship between wages and prices,

[1] Complete results are to be found in Cantril and Strunk, pp. 1004-1005, 1023, and 1025.

sentiment opposed to wage increases and favorable to wage controls has at times been expressed. *Despite* this presumed relationship, attitudes favorable to wage increases and opposed to controls have been voiced at other times. It is important to observe the chronology of the polls available on this issue. And although the interpretation of the apparent shifts in sentiment may be disputed, it is the shifts themselves that are more significant.

The only prewar poll on this matter goes back to June 6, 1937. To an AIPO question, "Are you in favor of higher wages for employees if higher wages mean higher prices?" 66 percent of those expressing an opinion replied Yes, 34 percent No.[2] One might surmise that these results reflect the reaction from a period of depressed incomes, a willingness to gamble on the possibility of price advances following a certainty of wage increases. However that may be, the war years brought a distinct contrast in attitude. Opinion markedly supported a limitation on wages. In two NORC and one AIPO polls of 1942 between 71 and 87 percent believed that wage controls were desirable or necessary to restrain a rise in prices.[3]

Nevertheless, these majorities do not seem to have indicated support for a rigid wage policy. On the contrary, there is evidence of a discriminative attitude. Not all wages should be frozen, nor should all be allowed to increase. No basis for determination of wage actions is identified, however. (It is entirely possible that each respondent primarily had himself or the family breadwinner in mind when replying that *some* wages should be allowed to increase.) Evidence of this screening approach to wages is supplied in one of the polls cited above. The further question was asked of the 85 percent who had expressed themselves *in favor* of a wage ceiling, "Do you think all wages and salaries should be kept where they are now, or do you think some should be allowed to go higher?" Of the *total* sample, 57 percent would have allowed some wages to go higher; only 21 percent wanted all wages kept at existing levels. (The "don't know" category was 7 percent.) In the June 2, 1943, poll of the AIPO on the question, "In the present coal strike do you think the miners should or should not be given a wage increase?" 58 percent said Should, 30 percent Should not, with 12 percent offering no opinion. And in a November 21, 1943, poll by the same agency on the causes for strikes, more respondents pointed to

[2] Cantril and Strunk, p. 1023.
[3] Cantril and Strunk, pp. 141, 1004.

justified wage demands than to unjustified wage demands (15 percent as against 10 percent).[4] There is no evidence here of a dominant attitude unfavorable to *all* wage increases, whether or not inflationary.

In the postwar years, there appeared an increased willingness to support pay advances and, consistent with such a change in attitude, a greater opposition to wage controls. Majorities still favored stable wages, but were significantly reduced; a substantial segment of the sample, at times approaching the size of the majority, supported pay increases. It may perhaps not be reading too much into the data to infer some uncertainty of opinion from the shifting size of the groups favorably and unfavorably disposed toward wage improvements and in particular from the greater number of qualified or "don't know" responses.[5] In five polls taken between January, 1946, and March, 1948, from 30.5 to 42 percent expressed themselves as favorably disposed to granting union demands for higher rates. The 42-percent response, moreover, came in answer to a question whether "workers should be given another wage increase of about 20 percent." Opposition to pay increases was expressed by from 45 to 55.1 percent. The group voicing no opinion or qualified judgments ranged from 12 to 21 percent.[6] It would appear, in general, that slim majorities still favored a policy of stabilizing wages, while a substantial minority would have supported a rising wage level.

That public opinion relative to wage increases had grown more favorable since the war years—or was displaying some ambivalence—is further indicated by the *majorities* supporting "moderate" wage advances. That is, despite the fact that a larger number had expressed themselves as generally preferring wage stability rather than rising wages, when asked about wage increases of specific magnitude even larger majorities *approved* increases of about half the size that the unions were then demanding. It appears that the "greedy" wage demand was frowned on, but that increases of a more modest (yet still substantial) amount were accepted.

In a poll of November 4, 1945, AIPO asked the question: "Because

[4] For these last two polls, see Cantril and Strunk, pp. 822 and 821.

[5] The relevant polls come from Cantril and Strunk, pp. 1016, 1017, and 1024; and *POQ*, Spring, 1948, p. 176, and Summer, 1948, p. 369.

[6] A breakdown of the AIPO poll of January 12, 1947, demonstrates that one's attitude toward wage increases does not follow directly from one's belief in how prices will thereby be affected. The results showed that of those who thought prices must rise if wages do, only 68 percent definitely opposed pay increases for factory workers on this date (21 percent approved, 11 percent had no opinion). And of those who thought wages could be increased without affecting prices, only 57 percent favored increases (32 percent opposed, 11 percent had no opinion).

there is no overtime now, the total weekly pay of many factory workers is less than it was during the war. So that their total weekly pay will be the same as it was during the war, these workers want a 30 percent increase in their hourly rate. Do you think they should or should not receive this increase?" The answers broke down as follows: Should, 33 percent; Should not, 55 percent; No opinion, 12 percent. The 55 percent who had said that wages should not be increased by 30 percent and the 12 percent without opinion were then asked, "Would you favor increasing factory workers' hourly rates by 15 percent?" The replies showed: Yes, 64 percent; No, 27 percent; No opinion, 9 percent.[7]

The net result is a showing that 76 percent of the sample, presumably representative of the general public, favored a wage increase of 15 percent or more. Only 18 percent of the sample opposed such an increase. Six percent were without opinion.

The poll was repeated November 30, 1945. This time an even larger majority—81 percent—were willing to support a wage increase of 15 percent. (Opposed were 14 percent, with 5 percent having no opinion.)[8]

A similar question was asked by AIPO relative to the wages of automobile workers only, rather than of all factory labor. The answers (November 21, 1945) showed that while only 30 percent of the sample would support a wage increase of 30 percent, 68 percent favored a wage increase of 15 percent. (The number opposed to the larger increase was 60 percent, to the smaller one only 22 percent. Ten percent had no opinion, in both cases.)[9]

Two other polls produced similar results. In the winter of 1945-1946 there occurred the General Motors strike, which attracted nationwide attention through the insistence of the United Automobile Workers' president, Walter Reuther, that the union be given "a look at the books" in order to establish whether or not the company could grant the wage increase demanded without raising the price of its cars. The AIPO conducted two polls on public sentiment with respect to this

[7] Cantril and Strunk, p. 1015.

[8] Computed from Cantril and Strunk, p. 1015. On the question of a 30 percent wage increase, the answers were: Yes, 38 percent; No, 52 percent; No opinion, 10 percent. Of the 52 percent saying No and the 10 percent without opinion, 69 percent favored a 15 percent wage increase, 22 percent opposed it, and 9 percent had no opinion.

[9] Cantril and Strunk, p. 1015. It is interesting to note that when the order of the questions was reversed (respondents being asked first whether they approved of 15 percent wage advances, then whether they approved a 30 percent increase), the number of those favorably disposed dropped. Only 54 percent—still a majority—would have supported the 15 percent raise, while a 30 percent increase would have won the backing of only 19 percent.

strike. The first, dated December 5, 1945, indicated that 92 percent of the respondents had heard of the General Motors strike (an extraordinarily high proportion) and 88 percent of this number attributed it to a dispute over a wage issue. Asked whether they thought General Motors workers should "get more pay," 60 percent answered Yes, 22 percent No, and 18 percent had no opinion.[10] In a similar poll of December 19, 1945, 57 percent believed that workers at General Motors should be given a raise. (Opposed were 23 percent, with 20 percent expressing no opinion.)[11]

It appears inescapably paradoxical that majorities could support a policy of wage stabilization while at the same time recording themselves as favorably disposed to "moderate" wage increases. Some explanation may be afforded in the polls which we are about to examine. Substantial segments of the population believe that business—particularly big business—earns profits sufficiently large to enable it to increase wages without increasing prices. It is too much to expect internal consistency in the opinions of a shifting sample of a changing total population over a period of time, but we may conclude that although people readily enough grant a necessary relationship between wages (as a cost item) and prices, they are not prepared to grant that the relationship is such that a given wage increase must necessarily be fully reflected in prices. The attitude favorable to "moderate" wage increases may thus indicate only that people believe that some wage increase can be given without requiring compensating price rises, or perhaps that a wage increase should not be kept from workers simply because a company may unnecessarily raise its prices thereafter.

On this point there are, first, a number of polls showing public opinion on who or what is to blame for rising prices.[12] In an AIPO survey of September 3, 1942, 27 percent of the respondents attributed the increase in food prices to "profiteers; wholesalers; retailers; big business," while only 16 percent of the total charged it to "the high

[10] Cantril and Strunk, p. 825. It is worth remarking that of those familiar with the strike (92 per cent of the sample), 44 percent "sympathized" with the union, 35 percent with the company, 10 percent with neither or both, and 11 percent had no opinion or fell into a miscellaneous category. The 44 percent sympathetic to the union from among those familiar with the strike represents 40 percent of the total sample. It thus appears that although only 40 percent of all respondents were primarily sympathetic with the union, 60 percent were willing to grant the union some wage increase.

[11] Cantril and Strunk, p. 1016.

[12] These polls are contained in Cantril and Strunk, pp. 216-217 and 669-671, except for the two polls in 1947, which are given in POQ, Fall, 1947, p. 492, and Winter, 1947-1948, p. 672.

cost of labor, wage increases and labor shortage; the failure of the government to put a ceiling on wages." In a NORC poll of May 22, 1943, based on a similar question, only 10 percent of the total answered "high wages and demand" or "labor cost." Again, NORC in a poll of May 18, 1944, asked respondents whether they thought food prices would go up or down in the coming year, and among the reasons given for the answers there is no mention of wages, labor, or the unions.

Food, however, is a category in which one might expect less tendency to charge the unions with responsibility for rising prices. And it is true that, in turning to the prices of all products generally, we find the unions being cited by substantial numbers as "mainly responsible" for the upward trend. It is perhaps more significant, however, that in most instances *larger* numbers name business as the responsible agent. Thus in the NORC poll of January 7, 1944, 19 percent of the respondents said that "profiteering and graft" were the cause of the wartime price rises, while only 12 percent laid it to "higher wages." In the AIPO poll of July 24, 1946, perhaps the most startling statistic is that 62 percent of the sample either blamed no one or did not know who was to blame. But 6 percent identified "big business; NAM" and only 4 percent "labor organizations; strikers."

In September, 1946, NORC asked, "Which one of these groups do you think is most to blame for the rising prices—business, labor, or government?" In the replies, 19 percent said business and 22 percent labor. (Government was named by 43 percent, with 16 percent falling in the "don't know" and miscellaneous category.) In an AIPO poll of June 6, 1947, of 49 percent who answered Yes to the question, "Do you blame anyone for present high prices?" 16 percent named "business and industry," and 10 percent identified "labor unions or leaders." In a similar poll of September 21, 1947, of the 50 percent willing to attribute blame, 14 percent laid it to business, 9 percent to labor.

Even more to the point, however, are five polls taken between 1944 and 1947 suggesting public placement of responsibility for price increases following wage increases.[13] To an AIPO question of whether wages can go up without prices going up, 49 percent said that this was possible, only 35 percent expressing a contrary opinion. In December, 1945, 46 percent of AIPO respondents said that the price of new cars should not be increased even if auto workers' wages were raised, in contrast to the 36 percent who believed that management should be permitted price increases to offset higher labor costs.

[13] These are to be found in Cantril and Strunk, pp. 1006 and 1023-1025.

A 1946 AIPO poll revealed that 38 percent believed that if price increases follow wage increases, "big companies are chiefly responsible because they could pay higher wages to workers without increasing prices." Only 29 percent attributed responsibility to the labor unions (25 percent thought both big business and unions were involved, and 8 percent expressed no opinion). NORC found that 56 percent agreed that "most of the really big industries could raise their wages without increasing the price of things they sell." Only 34 percent disagreed. In a similar AIPO inquiry, 47 percent thought wages could be raised by "most factories" without the need for compensating price increases, while 40 percent took a contrary view.

The seeming belief that companies *can* increase wages without a compensating increase in prices coupled with a belief that many companies would not do so, though they could, may explain the apparently conflicting views expressed in answer to two AIPO questions of the same date, October 17, 1945. In the first, respondents were asked, "Do you think that if wages to auto workers are increased by 15 percent, the price of new automobiles will be increased?" Replies were grouped as follows: Yes, 73 percent; No, 16 percent; No opinion, 11 percent.

On the other hand, the question was asked, "Some people say that automobile workers' pay can be increased by 15 percent without making it necessary to increase the price of automobiles. Do you agree or disagree with this?" Agree, 39 percent; Disagree, 33 percent; No opinion 28 percent. While it is entirely possible that the difference in tabulated results is attributable solely to the wording of the question, it also seems possible that some respondents were distinguishing between the necessary and the expected effects of wage increases, with more people expecting consequent price increases than believed them to be necessary.[14]

Whether a belief that companies can raise wages without having to increase the prices of their products is due to an assumption of rising productivity is difficult to say on the evidence available. Only two polls, both by AIPO, bear on this matter.[15] In the first, 43 percent agreed that "the way to keep prices down and wages high is to get each worker to turn out more work per day"—but 44 percent disagreed and 13 percent

[14] Cantril and Strunk, p. 1024. In an AIPO poll of October 19, 1945, substantially similar questions were asked with respect to a 30 percent wage increase. While 78 percent expected resulting price increases, 26 percent thought them unnecessary, 42 percent believed them to be justified, with 32 percent offering no opinion. Cantril and Strunk, p. 1024.

[15] The first (dated 1946) is in Cantril and Strunk, p. 1024, the second in *POQ*, Summer, 1947, p. 312.

had no opinion. In the second, 53 percent agreed that productivity must improve before wages can be raised, with 33 percent disagreeing and 14 percent without opinion. The most conservative inference to be drawn from these two polls—if indeed an inference is justified at all—is that a substantial segment of the public believes that wages can be increased out of some other source than rising productivity, presumably out of profits.

What conclusions can we reach, then, concerning the public attitude toward wage-price relationships? Obviously, conclusions must be treated as tentative, in view of the limitations of the data on which they are based. Nevertheless, we venture the following generalizations:

1. There is a recognition of some wage-price relationship but an uncertainty as to its nature.

2. This recognition leads to (a) an acceptance of wage controls as part of a price control program in times of emergency, and (b) some feeling at all times that unions must exercise a measure of restraint— the "greedy" demand is frowned on.

3. There appears to be, however, an unwillingness to saddle the unions with the sole responsibility for price movements. A large number believe that ultimate responsibility for price movements must rest with businessmen. There seems to be a rather widespread conviction that businesses (a) charge more than they have to charge, "profiteer," and (b) could pay higher wages without raising prices.

4. There is some tendency to be favorably disposed toward "moderate" wage demands by the unions, and without necessarily predicating them upon a prior increase in productivity.

This conclusion of a generally favorable climate of opinion within which unions may seek "moderate" wage improvements is not difficult to explain. The public appears to accept unions as *designed* to improve the economic position of their members. Unions cannot therefore logically be criticized for performing what may be regarded as their primary "natural" function. In a number of polls asking "What good things do you feel unions do?" (or some equivalent question), one reply at or near the top of every list has referred to their role in protecting or raising wages.[16]

This point should not be underrated. It is perhaps even warranted to raise the question whether the public accepts the profit drive of business as fully as the wage drive of unions. Here we may be en-

[16] Cantril and Strunk, p. 873 (Items 19, 20, 21), p. 875 (Item 41); also p. 878 (Item 52).

countering the old, old question of ethical justification. A large part of the public can accept the wage-raising function of unions as "good." It has a seemingly direct connection with mass welfare. Would an equally large proportion of the public accept the profit-making function of business as justified not by the system or by business needs only, but as somehow "good"? There is food for thought here, for both economists and business leaders.

These conclusions are speculative, but it can reasonably enough be asserted from the data cited that the public does not now mirror the alarm of some economists at the inflationary potential of wage increases. Though opinions may change over time, there is at present a tolerant uncertainty that does not add up to opposition. Nor should this be so surprising. In a nation composed largely of wage earners and their families, it may not occur to a substantial proportion of the public that wage increases are to be feared. The wage earner's worry may be his *relative* advance (or decrease), how well he is doing as compared with others. And if he decides that he is losing ground, his resentment may be directed not so much at those fellow wage earners who have won their increase (unless the increase is a "greedy" one) as at the employer who has not granted it, particularly if the latter is showing a profit.

None of this analysis is intended to approve or disapprove the opinions expressed in the polls cited. We have attempted only an objective reading.

PUBLIC JUDGMENTS ON WAGE PRICE RELATIONSHIPS 63

CHAPTER FIVE

Where the Public Stands on Strikes

W E COME now to the only remaining significant category of union behavior criticized on the four open-end polls ("What bad things do you feel unions do?") which we have been using as initial tests of intensity of opinion. This is the issue of strikes. Here we hit pay dirt. Strikes are a phase of union-management relations—and indeed the only identifiable phase—about which the public feels keenly critical.

In the AIPO poll on March 28, 1941, 10 per cent (the third largest group) named strikes as "the chief argument against labor unions."[1] In the remaining polls, strikes ranked Number 1 on the list of union practices found objectionable. In the *Fortune* poll of February, 1942, in answer to the question, "Generally speaking, what bad things do you feel labor unions do?" 40.3 per cent said, "They call strikes, interfere with defense, cause trouble." To a similar question on the NORC poll of May 30, 1942, 15 per cent replied to the effect that unions "call excessive unnecessary strikes." And of the 48 per cent who said that their opinion of unions had deteriorated since before the war, 20 per cent attributed their change in attitude to "too many strikes; strikes during the war," in the AIPO survey of March 20, 1945.

Nor need we rely solely on these four polls to establish with what degree of feeling the public has regarded strikes. On numerous occasions during the past fifteen years various polling agencies have asked respondents to name the most important problem facing the nation.

---

[1] Fourteen percent answered that they "take advantage of their power, never satisfied," and 12 percent that there were "racketeers, exploiters among the leaders." It will be recalled that these categories have not been analyzed because it is impossible to identify them as being associated only with the management relation, in contrast to relations with other groups such as members, nonmember workers, the public, or government.

Strikes have almost uniformly appeared on such listings,[2] often mentioned by only small percentages (from 1 to 9 per cent over the years 1935-1941, for example) but nonetheless ranking relatively high (from third to eighth most frequently mentioned problem in the period mentioned, for example). More significant than the frequency of listing, however, has been the fact that recurringly strikes have appeared at the top of the list as that problem named by more respondents than any other as the most vital. That this may happen under peculiar circumstances (as, for example, during the conduct of a war or in the face of the postwar pressure for the satisfaction of pent-up consumer wants) does not wholly reduce the significance of the fact. Of all aspects of the union-management relationship, strikes are the *only* issue which has been designated not only as a major problem of that relationship itself, but as a major *national* problem. Strikes (sometimes unfortunately coupled, in the system of classification, with "labor-management problems") were given Number 1 status in polls of June, 1943, February 26, November 13, and December 31, 1946, January 31, 1947, and November 25, 1949, by percentages ranging from 18 to 40, and were listed as the Number 2 national problem in polls of October, 1945, and September 25, 1946, by 18 and 32 percent of the respondents polled, respectively. It seems clear, moreover, that in a period when national security and welfare are likely to hang for an indefinite future on productive efficiency, the "peculiar" circumstances of the war and immediate postwar years are likely to reassert themselves, engendering the same public response to strikes.

We can, then, turn to the polls specifically relating to strikes with some assurance that these are not simply expressions of "general principle," but opinions carrying some degree of intensity of feeling. The number of polls relating to strikes is large, and for purposes of simplicity we shall classify them by major characteristics. The results of such classification suggest the following conclusions:

1. Substantial majorities favor rigorous wartime control of strikes.
2. Substantial majorities favor rigorous control of strikes occurring

---

[2] Cantril and Strunk, pp. 678-683. *POQ*, Summer, 1947, p. 293; Summer, 1948, p. 358; Fall, 1948, pp. 557-558; Winter, 1947-1948, pp. 657-658; Spring, 1949, p. 167; Spring, 1950, p. 182; Fall, 1950, pp. 602-603.

In a poll of October 15, 1947, 32 percent of the respondents named "labor troubles, strikes" as an important national problem, but not necessarily the major one. *POQ*, Winter, 1947-1948, pp. 657-658.

in peacetime under emergency conditions, such as preparation for defense or reconversion from war to civilian production.

3. Majorities would subject all peacetime strikes to restraints, and large minorities would outlaw all peacetime strikes.

4. There is a majority sentiment to prohibit strikes in essential industries or to subject them to restraints.

5. There is a majority sentiment opposed to sympathetic, jurisdictional, and general strikes and strikes in the civil service.

We shall summarize the poll materials prompting each of these conclusions. Let us turn our attention first to the data dealing with strikes in wartime.

At least ten polls were taken within the period February 23, 1942, through March 7, 1945, on the general question, "Should Congress pass a law forbidding strikes in war industries until the war is over, or should the workers in war industries continue to have the right to go on strike?"[3] The results are shown in the following table:

Date	Forbid Strikes %	Permit Strikes %	No Opinion %	Polling Agency
Immediately after Pearl Harbor	87.2	7	5.8	*Fortune*
February 23, 1942	86	9	5	AIPO
May 30, 1942	88	8	4	NORC
January 20, 1943	81	13	6	AIPO
June 16, 1943	81	19	—	AIPO
June 18, 1943	86	10	4	NORC
November 21, 1943	69	23	8	AIPO
January 4, 1944	76	15	9	AIPO
June 2, 1944	70[a]	15	15	AIPO
March 7, 1945	75	20	5	AIPO

a In this poll, of union members asked 64 percent replied that there was need for a law to prevent strikes in war industries. (26 percent said there was no such need, and 10 percent did not know.)

An overwhelming sentiment for outlawing strikes in war industries in time of war is evident. But this is not all. Substantial majorities expressed themselves in favor of outlawing *all* strikes in wartime. Thus,

[3] This was the form in which the question was asked by AIPO in seven polls. In an eighth by the same organization the question was phrased, "Do you think there is a need for law to prevent strikes in war industries?" In two polls by NORC the question was asked, "As things are now, do you think workers in war industries should or should not have the right to strike?" *Fortune's* question was in the form, "Do you feel that Congress should or should not pass a law forbidding strikes in defense industries for the duration of the emergency?" These questions are sufficiently similar in nature for us to consider the results to be comparable. The polls are to be found in Cantril and Strunk, pp. 818-823.

in the two NORC polls listed above (May 30, 1942, and June 18, 1943), those who replied that strikes should not be permitted in war industries were asked the further question, "How about workers who are not in war industries? Do you think they should have the right to strike during wartime?" Replies broke down into the following percentages of the total sample:

	Should	Should Not	Don't Know	Total Who Would Ban Strikes in War Industries
	%	%	%	%
May 30, 1942	11	74	3	= 88
June 18, 1943	9	73	4	= 86

Two AIPO polls support this result. In that of December 15, 1942, 89 percent thought that all strikes should be forbidden for the duration of the war, while in that of July 12, 1945, 78 percent believed that Congress should pass a law forbidding strikes in all industries during wartime. Some indication of the strength of feeling on this issue is perhaps afforded by replies to an AIPO question of May 23, 1944, showing 68 percent who would favor a law permitting local draft boards to draft any striker between the ages of 18 and 45.[4]

Finally, on the matter of wartime strikes, we have three polls which ask open-end questions on what should be done about strikes; that is, the respondents instead of being asked to favor or oppose some specific measure were asked to name the remedy they themselves would advocate.[5] Classifying replies to the first of those inquiries, we could say that 26 percent would forbid or "stop" strikes, 24 percent would take some punitive action against strikers, such as imprisonment or drafting them for military duty, and 22 percent would resort to government seizure of the company or compulsory arbitration. If we accept these three categories as all indicating a generally unfavorable attitude

[4] Cantril and Strunk, pp. 819, 824, and 468.

[5] These, in order, are from Cantril and Strunk, pp. 823, 824, and 824. The public has tended to favor almost any measure to control strikes about which it has been asked, even when these appear inconsistent. Although majorities had been expressing themselves as disposed to *outlaw* all strikes, in an AIPO poll of July 12, 1945, 77 percent answered that they would favor a law compelling employers and unions to submit their differences to a federal labor board *before a strike could be called* in war industries (Cantril and Strunk, p. 15). Respondents in these surveys have been concerned with only one result—that somehow strikes be rigorously controlled—and they would willingly support almost any measure which is designed to exercise some control over strikes.

One of the few questions eliciting a negative response to a proposed strike curb was that in the AIPO poll of April 30, 1941, in which 63 percent opposed a bill "which would treat any worker who goes on strike in a defense industry as a traitor, to be punished by one year in prison" (Cantril and Strunk, p. 819).

toward strikes, the total opposition is 72 percent of the sample polled. (At most, 15 percent indicated an attitude generally favorable toward permitting strikes to be conducted without interference, and 13 percent expressed no opinion.)

Replies to the second of these three open-end questions are less easily classified, but it appears reasonable to say that 32 percent would take punitive action against strikers and 13 percent would outlaw strikes, resort to government seizure or compulsory arbitration, suggesting 45 percent favoring a strict control over strikes. Perhaps 26 percent supported ameliorative action without controlling strikes ("give better wages," "treat workers fairly," "educate people on how to get what they want," etc.) while 4 percent would do nothing about strikes, for a total of 21 percent who may be said to oppose stringent strike control. The "no opinion" group is a sizable 30 percent.[6]

Finally, an AIPO poll of April 7, 1945, asked what the government should do "if the coal miners go on strike this spring." While the grouping of replies was poor, it seems clear that at least 74 percent of the respondents advocated strong action to prevent a strike in the mines.

On the basis of these data, the conclusion seems supportable that there is strong public opposition to *all* strikes during time of war. It likewise seems clear that the public is disposed to curb strikes in emergency periods, when a need for expanded production is felt, even though the nation is not at war. The two periods most nearly meeting this condition within the time when public opinion polls have been systematically undertaken are those of the pre-World War II defense preparation and the postwar reconversion to civilian production.

Public opinion regarding strikes in the months of defense preparation prior to the declaration of war in December, 1941, was not markedly different from opinion during the war itself. As in the latter instance there was in the former a majority sentiment, ranging from 58.4 to 78.3 percent, for outlawing strikes in defense industries.[7] In addition we have one AIPO open-end question, allowing respondents to name their own remedy for strikes during the period of defense build-up, "if you were in the President's position."[8] If we take the

---

[6] The figures add to more than 100 percent since some respondents gave more than one reply. The "miscellaneous" category has been arbitrarily included with the 26 percent opposing strict strike control.

[7] The relevant polls come from Cantril and Strunk, pp. 818-820, and *POQ*, Spring, 1942, pp. 166 and 167.

[8] Cantril and Strunk, p. 821.

replies advocating "anti-strike legislation," "government control where trouble is" or "of all industry during emergency," "compulsory arbitration," and "absolute authority to NDMB" as indicating a desire for strong governmental regulation of strikes, and add in the 11 percent of the replies that would punish strikers or their leaders, we have a total of 49 percent expressing a desire for strict control of strikes. The rest of the replies are really indeterminate. "Same as Roosevelt," "leave it to Congress," and even "arbitrate—no force" give little indication of respondents' attitudes toward the strike issue, nor does the miscellaneous category. We thus have 49 percent favoring strike control, 19 percent indeterminate, and 34 percent expressing no opinion, the total exceeding 100 percent since some interviewees gave more than one reply.

If these data support the conclusion that strikes in essential industries during a period of defense preparation are regarded unfavorably by public majorities, it likewise appears that numbers, ranging from between one third and two thirds of the samples, are in favor of stringent curbs on strikes in *all* industries during an emergency.[9] A *Fortune* survey of June, 1941, showed that *among factory labor only* opinions on this score did not differ much from the national sample. Proportionately as many were in favor of a compulsory settlement of union-management differences. Five percent more were opposed; 5 percent fewer were without opinion. That opposition to strike action during periods of emergency defense preparation was not confined to the pre-World War II mobilization is indicated by an AIPO poll following the outbreak of fighting in Korea. Seventy-nine percent believed that Congress should pass a law forbidding strikes in plants and factories that would be important in wartime.[10]

It is perhaps stretching the classification to speak of the postwar reconversion period as one of "emergency," and yet there is some basis for so doing. Consumers who had gone without many types of goods for as long as five years were impatient of further delays; many were disposed to think of their desired purchases as pressing and "necessitous." A smaller number may have been concerned about the actual process of reconversion, worrying that delays in that process might endanger continuity of employment. Some may have been troubled about the effect of labor disputes on that production which was to have been a counter to inflationary forces. Whatever label may be put upon

[9] Cantril and Strunk, pp. 15, 819-821.
[10] *POQ*, Spring, 1951, p. 178. The poll was dated October 8, 1950.

the period, it was clearly one of unusual pressures for uninterrupted production. It is not surprising, therefore, that the prevalent attitude was reflected in public sentiment with respect to strikes. Four open-end polls conducted by the AIPO over a fourteen-month period, September, 1945, to November, 1946, provide the supporting data.[11] Although the classification of answers makes conclusion difficult, it would appear that from 48 to 59 percent of the public was prepared to impose some limitation on use of the strike during the reconversion period. Another AIPO survey strengthens this conclusion. Some 70 percent concurred with Baruch's suggestion that all strikes and lockouts be called off for a year.[12]

We conclude, then, that the public is disposed to regard unfavorably strikes during wartime and during peacetime emergency situations, and substantial numbers (majorities in the former case and perhaps in the latter as well) would favor some form of control over use of the strike under such conditions.

What about strikes under normal peacetime conditions, however? Results from polls taken before the defense mobilization period beginning about 1940 and subsequent to the reconversion period, as well as from some taken during wartime but relating to time of peace, suggest that minorities ranging up to one third of the sample favor outlawing all strikes under normal peacetime conditions. Moreover, majorities have favored almost any proposal for postponing or resolving a strike situation.[13]

The sentiment with respect to restricting the freedom to strike (in contrast to forbidding strikes altogether) was given one of its earliest expressions in an AIPO poll of July 4, 1937, when 84 percent of those offering an opinion replied affirmatively to the inquiry, "Would you

[11] They are given in Cantril and Strunk on pp. 824, 826, 828, and 931.

[12] Cantril and Strunk, p. 826. This poll also points up that opposition to strikes cannot necessarily be taken to mean support for making them illegal. The further question was asked of the 70 percent who agreed that all strikes and lockouts should be called off for a year, "Do you think a law should be passed forbidding all strikes and lockouts for a year?" The affirmative answers fell to 54 percent.

[13] There is a problem in determining which poll materials should be included under this classification. Some surveys were made during wartime or emergency conditions but asked about peacetime situations. The results may easily have been influenced by the events at the time of questioning, however. Nor is it possible to draw any line separating the postwar reconversion period from postwar normalcy. In general, we have used such surveys as relate to peacetime conditions, regardless of conditions at the time of survey, and have construed the period of reconversion to have ended with 1946. These polls are found in Cantril and Strunk, pp. 396, 824; POQ, Summer, 1947, p. 311, and Summer, 1949, p. 353.

favor laws regulating the conduct of strikes?" Since that time numerous proposals, ranging from supervised strike votes to compulsory settlement, have been made the basis for opinion surveys. Without attempting to list them all, we may note that 86 percent of those giving opinions favored "a law requiring employers and workers to submit their difference to a federal labor board before a strike could be called" (AIPO, May 26, 1939); 70 percent of the total sample supported "a law requiring employers and unions to take their differences to a federal labor board before a strike could be called in any industry" (AIPO, July 12, 1945); 79 percent would require "employers and unions to take their differences to a government arbitrator for settlement before a strike could be called" (AIPO, October 3, 1945); 70 percent would require that threatened strikes be forestalled by a binding decision of a special labor court (AIPO, October 17, 1945); 75.8 percent would require the union to "let a management representative state the company's side of the dispute" when a strike vote is being taken at a union meeting (*Fortune*, November, 1946); 58 percent believed that strike voting should be under government supervision (AIPO, November 27, 1946); from 78 to 84 percent favored a thirty-day cooling-off period during which a fact-finding committee would prepare a public report (AIPO, in four polls from December 5, 1945, to February 13, 1946).[14]

In such expressions respondents may be more concerned with the "important" strike than with all strikes. The *Fortune* poll of November, 1946, suggested to the interviewee a number of possible ways of dealing with a strike situation, and then requested him to designate which method he would prefer, first, in the case of "a small electrical manufacturing company (employing about 200 people)," and then in the case of "a large electrical manufacturer like General Electric or Westinghouse."[15] The results suggest that the public would allow a greater degree of voluntarism in labor-management dealings in small concerns than in the case of large corporations. Of the total sample, 51.2 percent would have the government either stay out or simply offer its services when a small enterprise is affected. Only 37.3 percent would have the government forcibly intervene, and of these less than half (18.6 percent—still a sizable number) are favorable to compulsory settlement. But with respect to threatened strikes in a large corporation the proportions are virtually reversed. Voluntarism is supported by

---

14 Cantril and Strunk, pp. 817, 15, 16, 332, 829, and 16.
15 Cantril and Strunk, pp. 882 and 17.

only 33.6 percent of the total, while 54.3 percent would support compulsory government intervention. More than half of this latter group (30.2 percent, or close to one third of the total) would go so far as to advocate compulsory settlement. Moreover, in this poll a higher proportion of salaried executives than of union members is disposed to favor government intervention in both large and small concerns. Indeed, a higher proportion of salaried executives than of the general public would accept compulsory action. This attitude on the part of executives may reflect only the timing of the poll, however, since at the time of its taking—late 1946—the unions may have had some bargaining advantage due to the continued pressure of consumer demand for finished products.

If the size of an enterprise affects public opinion on strikes, the nature of a company's services is no less relevant. There appears to be a substantial sentiment for limiting or prohibiting strikes in enterprises supplying goods or services deemed especially vital to the community. In some cases majorities would support an outright ban on strikes in "essential" industries.

On at least three occasions AIPO has asked: "Should laws be passed to forbid all strikes in public service industries such as electric, gas, telephone and local transportation companies?"[16] Majorities of from 58 to 64 percent have supported such legislation. The opposition has been no more than from 29 to 32 percent. (From 7 to 12 percent were without opinion.) Separate totals for respondents who were union members, in two of the surveys, reveal that even a high proportion of their number would favor a prohibition on strikes in the selected industries (40 and 49 percent), and in the May, 1946, poll actually more union members voted to curb such strikes than to permit them (49 as against 44 percent). Separate totals for manual workers in the third of these polls, conducted in 1947, showed that a majority of manual workers would similarly have banned strikes in the industries named (52 as against 33 percent who would have allowed them). This result, which on first encounter may appear surprising, is more readily understood if we remember that among union members and workers, no less than among other segments of the public, strikes in the industries named—electric, gas, telephone, and local transportation—would have their adverse impact (by threat of loss if not by actual loss of the service) and that consciousness of this adverse impact may overcome feelings of "principle." A threat to one's supply of gas and electricity, and to a lesser extent to

16 Cantril and Strunk, p. 826, and *POQ*, Summer, 1947, p. 311.

his use of the telephone, implies almost a threat to one's family. Is it then so surprising that union members and manual workers generally would recognize the threat before a "principle," expressing in large numbers their opposition even to a weapon which so many of them had been taught to cherish, because it appeared to conflict with other more cherished values? The right to strike may be a sacred principle—until it impairs other rights of expectancy held in even higher esteem.

A *Fortune* survey of November, 1946, sought people's opinions concerning strikes on the railroads.[17] Approximately 42 percent favored voluntary settlement, but 45.6 percent would require compulsory arbitration. Of union members participating, almost 40 percent supported compulsory awards, though a majority of union members (54.6 percent) believed in voluntary methods of agreement. When the telephone industry is singled out for somewhat similar questioning, the results are less conclusive. Nevertheless, it is clear that sentiment for outlawing telephone strikes is likewise strong. In two polls of 1946 and 1947, 42.5 and 49 percent would have banned such stoppages, while 44.5 and 38 percent would have allowed them. (In both polls, 13 percent were undecided.)[18]

On the question of limiting the right to strike in vital industries, without actually denying it, the favorable majorities increase markedly. A 1949 AIPO poll showed 87 percent (including 81 percent of the union members participating) favoring a law requiring unions in "vital industries" to give sixty days' notice before striking, while a survey by the same agency in the same year indicated that 79 percent (including 74 percent of the union members participating) believed the federal government should be allowed the right of injunction against strikes in "public service" industries for a period during which the issues could be discussed.[19]

Finally, in our classification of strikes, we can record—on the basis of admittedly sketchy evidence but consistently with the general indictment of strikes—that the public appears to regard with disfavor sympathetic strikes, general strikes, jurisdictional strikes, and strikes of government employees.[20]

This condemnation of strikes under almost all circumstances may suggest that the American public is opposed to unionism or is at least

[17] Cantril and Strunk, pp. 882-883.
[18] Cantril and Strunk, pp. 827-828, and *POQ*, Summer, 1947, p. 311.
[19] *POQ*, Summer, 1949, p. 352, and Winter, 1949-50, pp. 731-732.
[20] Cantril and Strunk, pp. 821, 827-828; and *POQ*, Summer, 1947, p. 312, and Summer, 1949, p. 366.

opposed to the objectives which unions seek through strike action. Such a conclusion would be erroneous. There is no need to cite here those polls indicating that the American public has generally shown a favorable attitude toward unions.[21] More revealing is public sentiment toward the parties in actual strike situations.

If we go back to 1937, when the CIO was militantly seeking to organize basic industries, we find at least two polls taken during time of strike. The results show only a slight pro-management favoritism.[22] According to AIPO, 44 percent sympathized with "the John L. Lewis group" and 56 percent with the employers in the General Motors strike of 1937. In the steel strike of the same year, the sympathies of 46 percent of those expressing an opinion were with the strikers and of 54 percent with the companies.

Again in the postwar period we have records of public sympathies toward the parties to a strike situation. Again we find the public as inclined to regard the union's cause favorably as to support management's position. In two AIPO surveys of December 5 and 19, 1945, of those who had knowledge of the Automobile Workers' strike at General Motors, the further question was asked, "Which side are you more inclined to sympathize with?"[23] The responses divided as follows:

	Union or Strikers	Company or Management	Neither, Both, Undecided, or Don't Know
	%	%	%
December 5, 1945	44	35	21
December 19, 1945	36	40	24

On January 23, 1946, AIPO asked: "In the present General Motors strike, which do you think is more in the right—the workers or the company? In the meat packing industry strikes; in the steel industry; electrical industry?"[24] The results showed:

	Workers	Company	Both Right or Both Wrong	No Opinion
	%	%	%	%
General Motors	33	24	23	20
Meat packing	31	16	16	37
Steel	33	20	23	24
Electrical	28	15	15	42

[21] Some polls of this nature are to be found in Cantril and Strunk, p. 871 ff.
[22] Cantril and Strunk, pp. 816-817.
[23] Cantril and Strunk, p. 825.
[24] Cantril and Strunk, p. 825. The following *Fortune* poll is from p. 827, and the AIPO poll of November 27, 1946, from p. 829.

In a *Fortune* survey of November, 1946, of those who admitted to knowledge of postwar strikes in General Motors, the coal mines, and on the railroads, the further question was asked: "Which side did you favor more, that of the strikers or that of the company?" The responses broke down as follows:

	Strikers	Company	Don't Know
	%	%	%
General Motors	27.0	24.9	17.4
Coal	49.4	20.0	15.9
Railroads	31.1	32.7	20.2

Although almost 50 percent of those who were aware that there had been a coal strike sympathized with the miners, nevertheless an AIPO poll of approximately the same date (November 27, 1946) showed that only 20 percent of a national sample believed that the miners were justified in staying away from work. (65 percent said they were not justified, and 15 percent offered no opinion.)

The same contrast between sympathy for the strikers' position and disfavor over use of the strike weapon is shown in the AIPO poll of April 29, 1947, relative to the national telephone strike. Although twice as many respondents were sympathetic toward telephone workers as toward the telephone company (48 percent as against 24 percent), nevertheless more than half of all respondents (57 percent) believed that the United States government should require telephone workers to go back to work while the strike was being settled.[25]

The public's dissatisfaction with strikes thus does not spring from a procompany or antiunion bias. It appears to be rooted in a belief that in a great many instances strikes constitute a relationship between two parties, a union and a management, which somehow fails to fit into a comity of social relationships.

Summary

Let us recapitulate the findings of this and the two preceding chapters. We started out to identify the areas in which union-management relations were considered inconsistent with other rights of relationship in the community. To ascertain sentiment on this matter we resorted to the public opinion polls of the last fifteen years. Our investigation disclosed that there are relatively few aspects of the union-management relation about which the public feels strongly. Featherbedding and

[25] *POQ*, Summer, 1947, p. 312.

union security provisions are opposed "on principle," but the public appears not to feel sufficiently affected by such practices to take strong stands concerning them. On wage-price relationships there seems to be an ambivalent attitude—a recognition that rising wages as costs contribute to rising prices, on the one hand, and on the other a belief that businesses (and in particular the large corporations) can raise wages without raising prices. Except in periods when explicit government controls over wages exist, public sentiment tends to view favorably union drives for moderate wage increases, accepting the objective of higher wages as perhaps the primary purpose behind union organization itself.

With respect to these issues, featherbedding, union security, and wages, frequently mentioned in popular and professional writings as areas where the unions must exercise social responsibility, we can only conclude that any belief by members of the general public that their rights are thereby adversely affected is not sufficiently strong to require modification in the parties' conduct. The fact that a number of labor specialists or professional economists may believe that unions should (for example) forego wage increases in the public interest does not convert such a prescription into a social responsibility. When the public accepts or tolerates union activity, as to raise wages, there is little basis for condemning such activity as an evasion of *social* responsibility. One may argue that a union leader or a business manager who comes to believe that (for example) wages should be restrained in the interests of society should act on that belief regardless of public pressure. But this is to urge a kind of *personal* morality; the issue becomes one of an individual's conscience. It is not a social responsibility in any sense that exacts of him a course of conduct *regardless* of personal belief.

Only with respect to strikes do we encounter a union-management issue which seems to arouse widespread adverse criticism, presumably felt with some intensity. This criticism embodies more than lip service to some vaguely held principle—indeed among large numbers of union members it appears to override such a time-honored "principle" as the sanctity of the right to strike. Moreover, featherbedding, union shops, or wage raises—issues which do not much interest the public—may take on greater significance if tied into the strike issue. Public opposition to strikes may be intensified if the strike is over some matter which the public either deems inconsequential or opposes "on principle," but it is still the strike which is condemned under such circumstances and not the bargaining issue.

We hypothesize that the strike is stigmatized as a relationship between a union and a management which contravenes important rights of expectancy entertained by those not party to the specific union or management. It is our assumption that public opposition to strikes springs from a feeling that other people's rights are unwarrantedly trampled on by the particular union and management. Special-interest groups are viewed as unmindful of the rights of others, insufficiently concerned to bring their relationship into some reasonable consistency with the whole structure of relationships in the society. If our analysis is correct, we may expect that in time the parties will be coerced by popular sanctions into recognizing the social responsibility of achieving a compatibility between their relationships and other important relationships in the community.

Nor need we assume that it is necessary for the public to maintain its opposition to strikes at a white heat in order for it to become effective in forcing upon the parties a recognition of their social responsibility. If public opposition recurs frequently and with considerable intensity, that may be sufficient. But *recurring* condemnation or *waves* of intensity of feeling, in contrast to a persistently strong sentiment, may slow the process of change. Moreover, it may take time for sanctions to be mobilized, for the parties to learn their effectiveness, for particular solutions to be offered, weighed, and decided upon. There is no reason, then, to expect *imminent* modification of the union-management relationship as to strikes.

Nevertheless, it is in the matter of strikes, and not on any other issue, that unions and managements must *now* feel the weight of public opinion. If wages or union shops or other matters are brought into the picture and assume temporary prominence, their importance is based upon their relationship to the strike issue. It is the strike issue therefore that we shall examine more closely. We are interested in isolating the publics of specific strikes—those who are consciously affected. We want to know how their opinions come to be felt by the parties. What form may public sanctions against the parties take?

C H A P T E R S I X

The Real Basis for Public Opinion:
The Effects of Strikes

I F THE one aspect of union-management relations to which there appears to be general opposition is the strike, why does opposition arise here? What is there about strikes (and here the term is used broadly to include lockouts as well) that arouses public resentment?

The simplest answer is that a strike is likely to injure not simply the party against whom it is directed but the public as well. Before a strike leads to agreement, the public may have been subjected to substantial inconvenience. Indeed, at times the "innocent" public seems to be regarded by the parties only as a weapon or bludgeon to be used to force surrender; each side proclaims its sympathy for the public, which is being abused by the other's adamant refusal of concession, and seeks to align public support for its own position by expressing sympathetic concern for public welfare. But what is the basis for the public's involvement?

The structure of economic relationships in our society is based on specialization of services. In general, each individual becomes attached to a unit which is geared to produce services or goods of a particular, specialized type. So familiar are we with this specialization that we have taken certain corollaries for granted. One important corollary of specialized production is the mutual dependency of producers. Each individual can afford to specialize only because other specialists will make available goods and services which he demands. A worker can afford to be a full-time assemblyman in an automobile plant only because he knows that other workers will build his house for him; provide him with electric power, gas, and water; produce food and clothing for his use; and so on. In this mutual dependency, individuals come to experience a right of expectancy of the provision of the goods and services

78

on which they rely. Indeed, our material culture has built into it an expectation that electric power, telephone service, and fuel for heating and cooking will be with us each morning on rising as surely as daylight, and without any personal responsibility other than the payment of bills. In similar fashion if lesser degree, we all carry expectations that the local transit service will pick us up in the morning, that schools will take care of our children, that restaurants will feed us, theaters and movie houses entertain us, and so on.

While division of labor establishes our dependence as consumers on other producers, and it is this that we are most inclined to consider, it is equally true that the economy of specialization leaves us dependent as producers on other consumers. The lathe operator who expects to buy the goods of other specialists must himself have a market for his services. The trucker who is to enjoy the fruits of the work of others must be able to market his own skills. In the integrated pecuniary economy, our consuming capacity is largely dependent on our producing capacity. From our functions as suppliers of specialized services we derive the income permitting us to purchase the product of others' specialized work. All this is a familiar story, but it must be retold as a reminder that we develop rights of expectancy in the marketing of our own services no less than in the buying of the services of others. We entertain an expectation of continued income as long as we do our jobs adequately and as long as consumers demand our services.

But the strike sometimes frustrates such an expectation. When the struck firm suspends operations it ceases to buy materials, and the repercussions may be felt on many suppliers beyond the struck firm itself. The effects can spread by chain reaction. Each producer who is no longer able to sell to the struck firm, and who therefore reduces his own operations, curtails his purchases from others, and so on in almost indefinite regression. Numerous individuals whose livelihoods depend on continued earnings, and who have been performing their duties as required, and whose services are still desired by ultimate consumers, may thus suddenly find themselves cut off from a market for their labor because of a strike. In some types of strikes—notably coal and steel—the number affected as producers may actually be greater than the number affected as consumers. Once again, the expectations on which we assume our specialized producing roles are frustrated. Not only may a strike deprive us of the flow of goods and services on which we depend; it may also deprive us of an outlet for our own goods or services, on the sale of which we equally depend.

To the extent that a strike inconveniences us, then, it frustrates our rights of expectation, rights which are just as surely built into our culture as if they were matters of law. Only the fact that serious frustration of such rights has been sufficiently infrequent has permitted us to accommodate over the years two essentially conflicting rights—the right to strike and the right to expect continued provision of specialized services. Yet there can be little doubt about the inconsistency of these two rights, expressed as absolutes, and depending on the nature of their conflict some resolution may emerge, over time, which will reduce the content of one or both rights. One may interpret the critical content of public opinion polls on this matter as evidence that a rather large portion of the population recognizes an inconsistency between the right to strike (by others) and its own expectations, and that it would approve a resolution of this conflict which would modify the right to strike.

Nevertheless, although this may represent a satisfactory generalization, there is room for believing that the public does not regard all strikes in the same light. Strikes in wartime are condemned more unreservedly than strikes in time of peace; strikes in "essential" industries are viewed with less sympathy than strikes in general; strikes in large corporations are more frowned on than strikes in small enterprises. This discriminatory approach is, of course, a reflection of the fact that strikes affect the public in varying respects and degree, or, to put it more precisely, each strike affects differently a different public. To the extent that a strike affects a larger public or affects it more drastically, it arouses greater public opposition.

These observations are preliminary to the more difficult problem of distinguishing between strikes on the basis of their effects on the public.

Any strike has a potential effect on the household consumers of that product. It is this effect that we primarily have in mind when we speak of the impact of strikes. Yet this initial consequence is only one of a chain of effects and indeed may be the least important. In addition to household consumers, other individuals are affected in their capacity as producers or because of a relationship to producers. First, there are the families of the parties themselves, a group so intimately associated with union and management that we tend to identify them as one of the parties. Actually, families are party to the dispute only by relationship and deserve consideration in their own right. The striker's wife who struggles to make ends meet when her husband's income has been cut off, the manager's wife whose home may be picketed, are entitled to independent identification as an affected strike public. Their views with respect to the acceptability of the strike technique (in distinction to its specific issues) may differ from the views of their husbands. Second, there are the employees of the struck plant who are not actually party to the dispute—the clerical or sales force, possibly the maintenance employees, foremen, members of "middle" management. Third, there are the suppliers of goods and services to all the individuals who are members of the struck plant. These would include the local merchants, landlords, churches, outlying farmers, and so on, and their employees, for all of whom employment or income, or both, might be reduced in consequence of the strike. Fourth, there are the firms which supply goods and services (primarily materials, equipment, and transportation) to the struck plant, whose members (from owners to employees) may likewise be affected income-wise. Fifth, there are the firms which use the struck product in their own productive operations, and whose output may have to be curtailed if another source is not discovered. In all these cases where the strike has its impact on producers, the effect is transmitted not only to the producer as an individual (and "producer" includes, of course, all employees engaged in production processes) but also to his family. The number may run high of those who are thus involved not as household consumers of the struck product but as producers whose operations are somehow affected by failure of supply of that product.

But where can the line be drawn? The indirect effects of a strike may ramify throughout the economy. The producers whose operations are curtailed because of the strike likewise market goods and services. These too have their household consumers, their suppliers, their commercial users. The cycle continues. Each of these suppliers has its own suppliers. Each of these producers has its products, shortage of which affects their particular household and commercial consumers, as well as suppliers. There is an almost infinite regression of effects—potentially. Whether these effects appear, or the degree to which they appear, is dependent on such factors as the characteristics of the product, the extent of the bargaining unit which is struck (single firm or industry), and the duration of the strike, as we shall shortly see.

There thus emerges the notion of constructing a scale on which strikes might be rated in terms of their impact on the public, a scale which would take into account—for any given strike—the total effect on (1) household consumers of the struck product; (2) the "direct" producers, by which is meant (a) nonparty members and families of all members of the struck unit, (b) commercial users of the struck product, and (c) suppliers of the struck unit and its members; (3) the "indirect" producers, who are (a) the suppliers of the commercial users of the struck product and suppliers of the suppliers of the struck firm, and (b) commercial users of the products of the commercial users of the struck product; and (4) household consumers patronizing any of the "indirect" producers, whom we will refer to as "indirect" consumers.

The construction of such a scale has several uses. It requires an examination of what factors actually determine the impact on the public of any strike, which in itself is a useful task and not as simple as appears on its face. It also permits the ranking of strikes to show which are more public-affecting than others. Finally, it suggests the changing nature of public-affectedness of any strike as the strike continues, thus providing an answer to such a question as, What will be the impact on the public of a coal strike (which begins now) on the first day, the tenth day, or the fortieth day of the strike?

Another interest in the construction of such a rating scale is that by establishing the extent of a strike's impact on the public it reveals the "real basis" for public opinion concerning the strike relationship between unions and managements. It helps in understanding why public opinion should regard particular strikes as conflicting with rights of expectation of a continued flow of a product or service more seriously than in other cases.

In rating strikes by the extent of their effect on the public, we shall first evaluate separately a strike's impact on consumers and producers. Later we shall have to break these two broad categories into finer categories, in accord with the groups identified above, but for the moment let us concentrate on these two major subdivisions. In the case of each, we shall try to set up the principal considerations which determine how important the loss of the struck product is in the lives of those affected. These principal considerations will be set up in the form of continua, that is, scales on which any strike may be rated as affecting the public, in the given respect, anywhere from the least possible to the most possible degree, from 0 to 100 percent (though here we shall use a scale of 10 to represent all possible values). The significance of such continua will become more evident as the discussion proceeds.

Let us, then, consider the impact of any strike on the household consumers of the product involved. That impact is a resultant of three
considerations, which we shall here refer to as (1) the cultural necessity
of the product, (2) the stock effect, and (3) the substitutability effect.
We shall examine each of these.

By cultural necessity of the product is meant how important the
product is in the lives of those who consume it, how vital in their
structures of living. Here the term "cultural" is meant to subsume not
only the need which a given civilization has created for a particular
good or service (though that is frequently the relevant consideration);
it includes also the biological needs (as for water or food, without respect to form or variety). This cultural need for the product is easy to
confuse with a consideration which we shall examine later—the substitutability of other products for the given one. It may be thought, at
first, that no product is vital as long as there are adequate substitutes
for it, so that how vital a product is, in fact, depends on how satisfactory
are its substitutes. To avoid this confusion it may be worth while to
think of cultural necessity as how vital in the lives of its consumers is a
given product *or any satisfactory substitute for it.*

Examples may further help to clarify the significance of cultural
necessity. Let us say that the only newspaper in a town, the local transit
service, milk delivery, grand pianos, all have no very acceptable substitutes for most of their consumers. Although resort may be had to radio
news or out-of-town papers, walking or private cars, canned milk or
other beverages, upright pianos or harpsichords, none of these provides
a close enough approximation of the services of the primary product
to be counted as an adequate substitute. Despite this common degree
of substitutability (or lack of substitutability), we could not say that all
these products are equally important in the lives of their consumers.
Milk delivery and local transit services are evidently more vital than a
newspaper or a grand piano in the material culture of most consumers.
We would, then, say that a strike in either of the former services affects
a public more importantly than a strike in enterprises providing the
latter two. They would be rated higher on our continuum.

The element of deferability of consumption enters into this conception of cultural necessity. Regardless of how necessary a product is in
the lives of its consumers (if one thinks dichotomously of having it or
not having it at all), the consumption of certain kinds of items may be
postponed, making them less immediately necessary. Two products may

be equally necessary in the culture of a group of consumers, but one must be had now if its value is to be realized, while the other retains its value even if consumption is deferred. Admittedly, it is not always a simple matter to determine what consumption is deferrable and what is not. Suppose there is a strike of the movie houses in a community. Consumer A, who particularly wants to see the picture *West of the Smokies*, may be able to postpone seeing this film. The picture may be shown after the strike is over, and the timing is not important to him as long as he sees the picture *some* time. But consumer B, who during the strike simply wants to go to the movies as a form of relaxation for which the need is felt *then*, cannot postpone this consumption; a picture seen later is no substitute for a picture seen now, under the circumstances. If this pleasure is to be realized at all, it must be realized in the present. Despite such difficulties of determining whether or not consumption is deferrable, the principle is evident. Cultural necessity has two characteristics, then: it refers to the *dispensability* of the product in the lives of the consumers and also to the *deferability* of consumption of that product.

The cultural-necessity continuum may be thought of as ranging from products which are unnecessary (dispensable or deferrable) even for pleasure, with a value of 0, to products which are absolutely necessary to health and safety, valued at 10. In between these extreme values any product can be placed. The actual placement of any product is largely a qualitative judgment by the observer, but it would be entirely feasible to elicit—by opinion polls, for example—consumer responses providing a more objective determination. Tentatively, certain gradations of cultural necessity may be suggested, as guide points along the continuum, not as classifications.

Cultural Necessity to Household Consumers

0	1	2	3	4	5	6	7	8	9	10
Unnecessary		Necessary for pleasures and conveniences of varying degrees of importance			Necessary if hardship (physical, mental, pecuniary), in varying degree, is to be avoided				Necessary in varying degree for health and safety, ranging up to "absolutely necessary"	

The second factor determining how a strike affects household consumers is what we shall call the stock effect. Strikes differ in their impact because there are differences in the extent to which stocks of services yielded by the struck products are available for consumption during the course of the strike. A coal strike which begins with high coal stocks in consumers' bins and in retail yards holds less concern to the consumer than a coal strike which finds both bins and yards relatively empty. How large is the stock of any product depends in part on the physical "pile-upability" of the product (railroad services and electric power do not readily lend themselves to stockpiling, while coal, clothing, and some foods do), on the economic "storeability" of the product (some products, while physically capable of being stocked, involve excessive cost of storage—size 17 shoes, for example, for which demand is slight), on the "extendability" of products already in the hands of households (razor blades can be made to provide additional services even though normally they would have been scrapped, while food eaten once cannot be reused), and on normal accessibility (beehive coke ovens located close to coal mines do not carry large supplies of coal because the source of replenishment can be easily tapped). It should be underscored that the *services* of products rather than the products themselves are important here. Dial telephones, for example, can store up service for consumers in a manner which manual phones cannot, so that effects of a telephone strike differ depending on whether dial or manual service is involved. Similarly, a railroad strike is less damaging if there are large stocks of all types of goods which have already been moved to their destinations, thus providing a stock of railroad services already performed.

Stocks by themselves are not enough to give us the stock effect, however. Alongside the services of goods available during the course of a strike we must place the amount of those services which are being used up during the course of the strike. A given stock of coal has different meaning to consumers depending on whether they are then consuming coal at the rate of 5,000 tons or 50,000 tons a day. This relationship of stocks to consumption is typically expressed in the stock-consumption ratio. A ratio of 28 days for bituminous coal, for example, indicates that enough stocks are available to provide for normal consumption for a period of 28 days.[1]

[1] In the case of durable goods (for example, automobiles), the stock-consumption ratio may be computed by either of two methods. (1) The number of new automobiles available for use may be regarded as the stock, while the number of automobiles withdrawn from use (services completely exhausted, for which replacements may be presumed to be needed) plus the expected net increase in demand for automobiles would be considered as consumption, the two giving the stock-consumption ratio. (2) Alternatively, the total amount of services available in all cars in the hands of private owners, sales agencies, and producers would be considered as stock, with the total amount of services of cars consumed during the course of the strike plus net new demand for cars constituting consumption. Either method of computation is satisfactory, and choice can rest entirely on convenience.

The stock-consumption ratio is obviously affected by anything modifying the size of stocks or the amount of consumption. The most important modifications of amount of stock occurring during a strike are depletion due to consumption and additions due to increased production. The former is self-explanatory: the days of the strike pass and consumers continue to use up some portion of the stockpile, leaving less for the period over which the strike may continue.

The possibility of additions due to increased output takes into account primarily two factors: the proportion of the industry which is struck, and the proportion of industry capacity being utilized prior to the strike. If one firm contributing only 5 percent of an industry's output was shut down, the remaining firms would be able to make up the resulting loss of product more easily than if the struck firm had contributed 50 percent of industry sales. If the whole industry is struck, the possibility of additions due to increased production is virtually eliminated.

Nevertheless, in times of high production levels, the nonstruck firms in an industry may already be operating at peak capacity, so that they are unable to expand output at all. Regardless of the fact that the struck firm may contribute only 5 percent—or less—of the industry's output, the remaining firms may be unable to offset the loss of output by expanded operations. This is likely to be the case for many firms during wartime, though capacity operation is not confined solely to such emergency periods.

Modifications of the amount of consumption during the course of the strike are primarily a reflection of whether consumers, in anticipation of shortages, either voluntarily or compulsorily ration their use of the service. In the course of a coal strike, for example, householders may heat their homes at lower temperatures to conserve dwindling stocks; local governments may establish priority lists for sales from coal yards on the basis of need; apartment houses, schools, and other institutions have at such times limited their use of fuel.

It would indeed be convenient if we could use the stock-consumption ratio itself as a basis for reflecting the impact of a strike on consuming households. Large stocks relative to consumption would make a strike less severe than low stocks relative to consumption. The continuum would be set up to give increasing values for decreasing stock-consumption ratios, with a maximum of 10 for a ratio of 0. Such an approach is untenable for two reasons, however.

1. In many instances consumers will not feel the effect of a strike until stocks are exhausted or nearly exhausted. Whether the stock-consumption ratio of coal is 50 or 10 is not likely to affect a consumer's habits. Not until the ratio falls to a low figure is rationing likely to be instituted in many homes. If we use stock-consumption ratios, then, the effect on consumers is less correctly expressed as a continuum than as a turning point: up to some ratio, consumers have been unaffected; past that ratio they are affected. Increasing values for continuously decreasing stock-consumption ratios are clearly erroneous.

2. On the other hand, at the time that consumers' habits are affected, so that rationing is instituted, it is conceivable that stock-consumption ratios will conceal rather than reveal the nature of the effect. As rationing is instituted, consumption falls so that a given stock will last for more days. The more severe the rationing, the less will the stock-consumption ratio suggest the effect of the strike. Stocks will decline less slowly due to conservation, so that stock-consumption ratios (even though based on normal consumption) will similarly decline more slowly, concealing the actual impact which conservation may be having on the consumers. Consequently, we use a different basis for our continuum designed to show the stock effect.

Stock Effect: The Extent to Which Consumption Declines Due to Diminishing Stocks

0	1	2	3	4	5	6	7	8	9	10
0%	10%	20%	30%	40%	50%	60%	70%	80%	90%	100%

On this scale the effect of rationing is expressly indicated, and the lack of effect which diminishing stocks may actually have on consumer habits is provided for. Nevertheless, the stock-consumption ratio need not be discarded as useless. As a practical matter, it seems likely that a conversion table may be developed, showing—for a given product—the extent to which consumption declines are influenced by stock-consumption ratios. On the basis of experience, we may find that with coal at a stock-consumption ratio of five days (consumption being computed in terms of normal use), consumption may decline by 20 percent; while with stocks at three days, consumption may be reduced to 50 percent of normal. From such experience we would be able to estimate, from stock-consumption data, the actual stock effect on household consumers.

There is one weakness with this continuum: it does not take into account what economists refer to as declining marginal utility. The least important uses of a good or service are eliminated first; as long as some stock remains it is always the most essential uses which are satisfied. Increasing cuts in consumption of a good, then, result in more than proportionate hardship. A 100 percent cut in the use of electricity creates more than twice as much hardship as a 50 percent cut, yet we rate these as 10 and 5, respectively, on our scale. Ideally, the rating should increase more than proportionately with the reduction in consumption, where all individuals are affected alike by the strike. On the other hand, most strikes do not affect consumers equally. Some have large stocks and others none. In the first instance the proportionate hardship is considerably less than in the second instance. There appears to be no adequate way of estimating "average" hardship on a nonproportionate scale. Because we have been unable to accept any scale as indicating the effect of diminishing utility satisfactorily, we have retained the less satisfactory but simpler method of rating the stock effect as though hardship is equiproportionate to the reduction in consumption of the good.

We come now to the substitutability effect. By this is meant the extent to which consumers find another product acceptable as a substitute for the struck product. A strike at a theater is not likely to weigh heavily on its customers since they can turn to movies, finding these perhaps not as satisfactory as their original choice but sufficiently acceptable that the strike imposes no hardship. On the other hand, a strike in the local utility supplying electricity leaves its consumers relatively helpless, not simply because they are dependent on electricity for so many essential services (cultural necessity), but because its substitutes are relatively unsatisfactory. Local transit services probably fall somewhere between the two extremes of these examples. Increased use of private automobiles and cabs or walking provides acceptable substitutes for a substantial number of consumers but is not available to others, for whom no satisfactory substitute exists.

The measure of substitutability which ideally should be used here is perhaps the economist's concept of cross-elasticity of demand, which shows the proportionate change in the demand for one product (its price remaining unchanged) resulting from a small proportionate change in the price of another product. Thus if the price of theater tickets is increased and the resulting increased demand for movie admissions is proportionately greater than the resulting increased demand for night-club entertainment (the price of both remaining constant), we can say that movies are better substitutes for theaters than are night clubs. A small proportionate increase in the price of a given product has caused a larger proportionate number of consumers to switch to one alternative rather than the other. On the other hand, if the local transit fare is increased but there is no perceptible increase in the amount of gasoline sold or downtown parking space rented or in the use of cabs, we can say that the latter are not considered as satisfactory substitutes for public transportation.[2]

Unfortunately, no empirical estimates of cross-elasticities of demand exist, so that cross-elasticity is useful to us only conceptually, clarifying what we are interested in measuring. There is one deficiency which cross-elasticity, even as a concept, has for our purposes, however: it indicates nothing concerning the availability of the substitute products.[3] Goat's milk may be a reasonably satisfactory substitute for cow's milk for those who can obtain it, but it is not available in sufficient quantities to make it a practical substitute for most milk consumers. We are therefore forced to fall back upon an impressionistic judgment about the substitutability of other products for the struck product. Our scale, running from 0 to 10, simply reflects varying degrees of substitutability, ranging from very high to none.

Substitutability of Other Products for the Struck Product

0	1	2	3	4	5	6	7	8	9	10
Completely acceptable substitutes										No acceptable substitutes

These, then, are our three principal determinants of the impact of a strike on household consumers: cultural necessity, the stock effect, and the substitutability effect. But what of a strike's duration? Surely the length of time over which a strike extends is a principal ingredient of its impact on the consuming public.

[2] The stock-consumption ratio requires a delimitation of "the industry," in order to determine the proportion of the total amount of any given product which is withdrawn from the market. This is not a simple matter, in the face of product differentiation. We speak of the automobile industry, for example, but it is questionable whether we should include Cadillacs and Packards as well as Fords and Chevrolets in estimating the percentage of "the industry" struck, since the industry concept has implicit in it the notion of a high degree of homogeneity among a line of products. In elasticity terms, an "industry" would be composed of companies producing products having a very high (nearly perfect) cross-elasticity of demand in terms of each other.

Once it has been decided what firms compose the industry (that is, the units where products are considered homogeneous), then the acceptability as substitutes of all other (nonhomogeneous) products is, conceptually, measurable, and it is the adequacy of the "best" substitutes that is measured on our third continuum.

[3] Availability of alternative producers of the struck product has been taken into account in the stock effect, it will be recalled.

Duration is, of course, vitally important in determining the effect of a strike on consumers. But duration is significant only because it affects each of our three continua. It is not a separable measurement but, rather, something that enters into the measurements of cultural necessity, stock effect, and substitutability effect. How long a strike is protracted would be of no importance if the struck product was rated 0 on all three scales—as unnecessary (dispensable or continuingly deferrable), with loss of production having no effect on consumption of the product, and with highly substitutable products available in any case.

What we must do, then, is to measure the *changing* effect of our three principal considerations over the period of the strike. In some cases we must even extend our measurements to the period after the strike has been settled: declining stocks may have no effect on consumption during the course of the strike, but before depleted stocks can be replenished consumers may be deprived of the good or service even though production has been resumed.

The rating which is derived from our three continua is thus the rating of the effect of a given strike on the consuming public as of any given day of the strike. As the strike progresses, the cultural necessity of the product, the stock effect, the acceptability of substitute products —these are likely to receive changing values.

1. Cultural necessity need not remain the same over the duration of the strike: failure of garbage collection may be only a matter of inconvenience in the early days of the strike but a threat to health as the strike continues. The importance of milk to the consumer on any given day will depend in some degree on the availability of milk on previous days; the cultural necessity of milk to a housewife on the eighth day of a milk strike will be different depending on whether she started the strike with no quarts or a dozen quarts of milk on hand. This is not the same thing as the stock effect. It takes account of the stock effect on *previous* days of the strike, to be sure, but our stock-effect continuum is designed to show only the effect of the consumer's stock position *on the given day* of the strike.

2. The stock effect changes with the prolongation of a strike. Rationing effects are likely to be less noticeable in the early days of the strike but more significant as stocks decline. On the other hand, stocks may be limited in the early days of a strike but may subsequently expand after nonstruck producers of similar products increase their output.

3. Substitutability may change: what was acceptable early in the strike may cease to be acceptable with continued use, or what was unaccept-

able as a substitute at first may become acceptable with continued need; goods or services not available at the start may become practical alternatives when a little time has been allowed in which to organize their production.

The effect of time on the ratings is suggested by the following tabular form:

Day of the strike	1	2	3	4	5	6	7	8	9	10	11	..
Cultural necessity	—	—	—	—	—	—	—	—	—	—	—	—
Stock effect	—	—	—	—	—	—	—	—	—	—	—	—
Substitutability	—	—	—	—	—	—	—	—	—	—	—	—

On each day, the cultural necessity, stock effect, and substitutability effect would be separately rated to show these effects as of that day. This does not, of course, provide any measure of the cumulative impact of the strike. A given day's score does not reveal, for example, how long consumers may have been forced to curtail consumption. To show such cumulative effects, ratings would have to be added. As yet, however, we have not had occasion to discuss how the scores based on our three continua are used; we must still defer that question for a few paragraphs.

A rating of the changing impact of a strike on consumers, as it continues and as it is measured by these three continua, would presumably be made at or just before the start of a strike. Certain of the data might be difficult to acquire—such as stock-consumption ratios or the experience data necessary to convert these to percentage declines in consumption as a strike progressed. Judgments must reflect opinion where data are not available—as in the case of substitutability of other products. Nevertheless, there is no real barrier to establishing approximate ratings for all three considerations over any given duration. Such a rating would facilitate calculation of what strike duration is "tolerable" before public intervention is "compelled."

Up to this point we have been talking about the strike effects on household consumers. We have now to consider the effects on producers, if we are to observe the total impact of a strike on the public. For present purposes, let us distinguish between producers using the struck product (or some product of which the struck product is an ingredient) and producers supplying the struck firm (or suppying firms which use, directly or indirectly, the struck product). In both cases the same kinds of considerations apply as to household consumers, though with slight variations.

In the case of producer-users, it is not the cultural necessity of the struck product which determines need, but the production necessity. Some products are vitally necessary to a production process, so much so that without them operations must be suspended. Other products, while ingredients of the production process, can be more readily dispensed with. Floor brushes (or some substitute for them) are materials used in the course of production; the sweeping up of debris from factory floors is not a matter of aesthetics but of production efficiency. Nevertheless, most plants could continue operating for some time without benefit of cleaning apparatus. A steel mill could hardly get along so easily without coal (or some substitute). Our first continuum is therefore converted to measure the importance of the struck product (or some suitable substitute) to the production process.

Production necessity is compounded of dispensability of the struck product in the production process (indicating the extent to which production will be lost due to lack of the struck product or some substitute for it) and recoverability of the affected production (indicating the extent to which production lost during the strike can be recovered by make-up operations after the strike). Even if steel production is suspended due to a coal strike, for example, there remains the possibility that steel output lost now might be made up later. This possibility is best realized when the user of the struck product is operating at less than full capacity (so that operations subsequent to the strike can be expanded to recover lost production), when the user's sources of other necessary supplies can be expanded as needed, and when the user's customers are themselves willing and able to defer their purchases, the latter condition being most nearly met if there are no good substitutes for the user's product.

The assessment of recoverability is one of the most difficult aspects of estimating the real costs of a stoppage. There is frequently an uncertain connection between orders unfilled because of the strike and orders filled after the strike. Moreover, to some degree subsequent production is not an exact equivalent for strike-interrupted production. It may not forestall the need for resort to credit which would otherwise have been unnecessary, it may allow a time advantage to competitors which affects future business performance, it may not prevent customers from giving more serious consideration to alternative sources of supply or alternative products; for user employees it may not forestall hardship during the strike, and the lost output may be made up by fuller production schedules without a necessary accompanying recapture of wages. For these reasons it is not easy to determine to what extent recoverability should be viewed as mitigating the impact of a strike. Nevertheless, some judgment must be attempted in the light of all these considerations. Throughout this study whenever the term "recoverability" is used it should be understood in the special sense of the extent to which postponed operations are an offset to losses suffered during the strike, and we shall limit the period of make-up operations to the six months following the strike to avoid thin-spinning the result.

It will help to keep more clearly in mind the meaning of "production," in connection with production necessity, if it is identified with employment in the producing firm. We are interested in the extent to which output of the industrial user depends on the struck product on any given day, but output does not refer simply to the flow of finished goods from a plant. It includes no less the various maintenance and clerical services without which the plant could not, over time, operate. Even if a steel plant was deprived of coal, for example, so that the actual flow of iron and its products came to a halt, not all employees of the plant would be laid off. Some would be retained to keep plant and equipment in good condition, others to repair equipment, perhaps others to modify plant layout or to expand facilities, still others to continue to make out invoices, take care of continuing correspondence, keep records up to date, make payments, and so on. All these are aspects of the production process, over the long run. Nevertheless, such ancillary or facilitating operations cannot be continued indefinitely in the absence of the basic production process. Hence, production necessity, like cultural necessity, is a function of time, that is, the duration of the strike. During the first week, services such as those just mentioned may be continued even if the strike has shut down the plant, but as the strike progresses fewer clerical and maintenance employees will be required, until—if the strike lasts long enough—the user firm will reduce its employment to the bare minimum, the fixed labor charges that cannot be avoided, giving rise to services which, however, from the long view, must still be regarded as part of production.

There remains one final consideration under production necessity. If we think of production in terms of user employment, then such employment may be sustained by resort to temporary alternative jobs *outside the user firm*. To the extent that the decline in production employment in the user firm is thus offset by an increase in production employment elsewhere, the impact of the strike on producer-users is minimized.

To summarize, then, in the production-necessity continuum we take account of the degree of dependence of producer-users on the struck good, as if no stocks of or substitutes for that good are available, a dependence which is reduced by the extent of continuing sustaining operations, by the availability of temporary alternative employment, and by the amount of recoverability of strike losses.

The remaining two continua are virtually unchanged. The stock effect indicates the extent to which use of the struck product declines due to diminishing stocks (or the nonexistence of stocks). As in the case of consumers, producers sometimes ration their use of materials in short supply. Such rationing may be undertaken for several reasons. With a given stock of materials and no immediate source of replenishment, a producer may choose to allocate supplies primarily to high-profit or low-inventory lines, restricting their use in items which have a lower margin of profit or in which a substantial inventory has been accumulated. Complete shutdown may damage equipment (as in steel) or suspend production of goods or services deemed essential (as in railroads), so that partial operation over a longer period is preferable to full operation for a shorter time.

Finally the substitutability effect measures the adequacy of other products as substitutes for the struck product in the production process.

The tabular form on which we rate the effect of strikes on industrial users is then:

Day of the strike	1	2	3	4	5	6	7	8	9	10	11	..
Production necessity	—	—	—	—	—	—	—	—	—	—	—	
Stock effect	—	—	—	—	—	—	—	—	—	—	—	
Substitutability	—	—	—	—	—	—	—	—	—	—	—	

With producers who *supply* materials or services to the struck unit or to other firms using the struck product, the same three criteria of affectedness are used, again with slight changes. The supplier is concerned over outlets for its goods, rather than with materials to make them. The struck firm ceases to be a customer, with repercussions upon its supplying firms. If the struck plant does not resume operations within a short time, production in the supplying firms may have to be curtailed for lack of markets. "Market necessity" therefore replaces "production necessity" in our first continuum. Market necessity, like production necessity, comprises the two elements of dispensability and recoverability.

Dispensability relates to the dependence of the supplier on the struck unit—or on some substitute market—as an outlet for its production. The Chesapeake and Ohio Railroad is an important coal-hauling railroad, for example, supplying transportation services to coal-mining companies. Its dependence on the coal industry (or on some substitute for the coal industry) is great. The impact of a coal strike on it, due to market necessity, is more serious than for a railroad only 10 percent of whose services are taken for coal hauling.[4] As with user firms, so too with supplier firms, we equate production with employment; in consequence the dependence of the supplier's employment on the struck unit is reduced to the extent that temporary alternative employment is available outside the supplier firm. Recoverability measures the extent to which production not purchased by the struck unit during the strike will be bought by it after the strike, so that some portion of the supplier's output is not lost but only postponed.

Market necessity, like production necessity, is a function of the duration of the strike. A coal strike will not immediately affect all employees of a coal-mining railroad, since even if coal is not carried some portion of the labor force will be retained for maintenance and clerical operations. The longer the strike continues, the fewer such functions will be performed, however, so that the dependence of the supplier group upon the struck unit increases with the passage of time.

For the supplier, the stock effect indicates the extent to which his output declines due to inability to accumulate as stocks that part of his product which the struck unit would normally take. In some instances a supplying firm may be able to continue production and stockpile its product, while in other instances this is not possible. A railroad supplier cannot stockpile transportation services which are not currently demanded. A coal company is better able, in physical terms, to continue operations even if its market outlets are currently shut down. Whether or not stockpiling is physically feasible, however, there are sometimes economic reasons why it is not attempted.

[4] We take the ratio of purchases by the struck unit to total sales of the supplier as representative of dispensability in this sense. The procedure here would be as follows. First, we would break down the total purchases figure of the struck unit into its principal component categories, such as purchases of electric power or steel or railroad services, and so on. We would then take total sales of each of the supplier groups so identified and compute the percentage of its total sales normally taken by the struck unit. When reduced to our scale of 10, this would give us the first approximation of the market-necessity rating, which would then be modified to reflect the other elements of dispensability and recoverability mentioned in the text. In practice, however, as will be explained later, we have modified this approach for convenience.

In some cases a struck unit may continue some of its purchases from a supplier. If the supplies are of scarce materials, the struck unit may be reluctant to give them up even if it cannot use them until the strike is terminated. In the case of coal-hauling railroads, coal already mined enables the coal industry to continue purchases of coal-hauling services for a time. To the extent suppliers continue to provide goods or services to the struck unit, to that extent, of course, is the stock effect reduced. To that extent is its output *not* reduced by inability to accumulate stocks of its products.

The substitutability effect measures the extent to which a supplier can substitute another outlet for the one which has been struck. This is partly an effect of the level of economic activity. If any one automobile company had been struck at almost any time in the decade of the forties, steel companies would have had little difficulty in substituting other outlets for their steel. In times of slack production alternative buyers may not be so readily found, however. Substitutability of markets is also a function of the degree of specialization. If one company is geared to supply a particular product to another producer, made to the latter's peculiar specifications, it increases the difficulty of finding another purchaser whose needs are precisely the same. Some suppliers are so closely linked to producer-customers that a strike in the latter's plants will force a shutdown in their own. One example of such a close relationship is that between Briggs and Chrysler, with the former geared to produce to the specifications of the latter. The result is that a strike at Chrysler can be predicted to have its effect on Briggs. Finally, it is not always as easy for one firm as another to find temporary substitute outlets. If the steel industry is struck, it is not as simple for coal companies to find alternative buyers as it is for meat dealers in the event of a restaurant strike, who—by lowering prices—might induce more home consumption. The ability to exploit substitute markets is thus a function of the short-run price elasticity of demand for the product being supplied.

For suppliers of the struck firm, then, our tabular form for rating the effect of a strike is as follows:

Day of the strike	1	2	3	4	5	6	7	8	9	10	11	..
Market necessity	—	—	—	—	—	—	—	—	—	—	—	
Stock effect	—	—	—	—	—	—	—	—	—	—	—	—
Substitutability	—	—	—	—	—	—	—	—	—	—	—	—

So far we have a set of three continua for each of three groups in the public which is affected by a strike. We must now consider the relationship of these continua to each other. The fact that each of our three primary determinants of the impact of a strike on the affected groups is expressed as a relative on a common scale facilitates the use of each with the others, on the basis of the rating given.

Our necessity ratings (cultural, production, and market) may be taken as indicating the maximum possible effect of the strike on the relevant public on the given day. They are a measure of what the relative effects of a particular strike on consumer and producer groups would be if there were no stocks of or substitutes for the struck good. Production necessity and market necessity have a statistical basis—they reflect the extent to which output would drop, in percentage terms. Cultural necessity has no such significance, but simply measures, on a relative basis, the hardship to consumers if a particular good or service was withdrawn on a given day without stocks or substitutes available.

However necessary the struck good or the struck unit is to the relevant groups, to the extent that stocks are available or substitutes are adequate, the impact of the strike is reduced. An example may help. Suppose that on the given day of the strike,

cultural necessity = 10 (the good is vital to consumers),
stock effect   = 4 (consumption declines by 40 percent due to diminishing stocks),
substitutability   = 8 (substitutes are inadequate to supply 80 percent of the "value" of the services of the struck good).

Substitutes will be called on only to fill the gap left by the 40 percent fall in consumption due to declining stocks. We take 80 percent of 40 percent as the extent to which substitutes are inadequate to meet the effect of the decline in the consumption of the good, or 32 percent. The substitution effect thus diminishes the stock effect. We then take 32 percent of 10 or 3.2 (on our scale of 10) as the measure of consumer dependence on the struck good which neither stocks nor substitutes have been able to cushion. To this measure (which we have derived by taking the substitution effect as a percentage of the stock effect, and the resulting figure as a percentage of the necessity rating) we give the name *urgency rating*. The urgency rating indicates the degree of impact of the strike on the relevant affected public.

CHAPTER SEVEN

The Real Basis for Public Opinion:
The Number Affected by Strikes

W E HAVE now constructed scales on which to measure the relative extent to which individuals are affected by a strike, a measure which we have called the strike's urgency rating. Yet all strikes having the same urgency rating are not of equal importance. Obviously, the impact of strikes differs with the number of individuals affected. If two strikes have urgency ratings of 5, but one affects the city of New Haven while the other affects the city of New York, we would have to say that the latter had greater effect. From the point of view of the individual affected, of course, the number of fellow sufferers is not material, but if we are trying to calculate the effects of strikes we must take into account not only the character of the strike's incidence (as given by our urgency rating) but also the size of the publics involved. In each case, then, we are interested in the *number* of people affected, as well as in how they are affected.

In taking the absolute number of those affected, let us simplify matters by making the understood unit of account 100,000 people. Thus if a strike affects 5,000,000 individuals (both consumers and producers) we shall consider the number affected as 50. If the urgency rating of that strike, for all groups, was 2, then multiplying the numbers affected by the urgency rating would give us a score of 100 for that strike—a score which would represent the impact of that strike on the public, placing that strike relative to all other strikes with respect to public-affectedness.

For purposes of estimating the absolute number of individuals feeling the weight of a strike, it is necessary to segregate the public into categories. We deal here with seven major categories, as previously identified. Each of these involves something of a problem in estimation, and we shall have to make some tentative resolution of the problems presented. We shall briefly examine each of the categories for that purpose, but readers who are not concerned with this problem in estimation may prefer to skip this section.

First, we begin with the major subdivision of household consumers, under which we treat with direct consumers and indirect consumers. By households is meant not only private family units but also all non-profit institutions, such as hospitals, schools, churches, fraternal societies, service organizations, and so on. Direct consumers are those who normally would have used the product of the struck firm or industry. In the case of a strike at General Motors, for example, the direct consumers would be the absolute number of individuals who would have bought General Motors cars during the period of the strike. Indirect consumers are those who would have bought products which require the struck product in their making. If the coal industry is shut down by strike, individuals may not only be deprived of coal for residential heating purposes (direct consumption); they may conceivably be deprived of the services of coal-burning passenger trains or of the products which would have been shipped by coal-burning freight trains; they may be restricted in their use of electricity from utilities relying on coal-fueled generators; they may fail to get their local newspaper if its supply of newsprint is manufactured in a coal-powered paper plant. All these effects we refer to as indirect consumer effects.

Calculation of the number of direct consumers affected can be made in at least two ways. (1) We can take the expected number of sales of the struck unit for any given strike duration. "Expected sales" may be calculated on the basis of the sales of the same period in the preceding year corrected by trend and cyclical factors, or they may be estimated from the sales of the month preceding the strike, corrected by seasonal and cyclical factors. (2) Alternatively, one might take the expected number of sales of the industry as a whole (the expected sales of automobiles, for example) and reduce this figure by the proportion of total sales normally supplied by the struck unit. (If 1,000,000 people could be expected to buy cars in a given three-month period, and General Motors normally supplied one half the new car market, then the number of direct consumers affected by a three-month strike at General Motors would be 500,000 (or 5 when reduced by our unit of account).

A serious problem is presented by the fact that most companies produce not one product but a number of products. A company like General Motors, for example, may literally produce hundreds of products, not all but a great many of them consumer items. If the company is struck, all these goods are withheld from the market. How shall we treat such multiple-product firms in estimating the impact of strikes?

There seems to be no escape from the fact that each product deserves its own urgency rating and its own estimate of the absolute number of consumers who would have bought it over the course of the strike. It may be, for example, that the urgency rating for General Motors' new car output is low, since adequate substitutes are available. On the other hand, the urgency rating for its output of automobile repair parts may be high. Ford and Plymouth parts may be far less substitutable for Chevrolet parts than a new Ford or Plymouth is substitutable for a new Chevrolet. We should have to make a separate rating for parts, to add to the rating for new cars, then, in each case multiplying the relevant number of consumers by the relevant rating, in order to determine the total impact on direct consumers of a strike at General Motors, adding in as well the scores for all other General Motors' consumer items.

To follow this practice faithfully would involve, at least in the case of the large corporations, more of a search for obscure data than the results would warrant. As a compromise, which is not likely to lead to much distortion, we can group the output of multiple-product firms into major classifications, rating not single products but classes of products. It appears unlikely, even in the case of our largest or most diversified corporations, that their line of products would require more than ten product classifications, and in most cases fewer will be sufficient. To rate this number of "products" is not an unmanageable task.

The calculation of indirect consumers presents an even more difficult problem. With a product like coal or a service like railroad transportation, the number of possible indirect consumer effects is almost limitless. They would include all the products which consumers buy that are produced with the aid of the coal which is no longer available or distributed by means of the rail system which has been struck. Clearly we cannot consider all these. The solution which has been adopted here has been to limit ourselves to the two indirect uses of the struck product most obviously affecting consumers, unless the consequence is so to understate the indirect effects as to require consideration of additional indirect uses. Here too we can best proceed by defining user groups broadly. Moreover, if we are dealing with a strike at a multiple-product firm, then this requires consideration of the two most important indirect consumer uses of each of the struck products or product classes. In the case of all such indirect effects, we must first obtain the urgency rating for the "secondary" product and then multiply the number of affected consumers by this rating (using our unit of account of 100,000 persons). Those who are affected are the consumers of products which normally require the struck firm's output in their making.

If we encounter problems in trying to estimate the number of consumers affected by a strike, our difficulties are vastly increased when we seek to estimate the number of producers affected. Indeed, the effort would seem scarcely worth while except for the fact that it is precisely such producer effects that frequently magnify the impact of one strike over another. A strike in steel is likely to be so much more public-affecting than a strike in meat packing, not because consumers feel the effects more tellingly—the reverse would be true; when steel goes down, it is the number of producers affected which makes such a strike so costly to the public.

The term "producers" is used here to refer to all those involved in the production process, whether as owners, managers, or employees. Despite this inclusiveness, the most usable measure of the number affected in a producer capacity is the number of employees. This is the measure which has been used here. The primary justification for this simplified approach is that the urgency rating reflects the impact on production, and the immediate, most concentrated effects of any cut in production are felt by the working force rather than by owners and managers. There is no intent here to minimize the impact of a strike on these latter groups, but it is believed that, in terms both of strike-affectedness and the numbers affected, employees provide the most significant single measure of the importance of a strike to the producing groups.

Producers—thus defined—can be divided into five categories: the direct users of the struck product, indirect users, direct suppliers of the struck firm, suppliers of the direct and indirect users, and nonparty members of the struck unit. Each presents its own problem in estimation. Some of these problems can be resolved only expediently, with not very satisfactory results.

In the case of direct producer-users, we first identify the principal uses of the struck product. We then take the total number of employees in each industry so identified, reduced by the proportion of the industry which the struck firm or unit normally supplies, to obtain the number of direct-user producers affected by the strike. For example, if the railroads constitute one of the chief users of the coal industry's products, and if total railroad employment is 1,000,000, and if a strike in coal shuts down a portion of that industry which normally supplies one-half of the railroads' needs, we would say that 500,000 direct-user producers were affected.[1] We multiply this number (5, when converted to our unit of account of 100,000 people) by the relevant urgency rating to obtain the score for the direct-user effects of the strike on railroads.

Indirect producer-users are those who use products which in turn require the use of the struck product, as in the case of a processor of foods who uses electric power which requires struck coal, or the farmer who needs a new motor for his truck or tractor which is made by an automobile company using struck steel. In the case of these indirect users we face the same problem we encountered in dealing with consumers, and we treat it the same way. We select those two groups (broadly defined) most obviously affected. (If this procedure too grossly understates the effect, then additional categories may be added.) We calculate the urgency rating of the product which they lack because of the strike (which in this case is not the struck product itself—or products, if multiproduct operations are involved—but rather a good or service of which the struck product is a component). We estimate what proportion of the tertiary product (processed food, for example) is normally dependent on the output of the secondary producers (electric power suppliers) and take the same proportion of the total number of employees in the tertiary (processed food) industry against which to apply the urgency rating to determine the effect of the strike (in the primary industry, coal) on indirect production users.

If the problem of estimating the number of industrial users affected is more troublesome than that of estimating the number of household consumers, the difficulties in calculating the number of suppliers affected by a strike are scarcely less. Assume, for example, a strike at General Motors. That company normally maintains relations with close to 13,000 subcontractors, all of whom—with their employees—must be counted as suppliers. To these must be added the number of suppliers of nonprocessed materials, like steel and electric power, which General Motors itself uses. Moreover, since we include employees as an integral part of the struck unit, we must include as direct suppliers all

---

[1] For our purposes, it would be immaterial whether the struck coal firms normally supplied one half the needs of all railroads or all the needs of one half the railroads. In the first case, unemployment would be spread among all the roads, while in the second case it would be concentrated in half the railroad companies. The actual amount of unemployment is likely to differ in the two cases, but not by enough to warrant a distinction.

those merchants who provide goods and services—food, clothing, en-tertainment, gasoline, and so on—to General Motors' workers.

The procedure for calculating numbers affected, which corresponds to that adopted for other strike-affected categories, would be as follows. First, we would identify the principal suppliers of the struck unit. For each of these supplier groups we would calculate an appropriate urgency rating, the market-necessity component of which would reflect the ratio of purchases by the struck unit to total sales of the supplier group. This urgency rating would then be applied to the number of employees of the supplier firms in each group. Unfortunately, however, we have no way of estimating the total number of employees in those firms actually supplying steel to the coal industry, for example, or coal to the railroad industry. We have therefore adopted the expedient of using the ratio of purchases by the struck unit to total sales of the relevant supplier *industry*, and applying the resulting rating to the number of employees in the whole supplier industry.

Further, we have a choice of two possible methods of calculating the direct supplier effects of a strike. Overlooking for the purposes of ex-position the fact that the stock and substitution effects must modify the market necessity effect, let us consider that the urgency rating (by which we multiply the number affected) is given solely by market necessity, and that market necessity is unmodified by any other considerations of recoverability. Our strike effect for the supplier category would then be given by the formula:

$$\frac{\text{struck unit's purchases}}{\text{total supplier industry sales}} \times \text{total employment of the supplier industry}$$

But this would be the same thing as to take the equivalent of the num-ber of full-time employees who are wholly engaged in producing for the struck unit and for whom market necessity would then be at a maximum (100 percent, or 10 on our scale). The equivalent formula would be:

$$10 \text{ (that is, 100\%)} \times \left(\frac{\text{struck unit's purchases}}{\frac{\text{total supplier industry sales}}{\text{total supplier employment}}} \right)$$

By adopting this latter formula in preference to the former, we avoid the inconvenience of having to work with minute fractions. The ex-pression below we call the employment divisor.

$$\frac{\text{total supplier industry sales}}{\text{total supplier employment}}$$

It gives us the volume of sales of the supplier industry which is attributable to one employee. By dividing the purchases of the struck unit by the employment divisor, then, we obtain the equivalent of the number of full-time employees wholly engaged in servicing the struck unit, which we use for our number affected. (The market-necessity rating must then be 10 except as modified by other considerations of dispensability or deferability.)

Next we turn to the indirect suppliers, which consist of those business firms supplying goods and services to direct suppliers of the struck unit (in the case of a coal strike, for example, a telephone company supplying communication services to a coal-*hauling* railroad);[2] those supplying goods and services to direct commercial users of the struck product (for example, a telephone company supplying communication services to a coal-*burning* railroad); and those supplying goods and services to indirect commercial users of the struck product (for example, a telephone company supplying communication services to manufacturing firms which ship goods and receive materials via coal-burning railroads).

How seriously indirect suppliers are affected by a strike depends largely on how vitally affected are their commercial customers in all three of these categories. We cannot assume that the urgency rating of indirect suppliers is equal to that of their customers, however, for there are the possibilities of stockpiling of, and substitution of markets for, the supplier's own product, which are likely to cushion the effect, and of further reducing market necessity by diverting employees with reduced production workloads to maintenance and improvement operations. We have no way of estimating the number of employees involved, even of judging whether it is smaller or larger than the number of employees of their customers. Nevertheless, our best expedient appears to be to make the indirect-supplier effects of a strike a direct function of the strike's effects on their customers. The following procedure, which, though arbitrary, is probably conservative, has been adopted.

We arbitrarily enter a final score for indirect-supplier effects equal to one fifth of the combined scores of their three customer categories. This reduction should be adequate to allow for the possibilities which indirect suppliers have of cushioning the strike effects and for the contingency that total employment in the supplier firms, as a group, may

[2] Moreover, since our term "producers" includes employees, "indirect suppliers" embraces, too, those who supply goods to the local merchants supplying the strikers.

be considerable smaller than employment in the user firms (relying on the struck product) which normally are their customers.

The final strike-affected producer category is that of nonparty members of the struck unit itself. Obviously this includes all the employees who are not themselves striking but whose employment or income is curtailed because of the strike. A walkout by a key group of workers may force a shutdown of all production operations. A strike of railroad engineers, for example, may mean the layoff of many more nonstriking employees than the actual number of strikers. Since the nonstrikers are not parties to the dispute, they must be included as part of the affected public. While properly they are direct suppliers of labor services to the struck unit, we have segregated them because of their peculiar status.

The three continua from which are derived the urgency rating applicable to other suppliers cannot be transferred to nonstrikers. For other suppliers, market necessity reveals the maximum potential effect, on the assumption that production for and sales to the struck unit (or some substitute market) are completely discontinued. This maximum potential effect is reduced to the extent that production designed for the struck unit continues to be produced either for inventory (stock effect) or alternative markets (substitutability effect). But when it is the struck unit itself which is the market for nonstrikers' services, these latter two effects lose their meaning. The relevant consideration is the extent to which the struck unit continues to produce—not for stock, not for substitute markets, but simply to supply as much of its normal trade as possible. In the case of nonstrikers, then, our urgency rating will constitute a measure of the extent to which their employment is reduced by the strike, on the assumption that no final production is undertaken (an estimate which takes into account that some of their number are retained for supervisory, clerical, maintenance, and stand-by operations, that others may obtain temporary jobs elsewhere, and that some portion of strike losses are recoverable), an estimate which is modified in whatever degree output is actually maintained. In most instances the struck unit will make no effort to produce; firms closed by a walkout attempt to continue operations more rarely now than formerly. Nevertheless, in a few important cases—notably, the supply of electric power or the running of trains—supervisory employees are called upon to keep some essential services functioning, and to the extent that output is maintained the potential impact of the strike on them is not fully realized.

One remaining step must be taken to make our estimates of producer effects comparable with those for consumer effects. In considering the number of consumers involved, each individual consumer counted for one. If in a family of five each is a consumer of bread, we count five consumers. A coal-heated house sheltering three people would give us three consumers of coal. In considering the number of producers affected, however, we have counted only the number of employees, without respect to dependents. Yet it is apparent that loss of income or employment makes itself felt not only on the breadwinner but on all who eat the bread that he wins. Consequently, it is necessary to multiply all our previous estimates of number of producers affected by some figure which will reflect this additional impact. Let us use 3 as our multiplier, thus allowing for spouse and one other dependent—child or parent—for each producer.

Moreover, as soon as family effects are introduced it becomes necessary to take account of strike effects on the families of strikers themselves, since the families are not themselves a party to the strike relationship even though intimately affected by it. This group may be viewed as another component of the category, "nonparty members of the struck industry": we have included the families of nonstriking employees in this category because of their relationship to members of the struck unit, and we may reasonably include the families of striking employees in the same category, by virtue of their relationship to members of the struck unit. By taking twice the number of strikers, we thereby allow for two dependents for each striker.

Those family members are dependent on strikers' employment income in the same manner that the families of nonstrikers depend on the latter's job earnings. The urgency rating, like that for nonstrikers, simply shows the extent to which strikers' employment has declined due to the stoppage, an estimate which takes into account the possibility of temporary alternative work and recoverability of strike losses. (Partial employment by the struck unit ceases to be relevant, of course.) There is one major modification, however.

The families of strikers are distinguished from other component groups of a strike's public in the respect that they are party-oriented in a way that none of the other groups are. They are not parties to the strike, since the members of a striker's family do not initiate strike action, may have independent views with respect to its conduct, and, in general, are involved only through association with the strikers themselves, just as in the case of nonstrikers. But though members of the public, they stand on a different footing from the other identified public constituencies. They are intimately concerned in the strike's success or failure. While not parties, they are peculiarly involved, in that its *outcome* is of immediate concern to them, whereas other parties are concerned only with its *termination*. As has been previously noted, there may be some who believe that the intimacy of association is so close that families of strikers should be classed with the parties themselves. The view adopted here is that such intimacy lessens but does not remove their nonparty characteristics. We would be unwarranted, then, in regarding strikers' families as affected to the same degree as the families of others idled by the strike. Unique compensating factors are present in their case. Such special offsets to the losses inflicted by the strike are sufficiently akin to our concept of recoverability (offsets to strike losses) to suggest the method of allowing for the peculiar status of this group: their recoverability of strike losses is set greater than that for nonstrikers. The nonrecoverable losses of the latter are, in the case of strikers' families, further reduced by 90 percent. By this procedure we cut drastically any score for the impact of a walkout on unionists' families but at the same time retain the recognition that this group is not actually a party to the strike, but a nonparty, even if unique in its nature.

We have now considered all the members of the public affected by any given strike.[3] The diagram below recapitulates the groups involved.

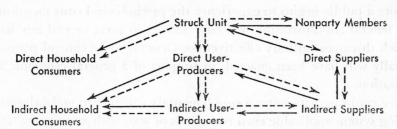

(Solid arrows show the direction of flow of goods and services between the related groups, while broken arrows show the direction in which strike effects are transmitted.)

[3] Because of the manner in which the criteria of strike-affectedness have been developed, an individual may be "counted" more than once in determining total strike effects. In the course of the same strike he may be counted as a consumer of the struck product (perhaps, indeed, of several products of the struck firm) as well as a producer. We believe that this "multiple counting" is desirable: presumably the more ways in which a person is affected, the more intensely is he affected.

For each of the affected groups we obtain a score derived from the urgency rating applicable to that group multiplied by the number in that group. But what weight shall we give to each of these affected groups relative to the others? How important is loss of goods and services to the consumer categories relative to loss of employment and income to the producing categories? We see no basis for attaching unequal weight to these groups.[4] We consider that the scores for all the affected groups, when added, give a measure of the total effect of a strike on the public. This measure has no meaning in itself, however. It simply places one strike relative to other strikes in terms of its impact on people, wherever and however they are situated. It enables us to say whether one strike imposes more hardship than another, taking into account both the degree of hardship and the number subjected to it.

One important limitation which lies upon this strike rating system is that it is inapplicable to wartime periods. In time of war popular antagonism to strikes arises not simply from the real costs, described in the preceding chapter, but from psychological costs that cannot be similarly measured. The feeling of potential danger to national security, the resentment over workers laying down tools when other men are shouldering arms on battlefronts, the possible danger to the security of loved ones—these are effects vastly different from loss of income or inability to secure some product or service. This limitation of the rating system does not appear to be a serious one, however. In time of war, it is not public costs which are crucial but military considerations. Even before a public begins to experience the psychological costs mentioned, the federal administration will have moved to avert or end any strike which threatens military effectiveness. General strike control programs usually will have been enacted, in support of a general economic mobilization.

We could perhaps enter a supplementary category to make the strike rating system applicable even to periods of war, with an urgency rating determined by military necessity, a stock effect, and substitutability, and with the number of persons affected graduated more than proportionately to increases in the urgency rating. Thus with a low urgency rating, we might presume that a relatively small number of the general cit-

[4] Especially in view of the fact that in the producer group we include the dependents of producers. Thus if there are three consumers in the family of a wage receiver (himself, his wife, and one child, let us say), there are, for our purposes, likewise three in the producer group, since we include those who are dependent on the producer's income.

izenry would be psychologically affected. With a higher urgency rating, reflecting a greater threat to national security and to the safety of family members in the armed services, the number of the general public psychologically affected would increase more than proportionately, until with an urgency rating of 10 we consider the entire nation to be affected. But such a procedure appears to be cumbersome and unnecessary. The fact is that when war is declared, any strike carrying any potential threat to the military program will fall under government proscription, with governmental sanctions becoming operative on its inception, without respect to relative strike ratings. It appears to be common sense, then, to admit that in time of war, strike effects on the public are likely to be vastly different than in time of peace, but that governmental sanctions operating on the parties are likely to render needless a rating system such as has been presented here.

Relative Strike Effects

This measure of the "public-affectingness" of strikes is based upon absolute numbers of individuals involved, whether as consumers or producers. For this reason it would be quite possible that a power strike which "cripples" a local community would rate lower than a national strike, say in automobiles, that actually affects people much less severely, simply because the latter affects more people. Such a result is, however, entirely consonant with the purpose of showing the total effects of any given strike. Similarly, it might also be true that on the rating scales here presented a railroad strike today would be more public-affecting than a railroad strike of 25 years ago, simply because the population served by the railways had grown and not because railways were any more necessary at the later date. The earlier strike may have, relatively, created hardships quite as great—perhaps even greater—than the later strike, but fewer people would have been affected, in absolute numbers. Again, this result is consonant with an effort to show the total effects of any given strike, since total effects are compounded of two elements, only one of which relates to the product itself (the urgency rating), the other being the number of affected consumers.

There are occasions, however, when it is desirable to calculate the relative impact of strikes that may occur in different communities, with populations of disparate size, or of strikes that have occurred at different times, with a population base of different size at each time. Such comparisons may be made by converting the population base from one of absolute numbers to one expressed in percentage terms. If we are interested in the relative impact of a power strike in New York City as opposed to a similar strike in Los Angeles, for example, we could calculate the urgency ratings for each of the strikes and then express the number of consumers and producers affected as percentages of the total consumer and producer populations of each community. We assume, as before, that all consumer effects should be weighted equally with all producer effects (both user and supplier) and the scores of the two categories added to obtain the total relative effect of a given strike.

Thus if a New York City power strike with a hypothetical urgency rating of 9 (let us say for all groups, to simplify the example) on the fifth day of the strike affects, hypothetically, 70 percent of the consumers in New York City and 60 percent of the producers (or 7 and 6 respectively if for convenience we use a scale of 10), our rating of the New York power strike would be 117. On the other hand, if the Los Angeles strike gave an urgency rating of 7 on the fifth day of the strike, with only 60 percent of the total consuming population affected and 50 percent of the producing population (or 6 and 5, on a scale of 10), the Los Angeles strike would have a rating of 77. The two ratings of 77 and 117 could then be directly compared, to give an approximation of the relative impact of a power strike of given duration on the respective communities. The same procedure would be followed for strikes separated in time. By thus converting our ratings into proportionate terms, we might say that a power strike of given duration is as public-affecting to a local community as a railroad strike of specified duration is to the nation, or that a local transit strike now inflicts proportionately less hardship on a community than a local transit strike of equal duration inflicted ten years ago, even though many fewer are affected in the former case and many more are affected in the latter case.

In making such relative ratings for local communities we do indeed drop out of the picture some of a strike's effects. Many local strikes do have their repercussions beyond local boundaries. Not all of a firm's consumers, both domestic and industrial, are located within a single city's limits, particularly when goods rather than services are involved. And the suppliers of a firm are likely to be spread, quite literally, throughout the nation, even though the amounts which they supply may be small. When, therefore, we concentrate on a strike's *local* effects we necessarily lose sight of the consequences which it has beyond the locality. We take into account only the consumer, producer-user, and supplier effects *within the local area.* Our justification for so doing is simply that, for some purposes, we are interested only in the local effects. One such purpose might be to gauge how a local strike stimulates public opinion.

It is our assumption that the rating scales which we have developed establish the "real effects" of a strike on the public. Moreover, while these scales admittedly do not directly indicate the effects of a strike on public opinion, we assume that there is a close and direct correlation between the "real effects" which the scales do reflect and the state of public opinion.

This assumption has its weaknesses. Other factors than a strike's "real effects" are likely to influence public attitudes toward it. For one thing, it seems likely that there is a "cumulative annoyance factor" which our scales do not show—the greater displeasure with the inconveniences brought by a strike if it is one of a number of strikes occurring at the same time than if it occurs in isolation. It is also probable that there is a "sympathy factor"—individuals not themselves harshly affected by a strike may nevertheless strongly oppose it because of their sympathy for those who are more seriously affected. The usual willingness of a striking union to supply services for "hardship" cases appears to be designed to avoid the operation of this "sympathy factor" on public opinion.

Moreover, if some principle appears to be involved in the strike, on which significant numbers of the public hold conflicting convictions, a general desire to end the strike may be secondary to divergent interest in winning the contest over principle. The real costs of the strike may be accepted more willingly, as members of the public align themselves with one or the other of the parties, becoming interested in ending the strike on particular terms rather than in simply ending it.

From the evidence of Chapters 3 to 5 it appears unlikely that issues over which a strike occurs are in fact more important to the public "generally" than the hardships engendered by the strike itself. Nevertheless, there remains the possibility that particular segments of the public may respond to such considerations of principle, perhaps with some intensity. We may think of such groups as party-oriented members of the public in distinction to the "general" public. And we have already noted that public opinion is more than a show of hands, since the intense feeling of a small group may be more effective on the parties than the less intense feelings of a larger number.

Specifically, the more management-minded members of the community may be less interested in simply settling the strike than in settling it on management's terms, while the more union-oriented members of the community may similarly subordinate their interest in restoring normal rights of expectancy to an interest in modifying, through union victory, the existing structure of rights. This is perhaps the Achilles' heel of our assumption that public opinion follows the real effects of a strike. Granting this weakness, however, it is still arguable that such party-oriented interests, in most instances, will be set aside—at least for the moment—as the real effects of the strike become more severe. In particular, as real hardship increases, the sentiment of the "general" public will itself intensify relative to the sentiment of the party-oriented groups.

Despite the limitations of the scales as indicators of public opinion with respect to particular strikes or particular types of strikes, it does therefore seem reasonable to assume that the effect of a strike on public opinion will be highly correlated with the actual effects of that strike on the public. As a corollary we should expect that sanctions directed against the parties to a strike relationship will be the more effective the more public-affecting is the strike itself.

For the purpose of indicating the state of public opinion in *local* strike situations, it is the relative rather than the absolute effects of a strike which are important. A strike of the same absolute magnitude *may* affect opinion quite differently, depending on whether it occurs in a small community where its impact is concentrated or in a large metropolitan area where its impact is relatively slight. A strike in the Meriden, Connecticut, plant of an automobile parts manufacturer, for example, may affect no more people than a strike in a similar plant in Cleveland, in absolute terms; but in the former case a more substantial element of the town is affected, since the plant represents a larger proportion of its industrial operations and employs a higher percentage of its labor force, who constitute the principal customers for its merchants, while in the Cleveland case the operations affect only a small proportion of the city's population. Public opinion in Meriden is therefore likely to operate on the parties more effectively in the case of a strike than in Cleveland, though we still could not say *a priori* whether it is sufficiently effective to end the strike.

CHAPTER EIGHT

Union and Management Views on Public Opinion in a Strike Situation

B EFORE proceeding with an analysis of the consequences of a strike relationship which runs counter to the parties' social responsibility, we are warranted in seeking further confirmation of our conclusion that public opinion concerning strikes is as the polls have represented it. It is only the existence of a public opinion hostile to strikes, at least in particular circumstances, which gives rise to an unfulfilled social responsibility, as here defined. Despite the real basis which exists for an opinion adverse to strikes, there are some who have expressed skepticism that public opinion is actually significant in strike situations. They would contest our reading of the poll results and related materials. It is their view that public pressures do not operate on the parties, even in important strikes, because there is not that strong adverse opinion which is necessary to evoke them. The public will generally put up with the hardships caused by a strike, they argue, rather than resort to sanctions against the parties—whether from inertia or from an ideological acceptance of the role of strikes in our society. This view suggests that the substantial numbers of those polled who favored limiting the right to strike might have been voicing an opinion held with no more intensity than their opinions on featherbedding or union security. If opinions respecting strikes are so lightly held that they generally pose no threat to those whose conduct runs contrary, there is no basis for charging a social responsibility to the parties, in this connection.

To secure additional materials bearing on this question, we addressed a letter to representatives and independent observers of unions and companies inquiring whether, in their knowledge or experience, public opinion influenced conduct in a strike situation and, if so, how. This inquiry was sent to somewhat more than a thousand individuals whose names appeared on the mailing list of the Yale University Labor and Management Center, in the membership directory of the Industrial Relations Research Association, in the Directory of Labor Unions compiled by the Bureau of Labor Statistics, and in a listing of labor reporters of major metropolitan newspapers. Approximately one fourth of our inquiries brought responses, not all supplying usable material, however. This canvass—admittedly unsystematic—was undertaken after the analysis of the preceding chapters had been completed, so that analysis of our replies constituted a genuinely independent reexamination of the issues so far raised.

A view similar to that identified above, skeptical of the influence of public opinion in strike situations, was expressed by about fifteen of our respondents. Some of their comments ran as follows:

I feel quite convinced that public opinion exerts a rather negligible effect on the outcome of strikes, at least in Massachusetts.—*A Boston newspaper reporter.*

I believe I can say truthfully that I can't recall a single instance in my 32 years of connection with labor matters in which public opinion was a decisive factor in settling a strike. I cannot even prove that public opinion has been a factor at all in our labor disputes, but we must think it is because we have had occasion to go to the public with statements and paid advertisements in labor disputes.—*The industrial relations manager for a meat-packing company.*

We have played parts in a rather wide variety of strike situations, ranging from the big strike at [a farm equipment manufacturing company] to walkouts in factories, retail stores and similar enterprises. Even when the public has been somewhat inconvenienced it has been our experience that it is inclined to be rather apathetic.—*An industrial relations consultant in Chicago.*

In general it is my feeling, with respect to local strikes, that public opinion as such has little weight either way.—*Operating executive in charge of labor relations for a large Ohio electrical manufacturing company.*

Frankly, I think that both management and labor tend to exaggerate the importance of public opinion in a strike situation. If it is important, I do not find that they have effectively exploited it.—*Attorney active in labor relations work in the New York City area.*

The public is apathetic to strikes and seldom injects itself into labor-management disputes. Occasionally, small segments will do a little shouting when they have been pushed around for a period of time, and this shouting is generally directed against the strikers.—*Official of a Providence machine tool company.*

I would say that in general the San Francisco public is not subject to emotional disturbance about labor controversies and while they are not happy about them, they look upon them as inevitable results of our economy here, just as they bear without complaint the inevitable rainy season when it arrives each Winter.—*Attorney active in labor relations.*

Since the larger group of the public falls into the apathetic category, my observations seem to indicate relatively little effect by public opinion on the behavior of either managements or unions.—*Former supervisor of labor relations in the hotel industry.*

These comments are generally suggestive of the viewpoint that public opinion is inert and inoperative in a strike situation. Some of them, however, raise questions which must be clarified before proceeding further with our analysis.

1. We are not concerned about the opinion of any group except that which is affected by the strike—the strike creates its own public—and even with respect to the public in this limited sense we anticipate a predominantly adverse opinion only when the strike's effects are significant. The fact that public opinion is *not* discernible in certain situations not important to the public is *not* conclusive that public opinion concerning strikes is lacking. We need experience no surprise when the president of a corporation writes, "I have had firsthand experience with three strikes. In each case these were in small plants (100-300 employees) producing welding electrodes, used by such customers as industrial plants and shipyards, who usually carry stocks for their immediate requirements. In these particular cases I did not observe any effect of public opinion." In these three cases, the urgency rating on our strike scales would have been low. With a low urgency rating we would expect that public opinion would not be evident. We have explicitly assumed that the intensity of public opinion varies directly with the strike's effects.

Failure of a union or management to elicit public support for its strike cause is thus no indication that public opinion is generally of no significance in strike situations. "In a recent ship repair strike situation," a labor lawyer writes, "it seemed to me that the Union had the better case and they did the usual job of propaganda, but so far as we were able to determine, pressure on the public and public officials was

of little avail. It seems to me that the best that one gets in a strike situation is a sympathetic but inarticulate public opinion." This may indeed
be the "best" that a union or management gets where the public is unaffected by the strike; our interest, however, lies in whether certain
lines of conduct are *forced* on a union or management when the public
is importantly affected by a strike.

Our previous analysis closely coincides with the view expressed by an
attorney prominently identified with the labor movement in New York
and New Jersey: "It is my considered judgment, based upon years of
experience, that the public, amorphous as it is, does not respond to
union and management propaganda but does respond in a strike situation when the strike subjects it to any measure of inconvenience. I believe that public opinion only plays a part when the public is hurt and
its squeals attract the attention of government officials, otherwise it is
my conviction that the public remains completely apathetic despite
anything the union and the management might do."

Public apathy under circumstances where it is largely unaffected by a
strike is not germane to the question of whether public opinion can
secure the end of a strike which has imposed costs of a significant magnitude on the public.[1] Our inquiry is directed to the question of
whether there is public apathy even in strike situations which significantly affect it.

2. It follows from our concentration on how a strike affects a public,
as a prerequisite to a public's affecting a strike, that we are not concerned with whether public opinion as to the issues behind the strike is
well informed, impartially arrived at, or discriminating—we are interested solely in whether public opinion exists in a degree sufficient to
affect the conduct of union and management. We are not interested in
whether the public examines and decides on the controversy but only
in whether it opposes the strike itself as interfering with its expectation
of a continuity of some service.

[1] One of our respondents from the Philadelphia area commented: "It is our general
opinion that public opinion, as such, has little bearing on a strike unless the public is
seriously inconvenienced. Even in instances of such inconvenience, as in Philadelphia
when the transit workers have struck on various occasions, it was interesting to note that
many people, rather than being upset or inconvenienced, seemed to almost welcome the
changes in their usual routine resulting from the strike." Without necessarily accepting
his evaluation of the reaction of Philadelphia commuters, we can agree that public
opinion may fail to assert itself even in situations where we might have expected it, depending on the "real" costs which the strike imposes. It has been said that the prolonged
strike of the Eastern Massachusetts Street Railway Company in 1952 did not arouse a
public reaction which the company had anticipated, as riders quickly made alternative
transportation arrangements which proved relatively satisfactory even for months.

This point deserves stressing because of the attitude prevalent among union officials that most newspapers are biased against them,[2] and because of the belief among many management people that government officials who are often called in as third-party intermediaries representing the public are pro-labor.[3] These judgments may both be correct, but they are not relevant to the question of whether public opinion exists to influence the parties. Such public opinion may be partially molded by

[2] The executive vice-president of a key CIO union expresses this view as follows:

"What is public opinion?

"In the average community, as well as nationwide, it is the press, radio, television and other media of mass communication. Since, regrettably, by their very nature and size, these organs of public opinion are in the hands of interests who side with management, the weight of this opinion is generally reflected *against* labor.

"With few exceptions, the news columns are slanted against labor in a strike dispute. The editorial columns almost invariably are. Radio and television are loaded with commentators who reflect management's viewpoint. Labor's story is often a lone cry in the wilderness of fact and fiction disseminated by the commentators.

"Since access to the advertising pages or sponsored time on the air is a matter of money, labor cannot hope to compete with management in utilizing this medium in influencing public opinion. The telephone companies, the steel companies, for example, spend millions of dollars in institutional and anti-strike advertising. No such sums, or anything like it, are available to a labor union in a strike situation. For the companies involved in a strike, these expenditures are tax deductible.

"Thus we see that both the organs of public opinion and the money necessary to use them effectively are in the main strictly on the side of management.

"It is remarkable, therefore, that labor does manage to get its side of the story told, however ineffectually. We do it, of course, through our own labor press. We do it through mass meetings and the distribution of circulars. We try to avail ourselves of such little time as we may get on the air—usually granted because FCC rules make it mandatory to permit labor's story after management has gotten in its story.

"The unions of course, try to use as many of the modern techniques available to them—within their means. They try to do a consistent job of public relations, they try to keep an up-to-date research department making information available to all interested parties, they seek to integrate themselves into the community of which they are an essential part.

"Americans, fortunately, do not believe everything they read in the newspapers or hear on the air. John Jones on strike for a living wage is their next door neighbor. They know he is not a wild Bolshevik seeking to overthrow our economic system. He wants to maintain his family, clothe them decently and educate his children.

"In the last analysis, the organs of public opinion finally fail when they load the case against labor in a strike situation. The community *knows* differently. Otherwise, it would be hard to explain how labor has won so many strikes against tremendous odds, steadily improved the wage and working standards of millions of Americans and steadily increased its membership to an all-time high."

[3] Typical comments from people in management are:

"Union pressure on the government is so great that it is extremely difficult to secure impartial hearings."

"My own judgment is that public opinion has very little bearing on the acts of union leaders. The politicians are interested in votes only and will go where they feel votes are. The government officials are appointed by politicians and respond to their sentiments."

"It is manifest that there has been nothing impartial in the attitude of the administration at Washington in labor matters since 1932. I say this without heat, or partisanship, but the statement seems to me to be incontrovertible."

biased organs—the public which is affected may be urged by newspaper editorials to direct its pressure against the striking union, for example. Or public sentiment may be filtered through prejudiced officials, so that a community pressure simply to end a strike may be translated, by government representatives, into a pressure on management to come to terms with the union, in order to end the strike. In either case, however, it is the existence of public opinion, *however formed or transformed,* that we are interested in. If it exists, then we must explain under what circumstances it is effective or ineffective in influencing the conduct of the parties to the strike. If such an opinion does not exist, however, out of apathy or cultural conformance, then obviously it cannot be responsible for pressures on the parties.

We would expect that bias would direct the application of public pressure primarily to one party rather than the other, but it is not whether sanctions are fairly or justly applied that we are interested in. We are concerned with whether sanctions are applied to *either* party or to both parties, in an effort to terminate the strike. The presence of bias is thus not relevant since it concerns the wisdom or justice of the opinion formed, whereas we are interested in the force of public opinion, however prejudiced or unwise that opinion may be.

3. Public opinion may make itself felt through the actions of some intermediary. Public pressure to end the strike may not only be applied directly to the parties but also indirectly through the agency of some influential individual who himself responds to public sentiment. That third-party intermediary may be a government official, a newspaper editor, a church representative, another business or union leader. However, it does not follow, simply because public opinion *may* draw such agents into its service, that whenever such third parties intervene in a strike situation they reveal the existence of a significant public opinion concerning the strike. We are not warranted in deducing from the operations of so-called intermediaries the presence of a principal force of public opinion. The third party may be responding to self-interest (the effort to make a reputation or to please one of the parties which desires his intervention) or to his own inner compulsions to assist in a "just" settlement. The public may indeed scarcely be aware of the existence of the strike which he is trying to settle.

The executive vice-president of a Midwest firm manufacturing machinery provides an illustrative case. "The only pressure which could be brought upon either the company or the union in a situation such as ours would be in the nature of quasi-social service pressures. There was considerable pressure of this kind exerted upon us. . . . This pressure came from organized groups, some somewhat radical, some religious groups, and, at the request of the union, from the office of the Mayor."

Much of the intervention by government conciliators falls in the category of efforts at dispute settlement not prompted by any force of public opinion. It is the conciliator's *job* to intervene, whether or not the public is cognizant of the strike.

One of our respondents, an official of a Connecticut firm engaged in the dyeing and bleaching of textiles, submitted a detailed statement of all third-party contacts during a two-month strike in 1951. None of these, he reported, gave evidence of being in response to public pressure:

In arriving at the statement that public opinion had no influence upon the Company's behavior in the strike situation I have carefully gone over the record of the strike and examined each contact or communication that we had with any person other than union representatives, excluding only communications with representatives of press and radio. There were twenty instances. I have also examined memoranda of meetings of executives of the company held during the strike at which courses of action were determined.

The contacts included an Army Air Force representative, three different Assistant City Attorneys on different occasions, a representative of the State Mediation Service, the Manufacturers Association of Connecticut, representatives of the Federal Mediation Service, a panel of the State Board of Mediation and Arbitration, the Mayor of the city, the Chief of Police, police officers of lesser rank, the Social Relations Committee of the local Council of Churches, an inspector from the State Labor Department and an individual who acted merely as a private citizen.

In none of the contacts was there any attempt by any of the persons involved to exert any power of their offices or organizations to influence the conduct of the company in the strike.

At no time were there any representations to the company that might be considered directly from the public.

I found no decision taken in executives' meetings that bears any evidence of having been influenced by a concern for public opinion, or resulting from any direct pressure of public opinion on the company.

Without any consciousness of the public opinion factor we did, of course, in appearances before the State Board Panel and in conferences with others, state the case for the company and argue the company's position, but this was in the nature of advocacy.

To this extent our behavior in the strike situation was influenced by the presence of, say, the Committee from the local Council of Churches, in that we were glad to meet with them and to explain the company's position. Such behavior influence is probably too indirect and too far removed from what you are concerned with to be of any significance but I give it to you in order that you may have a statement of the facts as nearly complete as I can make it.

Our inquiry is now more precisely delimited. We are interested in whether the parties to a strike situation which significantly affects its public believe that public opinion exists in a manner that may influence their conduct during the strike. We are not concerned with whether such public opinion is the product of propaganda or whether intervenors, themselves responding to public opinion, apply their pressures impartially and without prejudice. Nor do we consider that the mere intervention by third parties is itself sufficient proof of the existence of a public opinion. Let us now proceed to examine the evidence.

Public Opinion and Public Relations

A number of managements and unions testify that public opinion influences conduct during a strike situation, in their experience. Of course public opinion is not a concrete thing, susceptible to certain identification. It is possible that managements and unions are being influenced by a belief in something which does not exist. On the other hand, it is somewhat more likely that their reactions are influenced by previous events. The assistant director of industrial relations for one of the nationally known distillers offers an example:

As you might expect, decisions made and actions taken by our company are influenced to a considerable extent by public opinion in view of the fact that the very existence of our industry on a legal basis is virtually in the hands of the electorate. The "great experiment" taught us the value of good relations.

When in the 30's labor organizations expanded like a brush fire, we pursued a clear-cut policy of non interference and, as a result, we found our production workers 100% unionized within a very short time. From that date to this we have had frequent occasions in the give and take with the bargaining agents representing our employees when our decisions and actions were influenced greatly by consideration of the effect of public opinion. . . .

During the 17 years of our experience with unions we have naturally had some important differences which have resulted in threat of work stoppage and actual strikes. While most of these have been over rates of pay, one important one occurred when we tried to avoid the introduction of a health and welfare clause in our contracts.

In almost every instance where a strike was threatened or occurred the possible effect of public opinion on our actions played a very important role. On more than one occasion the company acceded to the demands of the unions on that basis alone.

Other examples were reported:

I recall an incident which occurred in Texas, where a [utility] company was adamant in its position on contract negotiations. By personal contact of the union representatives with local merchants and businesses, a leaflet campaign and a radio campaign stating the union's desire to avoid a strike and describing the adamant position of the management of the company, which, incidentally, was of non-resident ownership, considerable influence was generated. It is my opinion that sufficient influence was brought to bear upon the public resulting in a sympathetic public reaction against the utility and bringing about a settlement with a very short strike.—*Attorney active in labor relations.*

A number of years ago I was in charge of Industrial Relations in a comparatively small company in Missouri, and the union struck to attempt to force management to grant the union shop although a contract was in effect which contained a no-strike clause. One of the plants involved was in a comparatively small community and the payroll of the plant was of real economic significance to the community. . . . After two weeks or so, when it became fully apparent that the International Union was supporting the strike in defiance of contractual obligations, we decided to publicize the facts in the local newspaper . . . in a series of full page advertisements. This situation, of course, was favorable to the employer because the company position was clear and decisive and the issue was clear-cut without the ordinary complications that exist during contract negotiations. . . . The President of the International Union became greatly agitated at the publicity and as he put it to us he thought it was very unfair "to wash our dirty linen in public." In any event the employees organized a back-to-work movement which was successful.—*Industrial relations manager of a cement company.*

Public opinion is a factor in almost all strike situations and oftentimes it is the determining factor. Of course, generalities may be misleading, but judging from my experience, public opinion strongly affects almost every local or regional strike in all but the large communities. Much of my early experience in labor relations was in fairly small towns in Connecticut and Pennsylvania. There the bulk of the community had decided opinions on all labor disputes of any consequence. The welfare of the community was deeply involved in such situations and they affected local and state political fortunes. Under such circumstances both employers and employees struggled to align public opinion on their respective sides. The success of these efforts oftentimes determined the outcome of the strike.—*The president of a coal producers' association.*

The vice-president of a gas system reports that its companies "have experienced a minimum number of strikes, but I must say in every situation public opinion has had a definite effect on the decisions of management, and to a lesser degree on labor. I think I am also fair in stating that the effect would naturally be greater on management as they are looking into the future."

More commonly, however, the influence of a conceived public opinion is less pervasive than some of the above comments suggest. The director of industrial relations for a large glass company expresses a more prevalent view when he says, "We might make the general statement that public opinion in a strike situation is one of the major factors which might govern our decision in these circumstances, but it is far from the only consideration, and that our primary consideration is to achieve continuing, profitable operation by appropriate balancing of all of the factors that enter into decisions."

Even when the conduct of the parties is unmodified by public pressures, some of our respondents have testified to the existence of such pressures. The operating vice-president of one New York corporation writes that "probably all the pressure points in the book were in evidence during our work stoppage, to bring about early reconcilement of our differences. . . . We found the effects of them quite realistic and every so often had to go off by ourselves for a figurative inoculation to strengthen our resolve to maintain our position."

Union officials were less inclined both to specify and to generalize as to the direct influence of public opinion on their conduct in strikes, but newspaper reporters in two major cities pointed out that during 1952 the milk deliverers, members of the AFL Teamsters' Union, had been quick to deny threats of an imminent strike for fear that an aroused public opinion would be directed against them, as it had been in the past. A Washington reporter asserts: "The younger generation among the labor leaders places greater emphasis on public opinion values than their elders. I have heard a well known impartial chairman say that the public opinion argument in a jurisdictional strike situation was more persuasive with a certain union president than it was with his father who preceded him."

Among replies from management people, perhaps the most frequently encountered comment as to how public opinion influences conduct is typified by the statement of the director of industrial relations of one of the major automobile companies: "The importance of public opinion, in some strike situations, is evidenced by the closeness with which Industrial Relations people work with Public Relations people."

The close tie between public opinion and public relations, in a strike situation, was attested to repeatedly by our respondents. The following statements are suggestive of the management point of view and the type of public relations program to which it gives rise.

Frequently it is said that the parties to a labor dispute pay no heed to public opinion—that they assume an attitude of "the public be damned" especially when one of the parties is refusing to follow what may appear to some to be influential "public opinion." A moment's reflection upon the general course of conduct among employers and unions who become involved in a strike will indicate that this is not true. Perhaps in direct relation to the importance of a strike or labor disputes we see management and union directing a major portion of their arguments to one or more segments of the public. They show increasing evidence of being keenly and perhaps overly aware of the public—including all its segments—standing by as a sort of mass jury which would ultimately pass judgment. The extent to which management of this company is influenced by public opinion is observable from our effort to give the public the facts on which a sound opinion can be based.—*The vice-president in charge of industrial relations of a major steel company.*

[This] corporation at all times places a very high value on the good opinion of the general public. A strike would be considered a matter which must be handled properly from a public relations standpoint. Without going to the extreme of fighting our battle in the press, we would try to make our position as related to the points at issue in a strike clear to the general public; similarly, we would do what we could to correct any misinterpretation of the facts which might come from union representatives. —*President of an aircraft company.*

We have long recognized the effect of public opinion in connection with strike situations. On occasions where we anticipated serious labor difficulties in resolving labor-management differences, we have forwarded copies of letters addressed to all employees explaining the Corporation's position on controversial issues to a cross-section of the community thought-builders. —*Vice-president of a company in the oil industry.*

We make every effort to keep the businessmen and the general public in the plant community fully informed about the reasons for the strike and the details of the negotiations working toward a settlement. . . . We keep the public posted through articles in the local newspapers and send letters to the homes of businessmen, politicians, ministers, priests, and school authorities.—*Director of industrial relations for a processor of agricultural products.*

Unions are no less active in this effort to enlist public support for a cause.

Throughout the period preceding, during, and following the strike situations the Union is very conscious, at all levels of operation, of public opinion. This may be true to a greater degree than in other unions in view of the public utility nature of the communications industry, and in view of the industry's "service" tradition. Great thought, time, energy, and money, are devoted by the Union to the development and distribution of pamphlets, press releases, and other literature designed to acquaint all segments of the public with issues in dispute and the Union's position. The purpose of these publications is not only to set forth the facts, but to win public support and understanding of events leading up to and causing the strike. Whenever and wherever possible the Union attempts to obtain radio and television time, again to win public understanding and support. In many instances the Union must pay for this expensive communication medium.—*Research director of a national communications union.*

In our particular industry [the brewing industry] public opinion during a strike is of great importance. Both sides at the time of a strike attempt to gain public opinion through the use of newspaper stories and other media. In many instances where the union can show the justice of their position we have found that public opinion helps to a great extent in winning the strike for the reason that the public will not buy the products of the struck brewery, or other firm, as the case may be.—*General secretary of a national union with jurisdiction over breweries.*

Such comments of management and union representatives may or may not be the evidence which we seek, however. The fact that managements—and unions, too—have resorted to public relations programs in times of strike is not itself conclusive that public opinion with respect to the strike exists and is significant. The functions of the public relations department are varied. Without attempting to catalogue them, we can distinguish two relevant to our inquiry: (1) the party may attempt to overcome public apathy—the lack of a public opinion—and arouse support for its cause; (2) the party may seek to persuade an affected and concerned public *not* to pressure for an immediate settlement, enduring hardship or inconvenience in support of some principle which it is made to feel is important, or, alternatively, the party may urge an affected public to bring pressure on the opposing party, thus forcing a favorable settlement.

Performance of the first function of a public relations program (to arouse support for the party's cause) suggests that public opinion is *not* significant in the particular strike situation. It implies that the strike's urgency rating is low and that public opinion concerning the strike does not arise independently but must be stimulated by suitable "education" and information. It is only in connection with the second-mentioned function of a public relations department, to direct the course of a public opinion which is presumed to exist already in a degree sufficient to affect the outcome of the strike, that we find the evidence we seek.

If the strike is one which significantly affects the public, each of the parties may fear that pressures to terminate the strike may be directed primarily against it, leading to settlement on disadvantageous terms. In this circumstance each party may seek to channel public opinion primarily against the opposing party or to neutralize efforts of the opposing party to channelize opinion against it. The public relations program is here designed to justify actions which otherwise might be condemned; it is intended to deflect pressures which might force capitulation to the other party's terms in order to bring an end to hardships inflicted by the strike on the public. Opinion does not have to be aroused—because already aroused, it must be dealt with. The public interest does not have to be stimulated—because already stimulated to a degree capable of affecting the outcome of the dispute, it cannot be ignored.

In campaigns designed to channel a public opinion which is already aroused against the strike, argument on the basis of the equities of disputed issues is less likely to be effective than claims that the opposing

party is blocking agreement by an unreasonable or intransigent attitude, thus suggesting lack of concern for community hardship. Also
effective appears to be the publicizing of the use of violence by one's
opponent. Campaigns and countercampaigns of this nature (which on
their face may appear no different from those designed to *arouse* a
nonexisting public opinion in strike situations) do constitute (in distinction to those other efforts) evidence of the importance of public
opinion in a strike situation. An already aroused public opinion is seen
as a weapon to be used against one's opponent, if possible, and at a
minimum as a weapon which is to be deflected from use against oneself.
In these cases the actions of the party are suggestive of the reality of a
public attitude concerning the strike and a concern with the effect
which that attitude may have on it.

Public Opinion and Strike Strategy

Further inferential evidence of the reality of public opinion, to be
found in the actions of the parties themselves, is provided in the fact
that at times the parties build their strike strategy around it. The
attorney for a union in the utility field writes, "In many instances
public desire to avoid a strike is capitalized upon by the unions through
the enlistment of public officials who will request the union to postpone
or call off a strike, giving the union an opportunity to 'graciously and
with sincere desire to avoid deprivation of the public of the service of
a utility' postpone indefinitely a strike."

A strike is sometimes called only because it is believed that the
affected public will force an early settlement. The operating vice-
president of a company supplying construction materials reports: "It
was locally bruited around by the rank and file that 'This will only
last a couple of days—the company can't stand the interruption of
production and shipments because of customer demands—we'll be
called back to work with everything we have asked given to us.' After
the first payless pay day passed a certain restiveness developed in the
rank and file which gradually but inexorably burgeoned into a hostile
but recriminatory attitude toward the business agents of the local
union. After the second payless pay day, although I have no direct
evidence on this point, I suspect very definitely that International
representatives were themselves bringing pressure against the local
hierarchy to substantially modify their demands on the company. When
it became absolutely definite to the International representatives of

this union that the company's position would not be altered,[4] the crumbling walls of opposition disintegrated almost at once. A general meeting was called and quick concurrence given to return to work under the terms the company had specified."

A strike may be called because the union believes that management will go to any lengths to avoid an adverse public opinion which it believes will be associated with a strike, but the reverse is also true: a union may itself make sweeping concessions to secure agreement, rather than strike for better terms, because it fears an unfavorable public sentiment. A national official of one union writes: "We are very much concerned about public opinion in negotiations with hospitals. . . . We pay almost any price in order to avoid such strikes."

The actions of the parties thus provide some evidence as to the reality of public opinion in strike situations where the public is affected. The apathy or indifference which some have said characterizes the public in connection with strikes does not appear to be *generally* characteristic. Where the public itself is affected by the strike, the parties frequently seek to channel the resulting pressures or to incorporate them into their strike strategies.

Partisan Opinion Concerning Public Opinion

The above evidence is largely based on actions and experiences of the parties in strike situations. In addition a number of our respondents have volunteered opinions concerning the significance of public opinion. These beliefs may or may not have been the fruit of personal experience; in most instances, we have no way of knowing. The following are presented here as representative of a majority of those replying to our inquiry:

For many years and particularly in the last five years [this] Company has realized that public opinion is very influential not only in a strike situation but in any other matter affecting employee interest.—*Vice-president of a large electrical appliance company.*

Although I cannot point to definite instances, I do believe that it is important to have the community and, depending on the scope of the business, the public understand the dispute, the issue involved, and the attitude of the company concerned, for nowadays I find a growing feeling that we cannot regard disputes that affect the whole community as a private quarrel

---

[4] Despite the fact that the anticipated customer pressures did in fact develop and were keenly felt by the management.

between two interested parties.—*Vice-president in charge of public and industrial relations of a copper company.*

It is my well considered opinion that public opinion and, more particularly, community opinion has a most vital influence on the policies of both labor and management in their behavior during strikes or industrial disagreements.—*President of a New England manufacturing company.*

I believe that public opinion has a very strong influence with the management of industry in a strike situation, but public opinion does not command the respect of labor unions to any great extent.—*Vice-president of personnel and public relations of a major railroad system.*

I would say that almost all such public opinion reacts adversely toward the union that is on strike. This is simply because the public is not interested in issues but in the continued ability of the public to obtain the goods or services that are involved in the dispute. The union must, of necessity, bear the brunt of adverse public opinion in a strike because it is the party that is depicted as the aggressor by the newspaper, radio, etc.—*Representative of a miners' union.*

Our limited observation leads us to believe that public opinion is an important influence in settling strikes in communities where the strike affects the public, particularly the merchants.—*President of a paper-manufacturing company.*

We do feel that public opinion is a vital factor in the settlement of labor-management disputes. Certainly, where public service organizations are involved or where a strike involves products consumed by the general public, we feel that public opinion may well play a great part in the settlement of such disputes.—*Vice-president of a company manufacturing household goods.*

We very definitely believe public opinion influences both the Union and Management in a strike situation as well as other times of disagreement. —*Vice-president of a tool manufacturing company.*

Other respondents have defined their views more precisely. There appear to be two circumstances under which it is expected that public opinion will be a potent factor in a strike: when the struck product is vital to consumers, and when the struck plant is vital to a community, employment-wise.

1. Importance of the struck product to consumers as a determinant of public opinion significance:

The whole life and well being of a country is so dependent upon public services, such as transportation, telephone, light, power and other vital services, that the public interest is greater than that of any of its parts, and I think that this not only concerns public service but also the very large industries such as steel and oil, upon which the prosperity of the country depends.—*Copper-company executive (previously quoted)*.

It is my opinion that under ordinary circumstances the general public disregards any strike until it begins to affect the individuals directly. For this particular reason I believe that public utilities or public service organizations are affected greater by public opinion than any other companies. —*Vice-president of a utility*.

An overall generalization is that the type of industry in which a strike situation exists would be controlling to the extent public opinion would influence either party. For example, if a public utility would be involved, such as a telephone or a telegraph company, a commercial broadcast station, a transportation service or a distributor of facilities such as gas and electricity, ultimately the pressure would be great upon both parties because of the mass interference in the normal routine of the daily lives of the public at large. On the other hand, if the strike was in the plant of a manufacturer producing consumer goods, its effect upon the public would be limited to those contemplating purchase of the product and they might be content to defer their purchase until the situation cleared, unless confronted with an emergency in which event a second-choice product could be obtained. Yet, a manufacturer who is the principal employer in a small locality would be subject to public opinion and pressure even though very little of his product were used in that particular area. Generally, the effect of pressure would stimulate action to restore service or employment rather than provide a basis for settling the issue.—*Vice-president of a company manufacturing radio and electronics equipment*.

Workers in public utilities, especially, have found that strikes, unless won quickly, are not as productive of results as they used to be. The longer the strike, the shorter the temper of an inconvenienced public, including, unfortunately, workers themselves.—*New York attorney for a number of unions, chiefly in the utility field*.

It is my belief that public opinion with respect to the strike situation can have a very definite and significant influence on any strike situation if it is aroused to a sufficient extent. I would say that normally, unless the general public is directly affected by a strike as in the case of the shutdown of public utilities, there would be little interest on the part of the general public in a strike unless either management or labor or some other force as the public press would make a deliberate attempt to arouse the interest of the public.—*General president of a CIO union in the manufacturing field*.

I should say that the operation of public opinion in settling strike situations is directly proportional to the degree of public inconvenience.—*Labor reporter for a Midwest newspaper.*

2. Importance of the struck plant to the community as a determinant of public opinion significance:

The larger of our two manufacturing plants is in Louisiana, [at a location] where we are the second largest industry in town, with an annual payroll of many millions of dollars. If we were to have a strike, the economic consequences would be felt by almost the entire city, and the local merchants and other business and professional men would feel the pinch almost immediately. Consequently, it is my opinion that there would be tremendous public pressure on both the union and ourselves to get the strike settled, regardless of the nature of the controversy or the merits involved.—*Director of industrial relations for a firm in the oil industry.*

I certainly feel that public opinion is the single most important factor in any strike situation, particularly in small and medium-sized towns and in situations where the company is not part of a nation-wide series of plants. In a town like [this], I don't believe that a strike can be successful for the side which has public opinion against it.—*President of a ball-bearings manufacturing company in a town of 50,000 population.*

In a community of 150,000 within a 30 to 40 mile radius, with the company representing one-half the local employment, in a nine-week strike the community pressure becomes terrific. The mediator suggested 13½ cents, whereas the company had offered 10 and the union wanted 15. The mediator said if either party turned his proposal down he would make it public. Neither side felt they could risk turning it down.—*Director of industrial relations in a plant making heavy equipment (oral remarks).*

Public opinion definitely does influence management in a strike situation. Public opinion operates directly on the company, at least in a situation such as exists in [this small town] where the company is predominant in the community. In our situation we feel that the continued success of the company requires continued local favorable public opinion.—*Director of industrial relations in a textile company.*

It has been my experience that public opinion works strongest in small town labor problems. Here all the participants are closely connected and quickly and directly affected. The merchants must extend credits and forego collections, the general atmosphere of the town changes affecting the ministers, schools, and politics. In such cases, there is very direct (person to person) counseling, generally with both the management and the employees. . . . In larger cities the reaction is more indirect and therefore less potent.—*Vice-president in charge of industrial relations at an Ohio machine parts company.*

Our feeling is that in case of a strike public opinion would be non-existent, since we are a company of only about 1000 employees in a city of 3,000,000 inhabitants; and a large percentage of the employees do not live in Brooklyn. The local public would not be inconvenienced if we were struck forever.—*President of a Brooklyn metals fabricating company.*

In an overwhelming number of New York strikes in the metropolitan area, the public has no influence and, in fact, seems to pay little or no attention to stoppages. We may have a somewhat unusual situation here as many of the businesses are comparatively small operations and their individual troubles get lost unless they are parts of employers' associations.—*Member of New York State Board of Mediation.*

I have noted that in some of our smaller, so-called plant cities where we have one operation which perhaps supports a fourth or a third of that city's population, there is a much faster crystallization of public attitude than in our larger areas. While I can recall no instance where we acceded to public pressure in these smaller areas and settled a strike on terms which we did not like merely because of it, I cannot deny that the pressures aren't pretty rough at times. Usually it is not a question of the public in these smaller areas taking sides in the disputes. In most cases it represents self-interest or community-interest. The banker is worried about mortgage payments; the merchant is worrying about declining business; the mayor is worrying about the whole town falling apart and industry either moving out or refusing to come in; the minister is worrying about the families going hungry, etc. All they want is the men back at work, the merits of the dispute regardless.—*Member of the department of public relations in a major automobile company.*

It is our opinion that, except in the largest companies or those in which a strike affects the general public welfare, the effect of public opinion as it relates to either a Union or a Management in a strike situation is negligible in large cities. It is a potent factor in small towns.—*Director of industrial and public relations in a copper-tubing company.*

We have conducted many interviews with our representatives who have recently experienced strike situations. The results of these interviews firmly establish [that] there is a direct correlation between public opinion and its effect upon a strike situation and the size of the community, i.e., scope and limit of personal relationships. It was in the small community that we could isolate public opinion and note most clearly its effect upon the strike situation.—*Research director for a large national union with contracts in a number of manufacturing industries.*

The focusing by union and management representatives upon these two circumstances under which a strike is likely to evoke a potent public opinion—when the struck product is vital to consumers, when the struck plant is vital to a community—is what our prior analysis would have led us to expect. In the first case, it is the urgency rating which is determinative. The higher the urgency rating, the greater the effect on a given public (including not only the household consumer, however, but also the industrial consumer), and the stronger the opinion with respect to the strike. It was for this reason that we posited that the strength of public opinion in a strike was directly dependent on the "real" costs which a strike imposed on its public. In the second circumstance, involving the size of the community, the strength of public opinion is once again related to the "real" costs which the strike imposes, but the same real costs are *relatively* far more important in a small community than in a large city. A strike of one thousand employees in a town of 10,000 may involve no greater absolute costs than a strike of one thousand in a city of a million, but the effects on the smaller community will be proportionately much greater. Similarly, we might say that a strike of a company which supplies 25 percent of a small town's employment is *not* likely to arouse any more adverse public opinion than a strike at some hypothetical company employing 25 percent of a large city's labor force. It is not actually a small-town–large-city dichotomy which is a determinant of the strength of public opinion but the *relative* effects of the strike on the community. It was for this reason that, in Chapter 7, we converted our strike rating scales from an absolute measure to a comparative measure for purposes of contrasting different localities and different times.

Conclusions

We set out to analyze the views and experience of representatives of unions and managements as to the significance of public opinion in a strike situation. Admittedly, the conduct of our respondents in strike situations, as exemplified by their efforts to win public support or to use to their advantage a public opinion which they believe exists or which they anticipate will be aroused, and the beliefs of our respondents, however much founded on experience or thoughtful observation, are not conclusive evidence. When added to the conclusions derived in Chapter 5 from the poll materials, however, the total effect is quite convincing.

From our survey two primary conclusions stand out: (1) the parties believe that public opinion is a potent force in at least *some* types of strike situations and that it can significantly affect the conduct of a strike; (2) the significance of public opinion in a strike situation, or, to put it differently, the determination of *which* types of strike situations are affected by public opinion, depends on the "real" costs which the strike imposes, considered relative to the size of the community or communities principally affected.

While the replies of the union and management people do focus on these two conclusions, it is worth recording that a number of them suggested another ground determining whether public opinion became influential during a strike. This additional ground is whether some "incident" unrelated to the "real" costs which the strike imposes serves to arouse public opposition. The most frequently suggested incident serving this function was violence, though others which were mentioned were refusal to interrupt a telephone strike to provide emergency service during a disaster except upon stated conditions and the revelation of alleged Communist connections of the strike leadership.[5] Despite the fact that numerous respondents referred to the importance of keeping the public informed about the issues of a strike, there were few who expressed or implied a belief that an aroused public opinion sought to terminate a strike primarily on the basis of which party was in the "right" on the issues.

The findings of this chapter are nicely recapitulated in two statements received from respondents. The first is from the executive secretary of a mediation agency:

It has been our experience that public opinion is interested in strike situations normally to the degree in which the effects of the strike inconvenience the citizens as a whole. Where the inconvenience is considerable and direct, the influence of the people themselves as individuals is quickly

---

[5] Factors of this kind, and in some instances ideological ties to one or the other of the parties to the strike, unquestionably affect public opinion. It will be recalled that these were specifically considered when we chose to adopt the hypothesis that the strength of public opinion concerning a strike was directly related to the "real" costs which that strike imposed on its public. For a discussion of this point the reader is referred to the final pages of Chapter 7.

conveyed to both the company and the union by customers, by neighbors, and by the public as a whole conveying their wishes to their local governmental units in appeals to do something.

Where the effect is indirect, but where the dispute is long-drawn out or results in violence to individuals or destruction of property, public sentiment is inclined to be aroused at a much slower pace. In such instances we find that the element of personal interest or inconvenience is superseded by a sense of shock at actions committed by the parties.

Where both sides conduct themselves with a minimum of strife, where the public is not directly inconvenienced, the ratio of public opinion is pretty well limited to the parties concerned, those interested in settling disputes [such as mediation agencies], and those neutrals having some association or business contact with them.

And from an attorney active in labor relations in the Cleveland area:

1. The size and nature of the community has an inverse relation to the influence of public opinion. A strike which will arouse wide-spread interest in a small community will escape virtually unnoticed in a city like Cleveland. The interest in and knowledge of the strike in the former case will generate opinion which will be felt by both parties to the dispute. So also a strike in a highly industrialized community may attract little or no attention, whereas it would be a dominating event in a rural community.

2. The economic dependence of the community upon the strikebound industry is directly related to the influence of public opinion. In three recent cases of which we have personal knowledge, the town was small (under 5000), the company was substantial (300 to 1000 employees), and the economic dependence of the community was great. In all three cases, the influence of public opinion was substantial.

3. The nature of the issue or issues involved in the strike is related to the influence of public opinion. A strike over learners' rates will excite little sympathy for the Company, because the issue seems small, vague and unimportant. A strike over the Company's desire to reduce hours rather than to lay off employees is likely to have the Union on the defensive. Super-seniority for union officers may lie somewhere between these two cases. Perhaps it should be specifically noted that the nature of the issue relates more to the direction public opinion takes than it does to the question whether or not public opinion becomes a recognizable force in a particular strike.

4. The nature and location of the Company's customers are related to the influence of public opinion. Dramatic examples of this point are a Cleveland Transit strike, a power company strike, and a Union Commerce Building elevator operator strike. Here the customer is sharply and promptly affected by the strike, is close at hand to the strike, and usually becomes

vocal. In cases like these, public opinion is less likely to be partisan; the pressure is to *settle* without regard to issues or merits of issues.

In a sense this point is related to the point concerning the economic dependence of the community upon the strikebound industry. In the one case, dependence upon the industry is for a source of community income. In the other, dependence upon the industry is for a source of products or services.

The nature and location of customers as a factor in the influence of public opinion are further illustrated in situations where the strikebound industry is the sole, or virtually the sole, source of supply for other industries, or where customers typically do not buy much in excess of daily requirements, or where the product is in short supply, or (today) where the product moves into the defense effort. In these cases, customer pressure mounts rapidly and, in our experience, exerts a sharp influence upon the settlement of strikes.

5. Anticipated or apprehended public opinion is a factor which, in our experience, is frequently important in the settlement of strikes and in attempts to avoid strikes.

In a fair number of cases we find responsible managements attempting to determine whether public opinion will develop and what it will be if a strike is allowed to occur, or to continue. Customer opinion is customarily and carefully studied, and in many cases the expected reaction of the general public is also appraised.

Within the last month we had a good example of this. A strike of truck drivers brought building construction to a virtual standstill. The Union sharply reduced its demands. The employers felt that further reduction in demands was necessary. But it was widely believed by the employers that another week of the strike (which would have been probable before the Union would make further concessions) would cause public opinion (general and customer) to swing sharply to the Union because the amount of money separating the parties was only 2½¢ per hour.

In short, we think that the fear of public opinion not yet expressed is frequently an important, even though self-imposed, factor in settling and avoiding strikes.

6. A final, general comment is in order. It has seemed to us that, in its effects, public opinion is more likely to be non-partisan than partisan. We think we have found that where public opinion about a strike clearly had developed and was exerting pressure, its direction was largely toward *settlement* rather than settlement *in a particular way*.

Seldom have we felt that public opinion involved a conclusion that the Company was wrong and the Union right, or vice versa. Normally we feel, rather, that public opinion is that the parties should terminate the strike. Since this involves settling their differences, the result, of course, is that the merits of any particular issue must be resolved or compromised. But public opinion, more often than not, leaves this to the parties.

So similar are these conclusions to those presented earlier that it is worth repeating that they have no common origin. The earlier conclusions were reached by deduction. The conclusions just presented were the product of experience. By both routes we arrive at the same terminus: public opinion is significant and influential with respect to the conduct of parties to a strike in those situations where the public is itself significantly affected by the strike.

CHAPTER NINE

Social Control of Strikes: A Hypothesis

THE sanctions which are directed against union and management in a strike situation will be the more effective the more heavily a strike weighs on its public, according to the hypothesis already developed. In terms of our strike-rating scale, the higher a strike's rating the more likely that public pressures will be forthcoming to induce settlement.

We now proceed to a further hypothesis, which we shall wish to test before accepting: If the effects of a strike on the public reach some "critical" rating, beyond which the strike relationship is viewed as inconsistent with public rights of expectation to a continued flow of vital goods and services, then public pressures on the parties will be sufficient to force termination of the strike. Relationships in the society need not and cannot be perfectly harmonious. It is enough if reasonable compatibility exists—reasonable in the sense that the degree of incompatibility (of frustration of rights) is tolerable. We are hypothesizing that there is some strike rating which marks the dividing line between what a public conceives as being tolerable violation of its expectations and intolerable violation, and that any more onerous strike effects can be counted upon to evoke sanctions adequate to force a resumption of the supply of services or goods which have been withheld by the strike. We should not, indeed, expect to find some precise score which marks a fine separating line between tolerable strikes and those considered intolerable, but we might well expect to find some range of tolerance within which a forced strike settlement is probable and beyond which it is almost certain.

The significance of this hypothesis requires no elaboration. It would, if validated, suggest that at least one of the parties to a bargaining dispute must be confident that its relative bargaining power will permit the winning of a strike before the critical rating is reached, or else be equally confident of the disposition toward it of any third-party inter-venors responding to public pressure after the critical stage of the strike has been passed. It would likewise suggest that we already have built into our social system strike controls of a sort, called into play whenever the occasion actually demands their use and at that time capable of solving particular issues of inconsistent rights of expectancy. The need for additional forms of strike control may thus be considerably exag-gerated. The system may actually now be working practically if not perfectly through devices more subtle than some appreciate, to assure the objective of continuous provision of important goods and services. Indeed, the bargaining parties may actually have less leeway than the hypothesis as formulated suggests, since if from experience either the public or their third-party intermediaries believe that the critical stage of a strike will be reached quickly, sanctions may be applied to forestall the strike entirely. Such an implicit system of strike control has an appealing flexibility in that its application can be tightened or loosened in response to changes in public attitudes, and this itself carries an additional appeal for those who link response to public attitudes with democratic methods.

It is, of course, possible that the sanctions may be ineffective to end a strike in particular situations, because the parties elect to accept the penalties rather than settle on terms distasteful to them. In such a case we can hardly consider the system of sanctions *generally* ineffective, however, as long as they do impose a penalty on the party ignoring the pressure for settlement and as long as this penalty is appropriately severe so that it discourages unions and managements in other strike situations from preferring penalty to settlement.[1]

It may be objected that the parties are not penalized for single courses of action; that a union and a management engage in a variety of courses of conduct, some of which may be approved, others disapproved. Pressures for settlement of a strike which are ignored by the parties may not bring penalties upon them if they have, by prior beneficial behavior, built up a fund of good will. Hence the system of sanctions—while

---

[1] This is perhaps a proper place at which to insert a reminder that in this analysis a discussion of the effectiveness of sanctions is not to be construed as an acceptance of the desirability of applying them, nor is an examination of the requirements of effective sanc-tions to be regarded as implying that sanctions should be "improved" or made more effective in these particulars. The purpose of this analysis is the testing of hypotheses sug-gested by an examination of the data in the area of our inquiry, and an interpretation of the results, in an objective manner rather than as one pleading a case.

existing and genuine—may often be ineffective, failing both to end the strike and to impose penalties on the parties for not ending it. Such an objection misconceives the nature of sanctions, however. If sanctions are to be effective in preserving *specific* rights of expectancy, they must be geared to particular conduct which violates those rights, so that sanctions cannot be easily evaded by generally satisfactory conduct. To the extent that *generally* satisfactory behavior becomes an excuse for violating specific rights of expectancy, the sanctions are ineffective (by definition), just as enforcement of laws against robbery or shoplifting would be ineffective if a person's otherwise blameless conduct were to be accepted as excuse for engaging in those activities. The test of effectiveness of sanctions in a strike situation, then, is whether they secure a resumption of the discontinued service before the strike's effects are viewed as an unreasonable violation of expectations, except in a small minority of cases—decidedly unrepresentative—where individuals may prefer to accept appropriate penalties rather than submit to a settlement which they find unusually obnoxious. And it is our hypothesis that there is some critical strike rating (or definable range) at which sanctions become effective in this sense.

This hypothesis is difficult to test. It would require a penetrating examination of a variety of strike situations in which the attempted application of sanctions was studied simultaneously with a running calculation, day by day, of a strike's effects on the public. From such an extensive examination some conclusion might be ventured. The data necessary for a testing of this sort are simply not available. A less acceptable procedure has thus been adopted. We have studied in detail the nature of the effects on the public of strikes in three vital industries —coal, railroads, and steel. Of the strikes so studied, we have rated eleven in coal (omitting four wartime stoppages) and three each in railroads and steel, using the scales previously devised and basing our calculations on the last day of the strike (or on a day close to the strike's end where there has been some reason for such a choice). The seventeen ratings are arrayed below in descending order.[2] We are interested in discovering whether in such an array of ratings there is evident any isolable range, suggesting a "critical" level of public affectedness at which point pressures to terminate the strike become

[2] For descriptions of the effects of these strikes on the public and the computations on which the strike ratings are based, the reader is referred to Chamberlain and Schilling, *The Impact of Strikes* (New York: Harper & Brothers, 1954).

effective. For this purpose we would be unwarranted in assuming that
all the strikes rated were ended by public pressure; some may have been
brought to a close by pressure of one or the other party in the bargaining process. This would seem most likely to be the case in those strikes
with low ratings, suggesting a relatively limited impact on the public,
hence—by our assumption—relatively light public pressure to terminate the stoppage. On the other hand, there is reason to believe that the
strikes with high ratings, indicating relatively greater public hardship,
might be expected to elicit substantially greater public pressure on the
parties, and thus that it is in the higher-rated strikes that we must look
for the "critical" rating, if there is one.

Strike	Rating
1. Bituminous Coal, winter, 1949-1950	492
2. Bituminous Coal, spring, 1946	338
3. Steel 1952	315
4. Bituminous Coal, fall, 1946	306
5. Steel, 1946	167
6. Railroads, 1951	161
7. Steel 1949	128
8. Railroads, 1946	111
9. Bituminous Coal, spring, 1948	101
10. Railroads, 1950	65
11. Bituminous Coal, spring, 1939	62
12. Bituminous Coal, summer, 1947	34
13. Bituminous Coal, spring, 1941	26
14. Bituminous Coal, spring, 1947	23
15. Bituminous Coal, summer, 1949	12
16. Bituminous Coal, fall, 1941	10
17. Bituminous Coal, spring, 1949	10

There is some indication of an isolable range of critical effects near
the top of the array. Strikes 2, 3, and 4 (the bituminous coal strikes of
spring and fall, 1946, and the 1952 steel strike) are within 32 points of
each other, lying within the range 306 to 338. Do we have here a tentative identification of a critical range of strike effects (calculated in terms
of absolute rather than proportionate numbers affected), critical in
the sense that when the impact on the public rises to this order of
magnitude public pressures will be aroused sufficient to safeguard
public rights of expectancy?

Our sample of strikes is, of course, too limited to permit any conclusive answer to that question. The *apparent* emergence of such a
range from our array may be only coincidental. While further and
more refined testing of the hypothesis seems amply warranted, on the

evidence adduced the most we can say is that the hypothesis has not been nullified.

A question can be raised concerning the bituminous strike of winter, 1949-1950, which far outstrips the three apparent range-fixing strikes in effect, by amounts about half again as large. Obviously this strike cannot be included in any purported critical range without abandoning the notion of an isolable range. Yet how can we account for its very high relative rating, far in excess of any apparent critical level at which public pressures can be relied upon to terminate the strike? There can be no question of the harsh impact of this winter coal strike. Households were cold from lack of coal. Railroad traffic, both passenger and freight, was sharply curtailed. An estimated 230,000 employees were reduced to idleness through user-producer and supplier effects. Throughout January many local and state officials appealed to President Truman to take emergency action. It was not until February 11, almost six months after the start of the strike, that a temporary injunction against the union was obtained under the Taft-Hartley Act, however, and not until threatened seizure of the mines on March 3 that the parties were pressured into settlement. The critical level had thus been reached and far exceeded long before sanctions were ultimately effective, if 338 be taken as approximating the upper limit of "tolerable" interference with the normal flow of goods and services. Is this circumstance compatible with the existence of a critical range?

This one exception is indeed compatible with our hypothesis if it is believed that either the parties themselves (union and management) or the third-party intervenor influenced by public pressure (the President) were penalized for failing to respond (or respond earlier) to public opinion, and penalized sufficiently to discourage a repetition of their conduct either by themselves or by others. There is no clear indication that sanctions of this order were actually imposed, though a subtle analysis of political effects might disclose them.

There are other admitted objections to a conclusion that an identifiable range of critical strike effects has even been tentatively identified. Four of these may be mentioned briefly.

1. The rating scales themselves may be poorly conceived, so that they do not measure, even with reasonable approximation, degrees of public-affectedness. A more satisfactory rating scale might destroy the illusion of a critical range (though on the other hand it might increase the apparent likelihood of the existence of such a range).

2. The scales may be satisfactory, but the data which we feed into them may be sufficiently unreliable to render suspect any conclusions derived from them. The information we require is information which is often unavailable in the form desired. Estimates have had to be made; judgments and informed guesses have had to substitute for facts. Any result which is obtained on the strength of such analysis must be treated with caution.

3. The hypothesis of a critical range may be a reasonable one, but the notion of what constitutes a critical range may be erroneous. It may be the cumulative effects of a strike rather than the effects on some given day which are determinative of public reaction. Two strikes with equal ratings on their day of termination may have in fact evoked pressures of considerably different magnitudes because of effects prior to that day. A strike which rates 50 on each of the first ten days and then 500 on the eleventh day may be settled less quickly than a strike which rates 400 on each of its first eleven days. The nature of our data have not permitted examination of this possibility. This is a conceptual issue which can be tested only with better data. It raises a question, however, as to whether the supposed range of 306-338 may not be only coincidental, since the ratings compared may not even be conceptually significant.

4. The notion of a critical range suggests that a strike will be terminated by public pressure when its effects reach some identifiable order of magnitude. When a strike will be terminated, however, depends on the cost to each of the *parties* of continuing the contest. The sanctions available to a public constitute only one element in the costs to the parties. Other costs—the possible permanent loss of markets, the continuing loss of income with attendant hardships—are present also and influence the timing of the strike settlement. It is the cost of public sanctions *plus* the cost of normal strike attrition which, it would appear, constitute the pressures on the parties to terminate the strike. If an isolable range of critical strike effects is assumed (that is, a range applicable to all strikes), this would appear to rest on any one of three prior assumptions: (a) The costs of attrition in all strikes, at the critical level, are relatively equal, so that total costs (sanctions plus attrition) are relatively equal. This assumption seems tenuous on its face. (b) The costs to the parties from public sanctions are so much greater than attritional costs that the latter, even though unequal as among strikes at their critical levels, are largely subordinated to the former. This too

seems unlikely. (c) The two kinds of costs, sanctions and attrition, are not really additive, and public pressures work more or less independently of private attrition, in the same manner that a persecuted individual might succumb to torture more or less independently of any fines imposed on him. This possibility would appear to have greater surface plausibility, but it requires testing.

There are thus substantial doubts as to whether an isolable range of critical effects not only has been but can be identified. It is not enough for the testing of our hypothesis, however, even to establish— if we could—that an identifiable range of strike effects exists beyond which public pressures force termination of the work stoppage. It is necessary to establish further that the range so identified is one that marks a dividing line between what the public conceives as admissible frustration of its rights of expectancy, since perfect compatibility of relationships is too much to ask, and what it regards as unwarranted and unreasonable violation of its expectancies. We have defined a critical range of strike effects as one which not only evokes sanctions sufficient to terminate the strike but to accomplish that result before strike-imposed hardship passes beyond the limits of public tolerance.

Once again we are in the realm of public opinion, and our judgment is necessarily inconclusive. It seems evident to us, however, even should we accept (as we do not) the surface suggestion of our data that a critical range exists in the sense that it provokes sanctions adequate to end the strike, that if that range is of the order of magnitude suggested by our array (that is, 306-338, or, more broadly, comparable to the effects of the two 1946 bituminous strikes and the 1952 steel strike), then this exceeds the level of effects which would make the right to strike tolerably compatible to the public with its own rights of expectancy to goods and services. It is our belief—but admittedly based only on casual empiricism—that strikes with effects rating considerably below the range identified in our array have aroused strong and even violent public reaction. In that event, one would expect that the critical range—if one exists—would be lower than that indicated by our data. This would leave us (1) without present evidence for the existence of such a critical range of strike effects, and (2) with a larger number of exceptions to be explained, even should such a range emerge from a larger sample.

There is one possible means of reconciling the existence of a critical range of strike effects of the order of magnitude suggested by our array of ratings with our conclusion that public insistence on the honoring of its rights to goods and services occurs at lower levels of strike effects. No allowance is made in our ratings for the *anticipated* effects of a strike. It may be public anticipation of effects, however, rather than actual effects, which calls forth pressures for settlement in the lower-rated strike situations. Rail strikes are illustrative. A characteristic of such stoppages is that their effects cumulate rapidly. The 1946 railroad strike, which rates only eighth in our array, if allowed to persist for even a week longer might well have advanced into or beyond the 306-338 range. More precisely, public anticipation—or third-party antici-pation of public opinion—might have been that a rail strike allowed to continue even briefly might threaten an impact roughly equivalent to the two coal strikes of that year or a steel strike such as that which came in 1952. If such anticipations could be taken into account, it is possible that the lower-rated strikes in which public displeasure was made evident would be promoted into the range identified in our array, which might then be called critical in the sense in which we have defined that term.

This is a possibility which should not be ruled out, but it does not appear to us to constitute a satisfactory reconciliation between (1) the existence of a critical range of strike effects of an order of magnitude approximating 306-338 on our scales, and (2) the existence of a public opinion hostile to a strike which imposes hardships of a lesser magni-tude. If anticipation is to be taken into account, it would appear neces-sary to increase the ratings for *all* strikes, including those which now identify the range 306-338, and in that case the gap between categories (1) and (2) may remain, still requiring explanation.

We are thus left with considerable skepticism regarding our hypoth-esis. At best, it seems to us that should a critical range of strike effects be found, covering approximately the range indicated by our data, this would suggest that sanctions are effective more as an ultimate resort than as a guarantee that public rights will be reasonably respected. Such a finding would not be without its own significance, and certainly warrants further investigation, but it is not the same as the hypothesis we sought to test. The sanctions available to the public or to those who intervene at its behest and on its behalf thus appear to serve as a safety valve preventing explosion, but to be relatively ineffective as assurance of social responsibility in the strike relationship, as we have defined that term. The adverse opinion of the public to a strike may be strong; its members may apply such direct sanctions as they can and demand third-party intervention to end the dispute which affects them critically, and these are the conditions under which we would expect our hypothesis to be substantiated. That even under these conditions our hypothesis appears of doubtful reliability suggests that the weapons at the disposal of the public or its agents are inadequate to the task. The spirit of the public is willing but its sanctions are weak. Except in desperation, its means of influencing the conduct of the parties are likely to be of uncertain effectiveness in ending a strike.

We cannot accept this as explanation for the apparent unreliability of our hypothesis, however, until we have explored the subject of sanctions. We shall do this first by a general examination of the types of sanctions available.

CHAPTER TEN

Direct Sanctions in Support of Public Opinion

EVEN where a dominant public opinion exists, it does not automatically achieve its objective. In some manner the opinion of the public must be translated into conforming action by the parties if it is to be considered effective, or alternatively nonconforming action by the parties must meet with penalties sufficient to discourage nonconformity of others in similar situations. If public opinion adverse to a strike is to be effective, it must force an end to the strike or, alternatively, penalize the parties severely enough so that in the future management and unions, under similar pressures, would be likely to call off a strike.

The effectiveness of public opinion thus lies in the penalties which it can impose. These penalties—the party's only alternative to conformity—we call sanctions. The effectiveness of public opinion, then, lies in the sanctions which are at its disposal.

Sanctions may be both direct and indirect. By direct sanctions we mean those which the affected public can itself impose on the striking parties. A threat of refusal to do future business with the parties if the strike continues, a loss of community respect, the nagging of one's striking neighbor, are all examples of sanctions which the public can itself impose if the parties fail to end the strike which is hurting it. Indirect sanctions are those which involve a third-party intermediary, some individual whom the affected public expects to "do something" about the strike and over whom it holds some influence compelling him to "do something," and at the same time an individual who in turn holds the power of sanctions over the striking parties. In this case the public's influence on the striking parties is mediated by some agent, hence indirect. These two types of sanctions might be diagrammed thus:

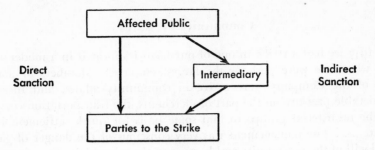

Actually, as we shall find, the indirect sanction may be more complex than the above diagram suggests.

Not all interventions by third parties come in response to public pressure, as we had earlier occasion to observe. When the mayor uses his office to end a strike, he may be responding to public opinion (an instance of an indirect sanction), but he may also be responding to pressure applied by one of the parties to whom he owes a political debt (in which event the sanction he employs is not in support of public opinion and hence is not the indirect sanction as we have defined it).

In this and the following chapter, we shall describe the principal penalties which an aroused public can impose on the parties to a strike. We make no effort to estimate the frequency with which any sanction is employed. These same sanctions may, of course, be used by other groups for other purposes—this does not concern us. Nor are we at present attempting to evaluate the effectiveness of these sanctions, a task which we shall undertake in a later chapter. Nevertheless, this catalogue of sanctions should impress the reader with the considerable arsenal of weapons available to the affected public and its agents. It helps to explain why such a seemingly empty threat as "the public won't stand for this" may have for even the hardened businessman and unionist a compelling effect, simply because it raises in their minds pictures of sanctions which *might* be imposed. The intangibility of the threat, if coupled with a knowledge of the numbers of ways in which it might be made tangible, may command reconsideration of the parties' positions. These sanctions which we are about to consider are the principal explanation for that respect for public opinion in a strike situation which, as we found in the preceding chapter, is held by many unions and managements. We turn now to consider the direct sanctions.

Community Pressures

In 1947 we had a strike in one of our factories located in a moderate size town where we were perhaps the largest employer. Members of management of the Company were active in community affairs, and there was considerable pressure on the part of merchants, the transportation company, and the ministerial groups to find some basis for quick settlement of the dispute. . . . The management was very conscious of the danger of gaining the ill will of the community and because of the community pressure exerted on both parties, the strike was settled in a reasonably short time.

This comment from a director of labor relations suggests that management, in the instance cited, was fearful of some penalty which an aroused community might impose on it. He speaks of "the danger of gaining the ill will of the community" as though this constituted a hazard seriously to be avoided. But wherein lies the danger? Admitting the fact that most people prefer to be well rather than poorly thought of, what hazard to a company does community ill will involve? What sanction can a hostile public impose on it?

The answer is not easy to come by. In part it is bound up with the intangible notion of "good will" which is so important a part of business philosophy. A businessman asked to define "good will" is likely to find himself groping for the right phrases to describe something which he knows is real and vital to the company's welfare but which has no certain form. He is sure it is real and vital because he spends money to create it. He believes it determines the value of the company's name or trade mark. It is the product of years of reputation-building. From the time the young career employee begins his rise up the managerial ladder, the chances are that he is made to feel the need for protecting company "good will" almost as he might protect his own honor. In some instances the jealous regard for the company's reputation is carried farther. The company's concern for its good name has at times led to an attempt to prescribe the private conduct of its employees. Behavior which is offensive to community standards has been made the basis for discipline or discharge, lest the offensive conduct of the employee be associated in the minds of the public with the name of the employer.

Good will is most commonly thought of as something existing in the minds of a firm's customers, but others are involved as well. A firm is mindful of the need for creating good will among its suppliers, too, not the least of whom are those from whom it hires its labor services. The reputation for fairness which a firm enjoys in its labor market— that is, in its local community—is something to be earned and safe- guarded. Good will in the labor market is gained not simply through the fairness of the company's labor relations, however, but through its general reputation. Workers prefer employment in a company which is respected for the quality of its product or service, for example. Where a company produces locally for a local market, then the community as both customer and supplier becomes the source of the company's good will.

It is because good will is valued so highly that managements fear any impairment of it. To the extent that a public opinion adverse to a strike is regarded as a threat to a company's good will, there is here an effective pressure on the management to seek a prompt end to the strike, a pressure over and above that provided by any economic losses which it is suffering.

Few types of enterprise are so subject to such pressure as are local public utilities. The director of personnel relations for an electric company remarked in conversation:

In a strike situation, an atmosphere of pressure is built up. The com- munity's leaders come in to see you about it. Customers who are particularly affected swamp you with calls and letters. The company is continuously deluged with reminders of its importance to the community. The result is to build up a general climate of opinion that is difficult to resist. Only if management believes some very important principle is at stake or if it conceives that the only alternative is concessions leading to financial dis- aster, can it withstand the barrage of public expression. But none of these pressures carries a "club." The only penalty on us is loss of good will, but that's enough. It's something the company has tried to build up over the years, and the need for which has been ingrained in every utility man.

Why is good will important? I suppose it's primarily that the company is dealing with people in the community every day, in their homes, on their property, and there is a strong desire to maintain a good relationship between you and them. It's as one of the men at the telephone company said to me the other day, "You let yourself get pushed around a good deal in this business because the customer can't go anywhere else"—a point of view which is just the opposite of that usually attributed to monopolies. It's because the customer can't make an effective substitution of service that it's so important to treat him well rather than leave him with a frustrated feeling of not being able to do anything about his gripes. So you feel a pressure to do things that you might not like to do, or that you might not do if you could tell him to go somewhere else. It's that kind of pressure we feel in a strike situation. I would say this is the most important way in which public opinion at such a time affects us.

The degree to which a company feels a threat to its good will is likely to be directly related to the urgency rating of a strike affecting it— that is, directly proportional to the "real" costs which the strike imposes on the public. A product vital to its consumers, a plant vital to its community, are conditions under which sentiment adverse to the strike becomes significant and hence are conditions under which the sanction of loss of good will is likely to be most keenly felt. Nevertheless, it is interesting to note that so jealous of their good will are some manage- ments that even when a company is submerged in a large city and its product is not essential to its customers, the fear of this sanction may still be present. There appears to be a compulsion on management to "justify" its position.[1] The vice-president of a company in the Boston metropolitan area, when asked why he should be concerned about his company's reputation during a strike when the strike would probably not even be reported in the local papers, hesitated and then replied that perhaps they could afford to take a chance on fighting the strike without respect to community sentiment but that they just did not want to take such a chance. "Bad news has a way of traveling fast."

Considerations of this nature give substance to what otherwise appear to be pious generalities: "The chief pressure of which we have been aware in management-labor negotiations is community status and public endorsement." "In my experience the concern of management is more likely to be with community standing than with the direct effect of consumer reaction on their product or services."

This concern by management for the company's reputation is far from impersonal. It involves their own individual standings and repu- tations in the community. If a company is known by the character of its people, it is no less true that its people are known by the character of the company. The status of a manager in his community is in part a reflection of the status of his company in the community. The company

---

[1] This compulsion is probably related to that function of a public relations program which in Chapter 8 we characterized as designed to arouse public support. It appears likely that such efforts are often undertaken not so much with the expectation of enlisting support that will bring an earlier end to the strike as to bolster community good will toward the company, however long the strike may last.

which enjoys the good will of the community—is known as "fair," "considerate," "reliable," etc.—endows its officials with a prestige that is lacking in enterprises, otherwise comparable, which are known as "tight-fisted," "tricky," "mean," etc. This means that the manager has a personal stake in the maintenance of his company's reputation. For his company to engage in a strike which works hardship on his community is to threaten him with a loss of personal prestige if the public condemns the company from which he derives, in part, that prestige.

Moreover, the manager's future may be linked to his company's standing. Prospects for recognition by other companies both inside and outside the local community, his chances for advancement by outside promotion, are closely linked to the reputation which his company enjoys. The individual who is sales manager for a company enjoying an enviable reputation is likely to receive more recognition in the sales fraternity than another individual, perhaps of equal ability, whose connection is with a company less happily known.

We have been speaking so far of company good will and the possible loss of prestige to management in a strike situation. What of the unions?

When a union goes on strike, with results that evoke a widespread public resentment, the striking workers must expect to feel that resentment even within their neighborhoods. To some extent public indignation may be deflected against the company, but if the strike really hurts the community it is likely to be the union members who, because calling the strike, are criticized as unmindful of the suffering of others. As pressure mounts and members become uneasy over the role in which they have been cast, there is a likelihood that they will generate pressures on their own leadership to end the strike. Even if the union leadership has maintained a resoluteness against community condemnation, it will be difficult for it to risk its position within the union by defying internal pressures to call off the strike. Certainly such a pattern is not discernible in every strike, and there is here implied no lack of purpose or resolve among striking union memberships generally. Nevertheless, union leaders who have conducted strikes significantly affecting the public will often relate that—however brave their public statements of union solidarity—there was a continuing concern whether the members would hold out against such direct pressures applied to them.

One observer summarizes the situation thus: "The average man or woman is not a crusader and therefore does not care to be aligned with an unpopular strike or issue. Therefore, as the neighbors and friends begin to criticize a particular situation as being futile, unnecessary, wrong, etc., the pressure within a union membership begins to build up and influence union leadership."

Not only are internal pressures effective on the union leadership, but, to a greater extent than with companies, unions are identified with their leaders. An unpopular strike threatens the reputation of both the official and his union.

Again, in the utility field such pressures are likely to be most intense. This is not the only area in which they become effective, however. Prolonged strikes of an industry-wide nature (whether industry-wide within a community, a region, or the nation) are likely to develop such pressures. In time of war any company whose production is related to the military program is almost certain to be the focus of bitter criticism, directed at either or both the parties. Special circumstances may affect the outcome. A labor reporter sends in the following example:

Some 1,000 street car and bus operators, working for a private company that furnishes all public transportation in this city, set a strike for May 1. That was also the date for a $50,000,000 city bond election. The City Council, by resolution at its regular meeting two days before the scheduled strike, called on the company and its workers to delay the strike for 24 hours (if it became inevitable to strike) so that public transportation would be available to take voters to the polls. The union belonged to the AFL Central Labor Council which already had endorsed the $50,000,000 bond program. In an "eleventh hour" vote just before the scheduled strike, the union agreed to postpone its strike for 24 hours. This postponement, I believe, was influenced by public opinion, because a previous bond election only two months before had failed to pass, and the public had begun to realize that it meant stopping the city's big public works program of building a new water plant, a new sewage plant, miles of street paving and laying of water mains and sewers. I feel sure the union wanted no share of the blame if the second election failed to pass.

One attorney well known in labor relations work concludes: "Very few citizens, regardless of their identification with management or labor, are impervious to the attitudes and evaluations of their fellows. When those attitudes and evaluations crystallize into a clearly defined expression of public opinion the response is, I think, inevitable." Whether or not the response is inevitable, it seems clear that condemnation of a strike by an aroused public carries a genuine threat to the reputation and prestige of the parties. This sanction imposes social costs whose reality has seldom been seriously questioned.

Where the parties are active leaders in other community activities— social, philanthropic, political, religious, educational—or aspire to recognition in such circles, a loss of reputation through identification with a burdensome strike may impose further penalties upon them, through loss of influence or prospective leadership positions in the organizational life of the community.

Family Pressures

In speaking of public condemnation of the parties, we have been referring to general criticism by all members of the affected public, whether affected as household or industrial consumer or as supplier. We turn now to direct sanctions imposed by particular segments of the strike's public. The first of these groups is the families and particularly the wives of the strikers, a group so closely identified with the strikers that, as has been pointed out earlier, there may be some who would prefer to construe them as parties to the strike.

Regardless of the wives' support of their striking husbands at the start of the strike, as it continues and family income dwindles or savings accounts are drawn down the wives may begin to apply pressure on husbands to "get the strike settled." This is likely to be especially true if there are children in the family who are made to feel the effect of the period of financial distress. Indeed, there are some who maintain that family pressures are often decisive in terminating a strike. An official of a large electrical manufacturing company writes: "The really beneficial pressures which develop in a long strike (here 'beneficial' is used in the sense of finding a solution rather than beneficial to either party) seem to come through the home. In two outstanding local examples, back-to-work movements were traceable to the wives of workers, notwithstanding the fact that those same wives had previously permitted their youngsters to take part in kiddy picket lines." An official in the lumber industry offers a similar example: "This particular strike happened in the summertime and the workers were able to exist by fishing and working for other industries during the strike period. . . . That strike lasted about four months and despite repeated attempts of negotiation, probably the main reason for the settlement of the strike was the pressure brought to bear by the families of the workers for them to get back to work."

The parties are aware of this potential source of pressure and each attempts to meet it with an appropriate program of public relations. The union seeks to enlist the support or even the participation of the wives in the strike, while managements often attempt to persuade the strikers' wives of the meaningless of the sacrifice. A railroad vice-president says: "The wives and children of employees involved in a labor dispute are part of the public, and in some cases when they are thoroughly informed, I think they have some influence with their fathers and husbands. That is why some companies mail to the homes of employees statements explaining the facts about labor disputes."

Such efforts at persuading nonstriking members of the family that the strike is ill-advised usually make two points: that the continuing loss of income to the family cannot be made up, and that the issue over which the strike has been called does not warrant this sacrifice. In one case of a strike in violation of contractual agreement, where the company publicized that fact by a series of advertisements, according to a company executive: "There was definite evidence that a substantial number of the wives of employees who read the advertisements made it uncomfortable for their husbands and questioned the integrity of the union organization."

The nature of the sanction involved scarcely requires any specification. The employee who loses the support of his wife, who is subjected to reproachful glances, to continued nagging, or—even worse—the "silent treatment," is being subjected to penalties which are real indeed and pressures which are sometimes difficult to resist.

Consumer Pressure

In discussing the direct sanctions available to members of the public let us start by delimiting the scope of our interest. We can do this by considering whether we shall include as sanctions (1) the pressure on management that comes from the threat that some of its customers may be permanently lost, as they go over to competitors, and (2) the pressure on management that comes from an organized boycott.

1. "In industries where I have been directly in contact with strike situations or know intimately the history of the strike situation, in the aircraft, petroleum, and flour milling industries, I can safely say that the biggest deterrent to continuing a strike, from management's viewpoint, is the loss of consumer acceptance through the unavailability of products and the consequent necessity of consumers purchasing other types of competitive merchandise." This comment of a director of

industrial relations has been substantiated by a number of other management members.

This type of pressure on management we do not consider a sanction in support of public opinion, however. It is a penalty imposed on one of the parties to a strike, to be sure, but it is simply part of the economic loss which management expects to sustain during a strike—whether or not the strike is public-affecting. Indeed the conclusion is unavoidable that under such circumstances the urgency rating of the strike—its importance to the consumer—is relatively low, since it is the availability of adequate substitutes which imposes a loss on management, an availability which, however, obviates consumer hardship. In this event we would expect no significant adverse public opinion. The instances in which we are interested are those in which the consumer segment of the affected public brings direct pressure on the parties because the strike is working hardship on it.

2. What of the organized boycott? Does this constitute a direct consumer sanction?

The research director of one large national union, after consultation with numerous of its representatives who had recently been involved in strike situations, sums up one conclusion of this group as follows:

Manufacturers and distributors of consumer non-durable goods were more susceptible to public opinion than producers and distributors of durable goods.

The threat of a consumer boycott exercised by the remainder of organized labor and others in a particular community has also been very effective in resolving a dispute. This type of boycott has been characteristic of the labor movement for many years and many central body newspapers have continued to list individual merchants who are presently unorganized or in whose establishment a strike exists. The effectiveness of such a boycott depends upon the size of the community and the historical tradition of organized labor in that community.

Specific examples of boycott action are easy to come by. One impartial observer in Louisville reported on the 1952 strike of two AFL unions against two of the city's largest hotels. "The unions struck for recognition shortly before the Kentucky Derby season. Until the allegedly low-paid strikers got violent in their desperation a month later, they aroused sympathy from the local press and groups like the Americans for Democratic Action. Organizations of Catholics, who make up a big proportion of the city's working class, withdrew important meetings from the hotels. So did other groups—even the Republican Lincoln Club." An official of a distilling company writes that, in view of the fact that bartenders are AFL-organized, "the fear of a boycott of our product has always been a factor in our decision making," and adds that "the attitude of the consumer-voter has played a very important role in our relationship with labor."

Despite evidence that the organized boycott constitutes a genuine pressure on management to terminate a strike, we exclude the boycott from our present interest. The reason is similar to that which we considered in connection with the threat of loss of trade. A product which is vital to the consumer cannot be boycotted. It is only in cases of low urgency rating that a boycott is feasible—cases where the product can be dispensed with or where acceptable substitutes are available. The boycott is a penalty which can be invoked only when the public is *not* vitally affected in its consumer capacity, situations in which a strike imposes a negligible "real" cost on consumers. Boycotts are organized because of principle, not hardship—devotion to a union cause, sympathy with class interests, organizational ties. We dismiss the boycott from consideration only because our focus of interest is solely upon the sanctions which are available to a public that is aroused because of "real" costs which a strike imposes on it; we are only concerned with what a public can do to protect itself from strikes which bring hardship by interrupting a flow of goods and services on which it has come to rely as a right, a right of expectancy.

The consumer pressures can best be discussed under two classifications: household consumers and commercial consumers.

1. The nature of pressures from household consumers can perhaps best be shown by illustration. We shall draw on the experience of the dairies and milk drivers in the Pittsburgh strike of 1950.

The strike began on June 9, involving 68 dairies and virtually cutting off the delivery of milk in seven counties with a population estimated at about 2,500,000. Arrangements were made for "emergency" deliveries. Family physicians were to certify the "emergency" need for milk (for babies, invalids, and diabetics) to the Allegheny County Medical Society, which in turn was to transmit these names to union headquarters for service. It was agreed between union and management that three firms would continue operations to meet these needs. By June 14 the Medical Society had had to install seven new phone lines to handle the mounting requests, totaling 13,000 as of that day and 25,000 two days later. It was reported that producers were selling milk at fifty cents a quart to "thousands" who came directly to their plants.

It was on June 12, four days after the strike began, that consumer pressures began to be felt by the parties. The Allegheny County Federation of Women's Clubs, with 18,000 members, through its president wired the union that it was not in sympathy with the strike because of the hardship it brought to families relying on milk deliveries. The following day the Southwestern District of the Pennsylvania State Federation of Women's Clubs demanded the resumption of deliveries while the issues in dispute between the parties were submitted to arbitration. As events developed it became clear that these were not third-party interventions so much as direct pressures from housewives through their existing club organizations.

On June 14 a committee of three women representing the "unorganized housewives and club members" waited on representatives of the dealers to hear the defense of their position, and five days later a similar committee subjected the union president to a like quizzing. Telephone calls from irate housewives flooded in upon dealers and the union, and protesting letters were published in the newspapers. The union president is reported as saying he was "afraid" to go home because women were always calling his home to inquire or scold. Those union members who were making emergency deliveries were said to have complained at the treatment accorded them. According to a newspaper account, "they have worked long hours without pay since the strike began and the [emergency] system was inaugurated. . . . But the tongue lashing and the abuse they have taken from housewives and others of the public irate about the strike, they say, has been discouraging and disheartening." Two labor reporters covering the strike situation subsequently agreed that the women of the community had instituted "a thoroughgoing uprising" against the parties. As the strike continued, both union and management officials were said to have become more and more "jittery" at the ceaseless pressure.

Nor did these consumer pressures end with termination of the strike on June 30, after 21 days. The following effects were reported:

A number of customers switched from home delivery service to store buying of milk, even though milk had been unobtainable at the stores during the strike, as a form of protest against the drivers.

In some instances when the regular driver attempted to resume deliveries he was ordered off the premises.

There was a substantial switching of dealers, as housewives showed their displeasure with their particular drivers, even though their new driver had likewise been engaged in the strike. In this general reshuffling of routes not all drivers came out equally well. Routes which had been built up by drivers over a period of years were torn down in 21 days.

In negotiations two years later, with union and dealers unable to reach a quick agreement, the union membership delayed before voting strike authority to its leaders. When rumors of an imminent strike began circulating, the parties were quick to issue a joint statement assuring the public that at least 72 hours' warning would be given before a strike was called.

On a lesser scale, the same types of pressures were applied in an earlier milk strike in an Ohio community. An observer reports that the strongest pressures on the parties "were the calls of milk customers to the dairies involved and to the milk drivers as well as calls to the heads of the union. The willingness to settle changed markedly after the first two or three days of the strike as expressions from the public caused both parties to take a second look at the loss of good union and good company relations with the public."

A milk strike peculiarly invites consumer pressure. It involves a commodity the absence of which hits especially at children and which for that reason arouses the anger of women in a manner that few strikes can. Nevertheless, it is by no means the only commodity which, when withdrawn, gives rise to consumer protest expressed directly to the parties involved.

What sanctions are here involved? Again it is not easy to be precise. Loss of organizational good will again is involved, this time the good will of a particular segment of the public. A threat to personal respect and reputation are also at stake. And, finally, it seems reasonable to believe that, even when there is little actual present likelihood of loss of trade because of the very importance of the product to the consumer, most managements have a gnawing belief that an embittered customer can sooner or later find some way of dispensing with his services. Consumer sanctions are thus both social and economic.

2. The sanctions at the disposal of commercial consumers are less social and more distinctly economic than are those of household con-

sumers. They implant the same fear of loss of good will. They play upon the same lurking belief that however indispensable one's firm may be to a customer today, tomorrow may provide that customer with alternatives. Sometimes they involve the threat by an impatient customer of withdrawing his trade, even at the considerable inconvenience and expense of developing another supplier capable of meeting his peculiar requirements or specifications. The pressures for resumption of deliveries brought by the commercial buyer upon the management of a struck company are therefore more than polite requests.

Customer relationships assume many forms other than a direct buyer-seller relationship. To suggest the prevalence of this form of pressure we need only cite some of the more common variants. One is the contractor-subcontractor relationship, in which the contractor is the customer of the subcontractor. (A California attorney active in a strike in the painting and decorating industry writes that the pressures of the general contractors' associations "which controlled contracts awarded the painting and decorating contractors were a primary factor in compelling concessions to the strikers" to end the strike.) The dealers of a manufacturer constitute its customers, whose good will must be maintained if a satisfactory sales outlet is to be assured. (*The New York Times* of February 2, 1946, reported: "According to Ward's Automotive Reports, an industry trade journal, dealers' pressure on factory sales executives helped to bring about the Ford and Chrysler settlements, and similar pressure is now being exerted on General Motors.") Tenants and other renters are the customers of landlords and other rentiers. (During the elevator operators' strike of 1945, "Seventy tenants, comprising 90 per cent of the occupants of a building at 264 West Fortieth Street, signed an ultimatum yesterday to the building's management declaring that they would not pay rent while elevator service was suspended, according to Harry Hirsch, a child's sportswear manufacturer with offices on the fifteenth floor of the structure," *The New York Times* reported on September 27.)

The economic character of the pressures from commercial consumers is readily apparent in the comments from our management respondents. An attorney representing managements writes: "Customers normally exert great pressure. It is usual to find customers inquiring about the strike, what is at issue, how much separates the parties, when the strike will be settled. These inquiries alone influence managements."

Amplifying this, the representative of a rubber company adds: "Industrial customers may criticize a company as a source of supply and be very influential. This can take two forms: (1) That the supplier can't handle his industrial relations problems in a competent manner and thus is not dependable or (2) that the customer has granted company-wide bargaining, a union shop or a wage increase and, therefore, the supplier should not be stubborn according to their definition." In similar vein, the vice-president of industrial relations for one of the large steel corporations remarks that "customers and other businessmen may express their opinion that a particular employer should adjust his conditions of employment to conform with conditions applicable to the customer's own employees."

Another observer describes the possible form consumer influences may take: "The pressures operate through the customer's purchasing department contacting the sales department of the striking company, who, in turn, carry their story to the top management and industrial relations people actually handling the strike. If the plant management is also responsible for sales as well as production and labor relations, this customer-pressure might have considerable influence." An executive of a large Midwest manufacturing concern comments: "The threats or inducements which such persons can offer are concrete and to the point, such as the loss of further business with that industry or the loss of contracts or such arrangements." The attorney previously quoted on customer inquiries adds: "Threats to cancel and replace orders are severe forms of pressure. Actual cancellation, removal of tools, dies and moulds, recall of drawings and designs—these are ultimate means of enforcing opinion and, of course, may be very effective."

Even where actual threat is not invoked, however, "customer impacts are of greatest importance," a steel executive writes. "Even during periods of tight supplies companies are normally looking forward to the day when they must sell the product in a buyer's market. A pattern which will adversely affect customers is avoided wherever possible."[2]

[2] It would follow from our hypothesis that public opinion is directly correlated with a strike's urgency rating that consumer pressure would be greater where alternative supply was less feasible. Since trade cannot be diverted elsewhere, the customer's only hope is to focus whatever influence he has upon the struck supplier. Several instances confirming this relationship were supplied by respondents. One writes of "several short strikes by District 50 UMW against the Ethyl Corporation at a time when the corporation inventories were low because of the war." He comments, "The product being a necessity to the gasoline-producing companies who were customers, [the strike] put them in a position where they would find it necessary to assert considerable pressures. In a more competitive industry

We have been discussing pressures brought by business customers against business suppliers. More than the business customer's interests are involved, however. If, through lack of supplies, his plant does not operate, his employees are affected, too. The customer's employees thus have a stake in the settlement of the strike, and at times they have brought pressure on the striking parties to resolve the dispute. An example is provided by a neutral observer. Speaking of a ten-month strike at an oil refinery in an Ohio city, he says "While the public was not considerably inconvenienced, a large glass plant and its employees were affected somewhat by the cessation of a flow of gas, a by-product from the refinery to the glass plant. This caused pressures to build up from the glass union to the oil union and from the glass company to the refinery executives, resulting in an agreement by one of the parties, theretofore reluctant, to agree to mediation, which in turn resulted in settlement of all of the 90-odd issues . . . which the parties faced."

The sanctions which the customer's union can employ against the striking union in such a case are relatively weak. There is not the same fear of direct economic penalty which haunts management. The principal penalty which it can impose is the threat of fostering a break in the support of the strike by the local labor movement or of opposition to interests of the striking union in local labor councils.

Supplier Pressures

1. The suppliers of a struck company, as part of the affected public, may bring their own pressures to bear to secure settlement of the strike. Parts suppliers whose market is cut off by the strike at a manufacturing plant, or tomato growers whose normal crop outlet is cut off by a strike at a cannery, provide examples. The principal sanction available to them is the threat of diverting their supplies to other producers. Here again we must be cautious in our interpretation. If alternative markets are readily available, the strike imposes small cost on the supplier and

---

such as the paper industry one would think the [customers] would assert more influences, but my limited experiences indicate that the customer pressures are equally great in the noncompetitive industries."

Another remarks:

"We know of a strike in October, 1951, involving a company which holds a virtual monopoly due to patents and the excellence of its product. Airplanes were parked outside a factory waiting only for this Company's product. Other suppliers of subassemblies were almost at a standstill waiting for the one product. Non-defense industries were similarly affected. In these circumstances, public (customer) opinion crystallized rapidly and clearly forced an end to the strike."

he is unlikely to instigate pressure on his normal customer. If alternative outlets are not readily available, the threat of diverting his output is a relatively empty one. Nevertheless, there are circumstances under which threats of diversion may materialize in the former case and under which threats in the latter case may be potent. Even with substitute markets available, the supplier may have so geared his production to the specialized needs of his struck customer that there are substantial inconvenience and expense in adapting to new customers. He is therefore likely to pressure for prompt settlement of the strike rather than seek alternative markets. The unwillingness to adapt to new markets may be overcome by prolongation of the strike, however, and here lies the effectiveness of his pressure. On the other hand, even though the supplier has few alternative outlets, so that his pressures on the struck customer carry no threat of immediate diversion of materials, the buyer may be fearful of so embittering its suppliers that should the future provide them with the substitute markets now lacking, it may find a carefully organized supplier system crumbling away.

Occasional instances have been reported of farmers who have forced an end to a processors' strike which has prevented marketing of their crops. Here the sanction at times has been forcible intervention. A cryptic United Press dispatch from British Columbia, dated July 26, 1952, reads:

> The C.I.O. United Packing House Workers Union halted its strike against the Canada Packers Cannery at South Sumas today after enraged farmers had seized the plant and started processing their pea crops themselves. The 200 plant workers resumed production with the first shift today.

The instances in which such a direct sanction is possible are rare, however.

2. One other form of supplier pressure deserves separate consideration. It will be recalled that in our analysis of the costs of a strike, we consider the employees of a company as an integral part of the company. We must therefore consider pressures applied by suppliers of materials to the employees, principally merchants. The merchants who sell food, clothing, household equipment, entertainment, and other goods and services to the striking employees are an important segment of the affected public, in that their sales and income suffer. In this respect they are no different from the suppliers of goods for the struck company's operations. Correspondence and interviews suggest that while

merchants are generally willing to extend credit to regular customers who are on strike, at least for a time, in a number of situations shop-keepers have sought to induce a settlement by bringing pressure on the strikers. "Tradesmen, saloon keepers, bowling alley proprietors, etc., urged employees to 'get after the Union and settle.' " Inquiries as to how long the strikers can keep it up and whether the strike is worth while provide a subtle kind of pressure. "The first direct and telling influence brought to bear on the union was the action taken by local merchants who began to question employees as to the justification for their strike action." Behind such advice and inquiries lies the potential threat—evident enough to a hard-pressed striker—that credit may be withdrawn. Such pressures may be applied not directly to the striker himself but to his wife, in which event it may set in motion family pressures of the type already discussed.

These, then, are the chief direct sanctions at the disposal of the strike-affected public—loss of community good will by the parties, pressures from inside their own families, economic influences brought to bear by customer and by suppliers, the latter principally touching management. As we shall see in the next chapter, however, indirect sanctions, which the public activates, are a potent supplement to these direct influences.

Indirect Sanctions in Support of Public Opinion

SOME of the strongest influences operating on the parties to a strike come not directly from the affected public but from some intermediary who acts on its behalf. We label these indirect sanctions, since the power of the public is felt via a third party.

Pressures of this sort develop in almost every critical strike situation. A Chrysler strike runs for more than a month, and the Wayne County dealers of Chrysler cars ask the governor of Michigan to intervene, saying that unless the strike is soon ended they, as well as Chrysler dealers throughout the United States, will be forced to close their doors or greatly reduce their working forces, throwing thousands of employees out of work. An elevator strike occurs in New York City, disrupting operations in the garment district, and on the fifth day nine garment manufacturers' associations petition the governor and the senior United States senator, holding that continuation of the strike "for even a brief period will result in the complete destruction of the fall season for New York's major industry," with "the appalling prospect of the mass diversion of its business to other markets." Numerous examples are provided by our respondents. "Within the last three years there have been two local transportation stoppages. . . . In both cases as the disputes continued, downtown merchants, who suffered losses in business, brought pressure to bear on the City officials to try to resolve the dispute." "Officers of a local plant where the plant is the principal provider of jobs in the community and where it borrows its money from local banks feel, almost immediately, the effect of local pressures in the event of a shutdown. Calls on the plant by public officials, local bankers, local members of the board of directors and so forth would appear to be the most effective pressures exerted."

It does not follow, however, that every contact between the striking parties and such a third-party intervenor involves indirect sanctions. Such intervention may not be a response to public opinion but may be instigated by the parties or arise out of personal desire to make a name for oneself. As a first requirement, then, indirect sanctions must be in support of actions by intervenors which are prompted by public pressures. This means that the public must be in possession of direct sanctions with respect to the intervenor, that the intervenor responds to a public expectation that he exert his influence on its behalf, and that failure to respond subjects him to the danger of penalties which the public is in a position to impose upon him.

This does not mean, however, that the intervenor must wait for public pressure to develop before he acts. From experience or deduction he may anticipate the force of public opinion. If a milk strike threatens or breaks, for example, he need not wait for the passage of two or three days, during which public pressure builds up, before using his influence on the parties. He may act at once, in the knowledge that the pressures will come if the strike is not settled.[1]

As a second requirement, indirect sanctions must involve some influence of the intervenor over the parties themselves. If the indirect pressures which are initiated by the public are to affect the conduct of the parties, then the intermediary through whom such pressures operate must himself have some hold over the parties. A gas strike is threatened. The mayor intervenes "out of concern over the possible suspension of gas service for schools, hospitals, housing projects and other consumers in the area." Even though the mayor's action is stimulated by his response to public pressures, we cannot properly describe this as the application of indirect sanctions until we can explain why there is any compulsion on the parties to respect the mayor's plea for a strike-foreclosing settlement. If the mayor's attempt at settling the dispute carries no force behind it, it invokes no sanction. For this reason if an official responds to public pressure simply by sending conciliators in to help the parties resolve their difficulty, we would not construe this as the application of a sanction. The conciliators are intended to be an assistance to the parties, but they do not normally convey any threat to the parties if, despite their assistance, the strike continues.

There is, of course, no requirement that the intervenor be neutral

---

[1] An outstanding labor reporter writes of the oil strike of 1952: "The Secretary of Defense told the White House that if the oil strike were not settled within a few days he would have to requisition all available aviation gasoline as a precautionary measure. That would have meant shutting down the civil aviation industry, which was already curtailing operations. Whether, or how, the civil aviation industry was bringing pressure on the White House at that moment I don't know. At any rate, the White House could foresee a great deal of pressure and unfavorable public opinion if civil air transport was grounded and the government was apparently doing nothing."

as between the striking union and the struck management. His pressure may be focused on one to the exclusion of the other, constituting a considerable assistance to one and disadvantage to the other. So long as the exercise of his influence is in response to public pressure to end the strike, however, we consider such partisan intervention an application of indirect sanctions.[2]

[2] Indeed, the calculation by the parties of the nature of third-party intervention in response to public demand has become a necessary element of strike leadership. Oscar Smith discusses this matter in "Implication for Collective Bargaining in Quasi-Public Work," *Monthly Labor Review*, March, 1952, pp. 257-262. He notes that a considerable segment of private employment involves the furnishing of services or products which cannot be discontinued without substantial public injury, and that unions and management, in such instances, must expect government intervention. "The probable relative cost of Government intervention to each of the parties thus becomes an important consideration to them as bargaining progresses."

As noted in Chapter 8, sometimes strikes are called only because union officials anticipate an intervention which will be favorable to them. Several instances of this sort were reported (how accurately we cannot say) by respondents.

From a New Jersey utility executive: "I have the opinion that such strike votes or strike threats are to some extent influenced by the possibility or desirability (from the union's standpoint) of inducing State intervention. In other words, I suspect that some of the union representatives feel that they might get a better outcome from their standpoint if they succeed in bringing politicians or government officials into the collective bargaining process."

From a New York utility executive: "Despite the fact that the collective bargaining contract with the Union provided for method of arbitration, the Union threatened to engage in a strike in order to obtain its demands. Officials of the Labor Relations Department of the City of New York were advised of the situation by the Union, and both parties involved were called to City Hall. Several conferences were held with the Mayor's representatives and it was apparent from the start that these representatives were pro-labor. . . . In this case the politicians, at the behest of the Union, attempted to steamroller the Company into a settlement."

Strike votes on the railroads have sometimes been taken by the railway brotherhoods for the specific purposes of bringing in a fact-finding board. In such instances, the threat of strike can be counted on to force governmental intervention. Any pressures applied to the parties to secure a resolution of their dispute—however partisan—would be construed as indirect sanctions.

Where intervention comes not in response to public opinion (whether or not anticipated), but because of a self-serving interest or payment of a debt to one of the parties or a zeal to perform a public service, indirect sanctions are not involved since public opinion does not motivate such intermediation. The United Automobile Workers thus constituted a "citizens' committee" in the 1945-1946 General Motors strike and a "provisional citizens' committee," composed of churchmen, in the 1950 Chrysler strike. Whatever service the members of these committees may have believed they were rendering to the public, it is most unlikely that they owed their existence or could attribute their intervention to the pressure of public opinion on them. This is third-party intervention at the instigation of one of the interested parties, not intervention under public pressure. As one of our respondents remarked, "Public officials do intervene. It is certainly likely that many times the intervention comes, however, from union-exerted pressure to do so and the belief that the official is dependent upon substantial labor support to remain in office. A transit strike or a power strike illustrates a case, however, where the official responds to public opinion which is probably not partisan at all."

The sanctions which intervenors may impose on parties to a strike are numerous and sometimes subtle. Despite their considerable arsenal, however, one class of intervenors—government officials—remark that members of the affected public often credit them with greater power over the parties than they actually possess. It is often believed, for example, that a public official can compel arbitration even against the wishes of the parties.

Indirect sanctions, then, come into play when a third-party intermediary responds to public pressure and himself can apply pressure on the parties to the strike. In examining indirect sanctions, therefore, we require two explanations: first, what influence the public holds over the intervenor; and second, what influence the intervenor holds over the parties.

Intervention by Government Officials

Of all third-party intervenors, unquestionably government officials—whether city, state, or federal—are the most common. Their response to an adverse public sentiment respecting a strike has two primary motivations. The first is a fear that members of the affected public will retaliate at the polls if their elected representatives do not do something to end the strike which imposes hardships on them. Even in the case of an official who intends to retire from public office at the end of his term, the threat of a defeat at the polls for the political party to which he has owned allegiance is likely to carry substantial weight. The second motive for intervening is to protect his public record. Personal reputation is involved in whether he responds to the needs of his constituency or whether he is apathetic to its distress. Vague threats of a petition for recall have even been made where an official was believed not to have pressed sufficiently the public's interests in a critical strike.

A former corporation counsel for a major city was probably not describing a unique situation when he said that city officials are susceptible to individual letters of complaint from voters. Several hundred letters in a city of several hundred thousand will be regarded as a "flood" of sufficient proportions to induce anxiety in the minds of the mayor and his staff. Phone calls add to his discomfort. Newspapers, themselves interpreting public sentiment, may call on him to act. At some point the pressure on him may become too great to resist. The fear of unfavorable consequences should he continue on the sidelines may override any qualms that he may incur the political opposition of the striking parties by "meddling." The official intervenes.

But what influence does the official have over the parties to the strike?

The Influence of Office

A public official may be able to use the respect for his office to induce agreement. There are two general methods which are available to him. The first is persuasion, the second condemnation.

Using persuasion, the official may publicly ask the parties to postpone a strike, to submit the differences to arbitration, to settle on terms which he himself proposes. Any of these procedures will secure—at least temporarily—that protection of the public which is his objective. Public persuasion has been proved successful. "We have had two or three instances in Cleveland where a strike has been settled through the efforts of our Mayor. This I recall has occurred both in the administration of Tom Burke, who is presently Mayor, and Frank Lausche, who preceded him and who is presently Governor of the State. . . . The contribution they have made to settlement has been due to the respect that both parties have for the individual and his position." The vice-president of a major railroad system writes, "The President of the United States . . . has on several occasions forced settlement upon employers by his expressions of opinions. This was particularly true of President Roosevelt." A staff officer of a strategic national union reports that "a contemplated strike in 1950 was postponed twice at the request of the President of the United States."

The threat of public condemnation of the parties, or of one of the parties, is a potent weapon. The parties may be put on notice or left to infer that the official will point an accusing finger if they break off negotiations, if they refuse to accept arbitration, if a suggested settlement is not acceded to.

Threat of condemnation is the basis for effectiveness of the "wearing down" process, whereby the parties are brought together and told to negotiate until they settle, and that if either breaks off negotiations before a settlement is reached public announcement of its responsibility for the collapse will be made. One public utility executive describes the effectiveness of such pressure: "Suppose you have a strike in a utility. Immediately you get the mayor into the picture and probably the state conciliation service as well. You've already been through long, wearisome negotiation sessions with the union, aside from trying to carry on your normal business functions. Now you have to go through further sessions with the conciliation boys, always facing the charge of disregard of public interests if you walk out of the meetings. So there are more meetings, and then perhaps the federal conciliators get into the picture. The meetings go on and on, the issues are rehashed. If it's an important strike it may wind up in Washington, with the parties being called into some agency or even the White House. Through all this it has been meet, meet, meet, talk, talk, talk. The pressure to settle is enormous, and the management who through it all can continue to hold out is a strong individual indeed. Somewhere along the line it becomes easier to say Yes." Yet it is apparent that this procedure is effective only because there is the fear of being publicly condemned if the conferences are broken off.

The instruments of condemnation are varied. The official may write a letter to the offending party, which is released to the press. ("Is the company's stand a matter of principle or just bull-headedness?" Mayor O'Dwyer wrote to President Fairless of the United States Steel Corporation during the 1949 strike). A full press conference may be called, at which the denunciatory statement is made. The official may act as an agent for organizing an adverse public sentiment, aligning it more firmly in support of his stand. (It has been charged, by individuals familiar with the situation, that the Chicago "brown-outs" ordered by Secretary of the Interior Krug during the 1946 coal strike, ostensibly to conserve fuel, had as their primary function the hardening of public opinion against the union leadership.)

What, then, are the sanctions which the public official may invoke against recalcitrant parties to a strike situation? We can identify at least three.

First, there is the fear that refusal of public request to settle the strike, inviting official condemnation, will result in a loss of personal prestige. An individual's reputation is not enhanced when he is flailed by someone who himself stands high in the community's social system. One business executive remarked: "It is my opinion that the primary influence which other third parties such as politicians or government officials can exert on management in such situations is primarily one involved with prestige. The management does not wish to subject itself to criticism from others of high rank in the community, even though the criticism may be in part unjustified."

Second, there is the vague fear by the parties that to incur official opposition is to open their organizations to undefined and indefinite future penalties. In some instances, it may turn "friends in high places" into enemies. There is here the same uneasy presentiment which generally accompanies any challenge to authority, particularly if the exercise of that authority appears to be in a popular cause.

The potency of this sanction has seldom been better demonstrated than by Mayor La Guardia of New York City in the 1939 strike of elevator operators. On the evening of the second day of that strike the mayor and the borough president, accompanied by their assistants, met a joint conference of the parties especially assembled at City Hall. The conference was brief. The mayor demanded immediate settlement of the strike, "in the interests of the public." "I want those buildings functioning tomorrow," he told them, picturing the destructive effects of the walkout, particularly upon business activity in the garment district. (Three associations representing hundreds of garment manufacturers had been that day petitioning the mayor for relief from the strike.) Turning to the union leadership he reminded them, "You boys owe the mayor a lot." Reviewing the offers which had been made by the parties, La Guardia then outlined his own projected compromise settlement, saying, "I recommend this as being in the public interest and in the interest of business in the garment center. I want to make sure this evening that all these buildings will be functioning tomorrow. There are very many more people concerned in the operation of these buildings than in this controversy." As an alternative to his suggested settlement, the mayor reminded them, "arbitration is still open to you if you want it."

As the mayor left the room, a member of the State Mediation Board, who had accompanied him, took the chair and addressed the conferees grouped around the table, "Either party that refuses to accede to the Mayor's wishes will regret it. This is a command. I am using these words deliberately. I hope every one will take this as a serious moment and that no one will dare to inconvenience the public after this."

Despite protests that this was a "dictated" settlement and the use of "Hitler methods," the employers after a short delay agreed to the proposal and the union leadership promised to submit the terms to the membership for approval. At the membership meeting, facing catcalls from an opposition which favored defying the mayor, the union leaders strongly urged acceptance of the compromise: "Mayor La Guardia, in the early days when we were up against it, saved this union. . . . Never has there been a better labor mayor than Mayor La Guardia. . . . We would lose public support if we defied the mayor. . . . You cannot defy the City Hall. . . . Even though you don't like it, if you turn it down it is suicide for this union. . . . Yesterday we had the workers in the garment center with us. Yesterday we had the public with us. Today it is a different story." The membership was reported as voting "overwhelmingly" in favor of the mayor's proposed settlement. The strike was called off the evening of the third day.[3]

The danger in "defying City Hall" was never made explicit to the membership. It was clear enough, however, that the union's leaders were fearful of incurring the anger of an official whose power they had reason to know, since it had previously been exerted on their behalf. They wanted neither to lose its support nor to have it exerted against them.

The third sanction in support of an official's use of the influence of his office is the more effective mobilization and concentration of that very public opinion to which he is responding, with a consequent increase in the effectiveness of the direct sanctions previously described. We may diagram the flow of pressures in the manner shown below, in which the dotted line indicates not pressure but assistance in bringing pressure:

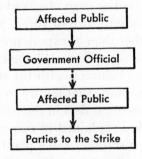

In terms of our earlier analysis, the official is here serving as an opinionative authority, lending the weight of his office and name to a particular view of the strike—how it should be ended; who is "responsible" for its continuance. Around such an authority public opinion can more readily focus, so that its direct weight is more readily felt by the parties. Condemnation of both the parties for refusal to accept his "reasonable"

<hr />

[3] This account of the strike is taken from issues of *The New York Times*, February 2-4, 1939.

proposal for settlement, or condemnation of one of the parties for standing in the way of that settlement which would bring an end to public hardship, is likely to firm public opinion in a manner discernible to the parties. Writes a member of management: "The concern about intervention by government agencies or government officials stems from the effect it may have on public opinion, rather than from any direct [punitive] act." Writes an attorney representing union interests: "Perhaps the clearest instance of the force of public opinion was the railroad strike of 1946. The President's address to the nation, which was more a reflection than a molder of national public opinion, effectively terminated the strike." We would modify that last statement. The President's address was *both* a reflection and a molder of public opinion.

Punitive Action Not Directed to the Strike

A government official bent on terminating a strike may engage in a variety of punitive actions which have no direct connection with the strike. They constitute punishments on the parties for conducting the strike in contrast to efforts directly to break it. In cataloguing these harassing actions, there is no implication that they are used with equal frequency. It is apparent from the replies of our respondents that most of them had not encountered or even observed at second hand the first type. It was mentioned by only two or three, and then as a matter of hearsay or expectancy rather than as experience.

1. Withholding beneficial action. Wherever the government—at whatever level—has placed contracts with the struck plant in the past, a suggestion may be forthcoming that failure to resolve the dispute may make it more difficult to secure orders in the future. The representative of an employers' association explained in conversation how this might work: "Suppose you have a shutdown in a plant that supplies most of a town's employment. The effects spread rapidly until the whole community is affected. There would be many who would be unwilling simply to accept unemployment or loss of income. It is likely that at this point some pressure would be put on their representative or senator to do something. The congressman might get in touch with company officials and inquire about the strike. He might make repeated inquiries. He might make suggestions. At any rate, he would make it known that he would like to have the strike settled. Why would the company respond to such pressure? Because government orders might be at stake.

It has been getting government business right along or expects to get government business in the future, but there are competitors to whom such orders might be diverted. Whether or not the threat would ever be carried out, it's likely to worry the management and give them more incentive to settle."

A related pressure is the threat of reallocating materials, in time of controlled allocation due to materials shortages, in case the struck plant does not resume operations.

At times legislative actions may be involved. During the 1946 steel strike, Democratic Senator Kilgore of West Virginia charged that steel management had flouted President Truman's wage proposal and deliberately "plunged the nation into an industrial war." He announced that he would press for repeal of "the tax rebate provision which permits United States Steel and General Motors to draw on the Treasury to finance their war on workers." He was supported by Representative Bailey, also of West Virginia, who offered a bill to that effect in the House.

Unrelated to any specific strike but in consequence of the postwar wave of strikes which were frustrating a pent-up consumer demand for commodities, a bill which would have liberalized the unemployment compensation program, supported by the labor unions and already passed in the Senate, was allowed to languish in the House Ways and Means Committee. A member of the committee, justifying this action, said: "We'll have to wait until the strikers get back to work. To extend the time for paying unemployment benefits would be to encourage idleness."

A neutral observer provides an example of such threats at the municipal level. "Recently, Minneapolis endured a long taxi strike—both the employers and the union leaders were set for a finish fight. . . . Company representatives began serious bargaining only after an amendment was introduced in the city council to remove the ceiling on the number of taxi licenses, thus threatening the near-monopoly the company enjoys on city streets."

In all these instances the danger of having certain benefits already enjoyed withdrawn, or of having certain anticipated benefits withheld, can be avoided by settlement of the strike.

2. Influencing rate actions in the case of public utilities. In those enterprises where a shutdown is likely to be especially disruptive to the community—the public utilities—a potent sanction is made available

to public officials by the influence which they may be able to exercise (or, equally significant, which others believe they may be able to exercise) over applications for rate changes. Such an influence is available to municipal authorities in some instances, to state and federal authorities in others. Among the types of business activity which are affected by this influence are power and light, gas, water, telephone and telegraph, local transit, railroads.

The vice-president of one utility, after first describing the activities of a municipal mediation commission in the city in which it operates, remarks: "This committee, when acting as a panel, is composed of two members of labor organizations, two members of industrial organizations and two public members. The Committee operates under the direction of the Mayor of the city with a full-time secretary appointed by the Mayor. Being a public service company you can well understand the pressure that can be applied against management by such a committee. Unlike many other states this state operates under home rule which gives the city officials the power of establishing public utility rates."

An alleged instance of the use of a state official's influence in such matters is reported by an attorney active on behalf of several utility unions:

In 1947 there was a national telephone strike. The American Telephone and Telegraph Company and its affiliated companies refused to make any wage offer whatsoever. The first break in the strike came in [one] state where Governor Blank called in officials of the [regional] Bell Telephone Company and the CWA Division to the State Capitol. The Company officials bridled at the invitation and threatened to leave the conference. Governor Blank, in my presence and in the presence of union officials, said that he would go to the people of the State if they left before he concluded the conference. They stayed on. However, they remained adamant regarding a wage offer until Governor Blank made reference to the fact that the Railroad Commission (which fixes telephone rates in that State) would unquestionably be interested in the Company's intransigence, when the company sought relief from the Commission with respect to rate revisions. The Company then made the first of the wage offers which came from the Associated Bell Companies before the strike was settled.

3. Miscellaneous harassing actions. A determined official can usually find grounds for a variety of sniping actions against parties which are reluctant to call off a strike. As one union attorney said, "There isn't

a company in the country that isn't continually breaking some law—usually unintentionally and unconsciously—so there's always some pretext." He claimed knowledge of cases where a recalcitrant employer was threatened with having a license revoked; another might be told that the Board of Health "might make trouble" or that he would be found in violation of a safety code. The personnel manager of a large consumption-goods company listed "some examples of the types of pressure which can be applied to management"; "Employers are always vulnerable to charges of violation of wage and hour regulations. Honest errors can result in charges of deliberate violation. State Labor Departments can always find violations of their regulations which normally are not significant. Fire Department inspectors can make it pretty difficult and expensive for even the most conscientious employers to comply with all of the technicalities imposed on them."

According to hearsay, the municipal mediation authorities of one large Eastern city, operating under the direct jurisdiction of the mayor, have in repeated instances walked into the shops of employers engaged in a protracted or damaging strike, looked at the ceiling, and commented, "My, your plumbing is in bad shape. If the inspector learns about this he will probably make you rip it all out, and that will cost you a lot of money—more than it would cost to settle this strike." Food-handling establishments were told that if the health department inspector learned of "violations" the required changes or new equipment could be "very, very expensive."

In the 1950 strike of elevator operators in New York City, it was reported that Mayor O'Dwyer was seriously concerned over effects of the strike on the health of tenants, telling reporters that a heart specialist had advised him that for four months after the 1936 strike physicians had been busy attending patients whose hearts had been affected by the unaccustomed climbing of steps. "It was reported that the Mayor had warned the landlords that unless they settled the dispute now by negotiation or arbitration, it might cost them more in the long run to hold out. He is said to have intimated that inspectors from the Health Department and the Department of Housing and Buildings might be sent into the struck buildings to look for violations."[4]

Actions of the above types are directed primarily against managements, since it is they who are most susceptible to harassment through ownership and operation of property. Union officials are not completely

4 The New York Times, April 28, 1950.

immune from such pressures, however. A labor lawyer reports that union leadership in a critical strike has been threatened with public exposure and even criminal prosecution where one or more of the leaders had a criminal record, "as sometimes happens."

Nothing in the above recital is intended to suggest that such harassing actions are frequent or prevalent. On the contrary, most of our respondents professed no experience and little knowledge of their use.

Punitive Action Directed to the Strike

Among the common official sanctions which may be invoked is the actual breaking of the strike. Here, in distinction to many of the threats discussed above, the penalty is usually directed against the union. There is no need to dwell at any length on the means available to governmental officials who are bent on bringing an end to a strike. Most readers will be able to supply examples from their own knowledge.

1. Taking over or ensuring the supply of services. A government official may threaten to render a strike wholly ineffective by seeing to it that the struck operations are resumed. Post-World War II instances of the use of such threats may be cited. The President ordered the Secretary of the Navy to recruit personnel to man merchant ships during a maritime strike. The governor of Michigan announced that the state stood ready to supply manpower to maintain services, if management asked for it, during a strike of a power company affecting more than 2,000 communities. The mayor of New York City publicly announced that he would employ civil servants to maintain operation of tugboats, subways, apartment elevators, and to provide plumbing services to postwar construction projects, when strikes were projected or called in these respective areas. Threats of this sort can be compelling.

In Newark, for example, the milk delivery men "know" that city authorities would break a strike after the second day by having city employees buy milk directly from the farmers and sell it on street corners. Bus drivers in the same area are fearful that in a strike the governor would send in state militiamen to drive the busses; they are not "sure" but consider such action "likely," and "a broken strike is a terrible thing to a union."

A related sanction is the provision of alternative services. In local transit strikes government officials have organized share-the-ride clubs; requested interurban and suburban bus lines to operate within areas normally not open to them; suspended city ordinances against in-town operation of out-of-town taxis; called on service clubs to organize their members into squads of roving "free taxis."

2. Police actions. Government officials can break strikes by their use of police or state militia. Picket lines can be rendered harmless. Under cover of preventing violence, strikers can be intimidated. The National Guard may be called out even though incapable of making any contribution except "patrolling streets." The president of one large national union writes, "The mere presence of uniformed police is coercive and operates as a restraint upon the enthusiasm of striking employees."

3. Court actions. Despite state and federal anti-injunction laws, an appeal for injunctive relief is still available to governmental units in many judicial jurisdictions. In some instances such relief is available only to governments which operate the struck properties, but this limitation is not everywhere imposed. The Taft-Hartley Act places with the President discretionary authority to ask for an injunction against parties to a strike which has been found to threaten the national health and safety. Failure by the parties to respect such injunctions may lead to contempt citations, jail sentence, and fine. The most celebrated instances of enforcement of an injunction against continuing a strike are perhaps the fines levied against the United Mine Workers and John L. Lewis, the union's president, in 1946 and 1948.[5]

4. Exercise of discretionary, emergency administrative authority. State legislation and wartime federal legislation have conferred on governmental authorities discretionary authority to seize struck properties or compel arbitration, under specified circumstances. Among the primary industrial states, for example, this authority has been exercised

---

[5] One case that may be cited for its novelty is that of *McCran, Attorney General,* v. *Public Service Railway Co.,* No. 54/300, 95 N.J. Eq. 22, 122 Atlantic Reporter 205 (September, 1923). Public Service Railway, which then served a million passengers daily in 142 New Jersey municipalities, refused to grant wage increases demanded by its employees and was struck. After two weeks of inoperation, the Board of Public Utility Commissioners ordered the company to resume service. The company did not comply, and the attorney general petitioned for an injunction to enforce the Board's order. The company's defense was that it could not afford to resume services as it could only operate at a loss during the strike. The court, in rejecting this defense, ruled: "The duty resting on a quasi public corporation must be performed, or its privileges and franchises must be surrendered. It cannot assume to discharge its duty to the public on and off, as it may find it profitable to do." Expressing hope that the effect of the decision might be "to stimulate negotiations to settle the many difficulties with which the Company is confronted," the chancellor nevertheless remarked that it was not for him to make an exhaustive investigation of facts to decide whether or not the Company could operate at a profit; it was enough "if it appears that it is obliged to operate under a charter which it has not surrendered."

during peacetime in Massachusetts and New Jersey. Since 1951 constitutional barriers have been raised to the exercise of such authority, both in federal and state jurisdictions. President Truman's seizure of the steel industry in the 1952 strike, undertaken on the presumption of inherent and implied constitutional authority, was nullified by Supreme Court decision. State laws empowering such actions were found to be in conflict with federal legislation. Nevertheless, it is reasonable to expect that valid legislation authorizing discretionary intervention by administrative authorities, designed to end strikes found to threaten public health or safety, will continue to be among the available sanctions.

5. Request for specific legislation. A chief executive in a political jurisdiction may threaten to request the legislative authority for specific power to break the particular strike. In the protracted 1952 strike of the Eastern Massachusetts Street Railway Co., Governor Dever asked for state legislation giving him authority to seize and operate the struck lines. (In this case, however, there is some reason for believing that such action would have been welcome to the parties.) In the 1946 railroad strike, President Truman asked for legislation enabling him to draft all striking employees into the Army; and in 1952, following the Supreme Court's rejection of the notion of inherent presidential power, he appealed for congressional action specifically granting the authority which he had previously assumed. In these three instances, the legislation sought was refused. Neither union nor company can count on refusal in advance, however.

6. Miscellaneous harassing actions. A government official may seek to break the internal unity of the strikers by investigating "rumors" that a strike is being agitated by a small group of active Communists disregardful of the interests of the rank and file, or by threatening punitive actions which, it is claimed, willful union leaders have "forced" upon him. In the latter category is the enforcement—sometimes compulsory in law but almost always discretionary in fact—of laws calling for the discharge of striking civil servants, such as the Ferguson Act in Ohio, the Hutchinson Act in Michigan, the Condon-Wadlin Act in New York. In some instances the official may threaten to appeal over the heads of local union leadership to national union officers, charging the former with incompetence and possibly damaging their chances of future advancement within the organization.

Besides actions such as the above, designed to break a particular strike, threats of a more general nature may be directed to the strikers.

The parties, and especially the union, may be advised that the government will sponsor general antistrike legislation or will be powerless to oppose such legislation unless the offending strike is called off. The possible effectiveness of such a threat is suggested by a resolution, adopted by the executive board of the International Brotherhood of Teamsters in 1947, which stressed that "restrictive anti-labor laws have resulted and may further result from the calling of strikes to the detriment of labor generally," and urging restraint in the use of the strike weapon.

One type of legislation mentioned in this category is compulsory arbitration. In the 1952 Baltimore transit strike, for example, the governor charged both company and union with "striking against the public" and threatened to ask the assembly to intervene by passing a compulsory arbitration law. Another instance in which such a threat has been employed is provided in greater detail by two writers who were involved in the proceedings described:

On April 7, 1947, the Traffic Telephone Workers' Federation of New Jersey, a labor organization consisting of 12,000 telephone operators employed by the New Jersey Bell Telephone Company, struck against that company. . . .

The Governor of New Jersey seized the facilities of the company on the afternoon of April 7, 1947, pursuant to a New Jersey statute. This statute did not forbid strikes or picketing in a labor dispute involving a public utility.

On the night of April 8, one day after the commencement of the strike, the New Jersey Legislature enacted a bill [popularly known as "The Public Utility Anti-Strike Statute"] within two hours after receiving it from the Governor and without any public hearings. The attorney for the union was forewarned that the bill would pass unless he persuaded his client to call off the strike. Before signing the bill, the Governor let it be known, through the Chairman of the New Jersey State Mediation Board, that if the strike were called off, he would not sign the bill. The Governor's ultimatum failed. He signed the bill on April 9, 1947, and it became effective as the law of the state upon signing.

The law provided for the outlawing of strikes against a public utility after its seizure by the Governor, for compulsory arbitration, and for exceptionally heavy penalties against strikers and their leaders in the event of strikes in violation of the act or the decision of the arbitrators.[6]

[6] Henry Mayer and Abraham Weiner, "The New Jersey Telephone Company Case," *Industrial and Labor Relations Review,* April, 1948, p. 493.

Because this catalogue of punitive actions which government officials may direct against the parties to a strike may suggest—as it is not intended to do—that direct actions of this sort constitute the usual type of official intervention, it is worth ending this section with the comment of a seasoned negotiator in a vital industry. "At the national level, at least, my experience has been that the intervention of government officials often is decisive. . . . And they do not have to be so crass as to threaten specific action. The power of government is so great, including the power to arouse public opinion, that it is not necessary to bring the weapons publicly into view. Everyone concerned is aware of the fact that the weapons actually exist."

Intervention by the Press

The role and influence of newspapers in strike situations are variously interpreted. Some identify the press with public opinion, while others carefully distinguish it from public opinion. In this study we treat the press as an intervening third party, distinct from public opinion. As such, the general preliminary remarks made with respect to all such intervenors apply here. (1) Newspapers which seek the end of a strike may be prejudiced against one of the parties and may seek to end the strike by securing its defeat. We are not concerned here with the nature of its bias but with the weapons it has at its command to force strike termination. (2) Newspapers which intervene may do so at the behest of one of the parties or on their own initiative, out of self-serving motives. We are not interested in such efforts but only in those efforts which are induced by pressures from the affected public which the journal cannot ignore without penalty. In addition, we adopt no view as to the general effectiveness or ineffectiveness of newspaper intervention, but assume that, like intervention by government officials, it may be one or the other depending on the circumstances.

What influence does the public affected by a strike have over a newspaper which would induce it to seek the end of that strike?

First, cynicism concerning class interests and financial influence notwithstanding, the newspaper is widely regarded as a representative of general community interests. Its function in the United States has come to be more than a purveyor of news; it is expected to perform a role of community leadership and to supply the closest approximation of a community conscience. Its editorial column is the most evident reflection of these latter functions. Usually capped with a defined program or platform, a scriptural verse, a proverb, or a slogan, the editorial column becomes the medium through which social policies are advocated or denounced, public officials are supported or criticized, actions are applauded or condemned. As an organ of lay ethics and morality, the newspaper is expected to speak out for the innocent victims of private aggression, to demand justice for those in the community who are unjustly subjected to hardship.

A public suffering in consequence of a union-management conflict is an almost "natural" cause for a newspaper to adopt. Indeed, it is an almost necessary cause. For a newspaper to ignore the inconvenience or hardship of a substantial public which is significantly affected by a strike would be almost certain to subject that newspaper to censure. A community which expects the championship of causes from its press would be suspicious and critical of a newspaper which remained editorially silent in the face of a serious strike. It is worth repeating that while a biased press may defend its public honor by singling out the union for vicious and prejudiced attack, it is not the bias which is significant to this study but the pressure on the journal to intervene to settle the strike. Failure to respond to public expectation in this regard would endanger a newspaper's position and influence in the community, and loss of standing in the community may affect its subscription lists, and a shortened subscription list may affect advertising revenues. The pressure on a newspaper to respond to the immediate interests of a public affected by a strike is probably of about the same intensity as that bearing on elected officials.

There is a second pressure which is likely to be felt by newspapers in strikes which have a general impact. The economic distress felt by merchants and businessmen generally, as the effects of the strike snowball, is likely to stimulate them into seeking active press intervention. Settlement—any kind of settlement—becomes important to their economic welfare. The influence which they possess over a newspaper is the influence of advertisers on whose patronage the newspaper relies. It is the influence of the customer whose trade is important. The newspaper cannot disregard such importuning without fear of customer—that is, advertiser—retaliation. Defection to a competing newspaper which is more sympathetic to their plight, to the local radio station, to display or handbill advertising, or simply the dropping of advertising altogether by the firm which had been wondering about its merits are all penalties to which a newspaper is subject.

Intervention by a newspaper can take several forms—public insistence that the parties resolve their dispute by any means, so long as they resolve it; editorial proposals which are urged on the parties as a basis for settling the dispute; public condemnation of either party or both parties for prolonging the strike; public insistence that other third parties intervene. But what sanctions support any of these efforts? We may distinguish three.

Influence on Personal Reputation of the Parties

A newspaper is in a strategic position to influence its readers' estimation of union and management leaders. Refusal to call off a strike or to cooperate in efforts to end it may subject them to sharp editorial criticism leading to their general opprobrium. Public castigation for one's indifference to community hardship can be punishing indeed. When newspapers describe in detail the nature of the suffering inflicted by the strike and charge the parties with responsibility for that suffering, there is no ground for partisan denial. The suffering is factual; the responsibility is immediate. Falling back upon one's "right" to strike or upon the "principle" behind refusal to agree on the other's terms does not lessen the reality of community hardship. No amount of rationalization can hide even from the participants their involvement in the cause of it.

Particularly if the newspaper concentrates responsibility on a single individual can the effect on personal reputation be most damaging. There can be little doubt, for example, that the name of Michael Quill, president of the Transport Workers Union, has been blackened by the attacks of New York City newspapers on him for his part in the subway and bus strikes of that city. The unfavorable reputation of John L. Lewis has been "made" to a remarkable extent by the editorialists and cartoonists of the nation's press in their repeated condemnation of him for his role in coal strikes. Whether such criticism is deserved is here irrelevant. The fact is that the power of the press to affect the honor of one's name constitutes a powerful weapon in support of its intervention to end a strike. It is all the more powerful because responsibility for the suffering of others is so difficult to defend. The best defense is to shift responsibility to others, but the effective means for such a defense may be denied by a hostile press. Union and management officials refuse to end a critical strike only at the risk of having their personal reputations pilloried, their names dragged through editorial mud.

Influence on Organizational Achievement

Because of its peculiar role in the community, the newspaper may be in a position to penalize intransigent parties to a critical strike by opposing them on other issues or by refusing them support at times when support would be welcome. Petitions for exceptions to zoning ordinances or for tax relief may be fought in the editorial columns; publicly regulated enterprises may fear newspaper opposition to requests for rate adjustments. Unions may be influenced by realization that antilabor legislation may be supported more vigorously by newspapers which they have antagonized.

A strategically placed observer reports an example of such pressures:

Within the last three years there have been two local transportation stoppages. In both cases public opinion and pressure from many sources in the community were brought to bear on the parties in dispute. The newspaper took an active lead in pointing out how the public suffered from the inability of the parties to reach a settlement. It urged various types of action to be taken by the City and came out in favor of compulsory arbitration of public utility disputes. . . .

The transportation company was well aware of the importance of the newspaper as well as the attitude of the City toward possible revisions in the fare structure which might be necessary if a wage increase were granted to settle the dispute. It had to pay attention to this pressure. The Union, on the other hand, was afraid of the possible implications of the compulsory arbitration, but in particular was conscious of the growing irritation at the public inconvenience and the unfavorable attitude which was being directed at Labor in general. . . .

In the second of these cases a tripartite panel from the community mediated the dispute. The Chairman of the panel was the publisher of the local newspaper. His suggestions for possible avenues of settlement were given very serious and careful consideration by both parties to the dispute because they were aware of his great ability and experience in mediation, and also because they were aware of the ultimate power which the newspaper could bring on the parties within the community. I think it is safe to say that in the case of the Labor representatives, it was their recognition of the over-all importance of the newspaper's attitude on labor-management matters in general, as well as their belief in the inherent fairness of the publisher, that compelled them to consider his suggestions in this particular dispute. I think it was the recognition of both the fairness of the publisher as well as his potential power on matters affecting the transportation company particularly with respect to increases in fares, that compelled the Company representatives to give great weight to his suggestions.

Influence as a Provocateur

The newspaper may bring pressure on others to intervene or may act as the organizer of more effective opposition.

In particular, the press may so insistently demand action by government officials that the latter are prompted to act sooner than they might otherwise have or even when disposed not to intervene at all. The nature of this pressure is diagrammed below:

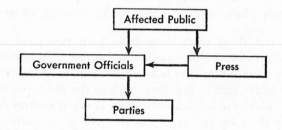

Intervention by government officials brings into play all those sanctions available to them, which have previously been discussed. Their response to newspaper pressure is likely to come from the realization of the importance of a favorable press if they are to continue in public office.

The newspaper may play an assisting role, acting as an effective aid to public opinion without itself invoking the sanctions it commands. In this role it seeks to focus the public opinion to which it responds, so that the public's direct sanctions are more effectively employed. It can do this by such simple devices as giving "scare" headlines to news stories, allotting a prominent and substantial space to pictures and reports of the strike, continuing an emphasis on the costs and burdens of the strike, selecting "human interest" stories arousing emotional resentment, and so on.

An outstanding example of the power of newspapers to mobilize the direct sanctions of a community against an offending party was provided by the Cleveland transit strike of 1949, in which the union struck the city-owned lines without warning shortly before Christmas, when last-minute gift shopping was at its peak. The *News,* the *Press,* and the *Plain Dealer* gave over their front pages to the strike. They headlined the belligerent statement of the mayor. Their news reports pictured a city beleaguered, some with the flavor of wartime communiqués. In this instance the role of organizer of public opinion was supplemented by editorial condemnation centered on an individual. The union president was singled out for bitter personal criticism. A five-column front-page editorial in the *Cleveland Press,* accompanied on the left by a picture of the union official, and on the right by a group of apparently frustrated people idly waiting around a transit stop, was headlined "One Man vs. The People."[7] In this case the mayor moved swiftly against the union and the strike was broken in five days by court injunction. There is little doubt, however, that this decisive action was possible only because public opinion in Cleveland had been so sharply focused and effectively organized by the local press. Under editorial leadership, there was a community "uprising," which could scarcely have been anticipated by union leadership, of a type which has probably not been duplicated in other cities where transit strikes have been called.

Intervention by Other Unions and Managements

Other unions and managements sometimes press for settlement of a strike because they are members of the affected public. The union's members may have been thrown out of work by the stoppage; the man-

[7] The text of the editorial read:

"Here are two pictures.

"They are the two sides of this community's disastrous Christmas present—the transit strike.

"One is Thomas A. Meaney. He and he alone is responsible, directly and personally.

"Month after month, day after day, he worked toward this strike.

"He has put the men and women who trusted him, the ones he was mistakenly supposed to represent, in a degrading position.

"When he finally saw the tide was turning against him, he began to pretend he actually didn't want a strike.

"But he wanted a strike and he got it.

*   *   *

"The other picture shows citizens huddled in the snow at a bus stop, waiting and hoping.

"It is a picture that now can be taken at any hour, in any part of Greater Cleveland.

"These are the victims of Tom Meaney's arrogant, unscrupulous leadership. They are the ones really hurt, the men and women and children all over town.

"The clogged streets, the spoiled holidays, the fire dangers, the reduced shopping, the stranded families, the empty pay envelopes—these are Meaney's monument.

"The people didn't ask any favors or any special treatment.

"All they wanted were their rights as self-respecting Americans.

"As long as Meaney is yelling and faking, no one is getting those rights."

In similar fashion the other newspapers took up the cudgel against "a wholly unnecessary strike, fomented by one utterly irresponsible and unscrupulous union leader."

agements may be unable to sell their products to or buy the products of the struck firm. Such unions and managements we do not consider intervenors; they are among those directly affected.

In still other instances unions and managements intervene in a strike not in response to public pressure but at the instigation of one of the parties. Sympathetic strikes and boycotts are examples of actions inspired by one of the strike participants. This kind of intervention falls outside our range of interest, since it is not a response to a frustrated right of expectancy but a mobilization of forces by one of the parties to the strike.

Third-party intervention by other unions and managements may, however, be stimulated by public opinion. The sanctions to which they respond are the fear that public resentment of the parties to the strike may be generalized to managements generally or to unions generally. In such an event public antipathy to one or the other of these interest groups may lead to loss of good will and perhaps to acquiescence in or even support of restrictive legislation or regulation. Unions in particular are conscious of the possible stigma which may attach to the labor movement as a whole due to the intransigence of one union in a critical strike.

Examples are not wanting. In the Cleveland transit strike referred to above, the Cleveland Federation of Labor, conscious of an aroused public opinion, fearful that it too would be tarred with a reputation of insensitivity to public interest, and—it was said—worried that a critical public would rally to the support of Senator Taft in the next year's election because of this demonstration of the need for legislative controls over unions, publicly disavowed the action of its constituent member. The officers of the Cleveland Federation wired President Green of the AFL to exercise his influence to have the strike called off, saying, "Unless we receive an immediate reply to our request for action on your part it will be necessary for us to call an urgent meeting of the Cleveland Federation of Labor to take action against the transit union." Green is reported to have wired the striking union that "it is imperative that you call off this mad strike." At the strike's collapse, the Cleveland central union suspended the president of the offending union "unless and until he explains his actions in the recent transit strike to the satisfaction of the delegates."

In a 1952 strike by garbage tippers in Louisville, leaders of the local labor movement, stirred by public opinion, brought pressure on the striking union to restore service. In a 1946 plumbers' strike in New York City, the president of the Building and Construction Trades Council assured the mayor that other unionists would work with nonunionists called in to perform plumbing work. In a 1950 strike of a metal fabricating company in Hartford, one of the principal pressures on the union came from other unions in the city which felt that a long strike would make those employers who were inclined to fight labor even "tougher" to deal with.

The rationale behind such interventions has been explained by Daniel J. Tobin, former president of the Teamsters, in criticizing the United Automobile Workers for prolonging the General Motors strike of 1945-1946: "Some in the Automobile Workers' Union may say that it is none of our business, that they are running the affairs of the union. That's true to a certain extent, but it is our business because every time a labor union makes a mistake or loses a fight, it weakens the whole structure of organized labor."[8]

Management pressure on management during a strike, while usually less publicized, likewise occurs. It has sometimes come through such business organizations as the local chamber of commerce.

The sanction which the intervening union or management holds over the strike party is the possible loss of the esteem of those who are part of his "class," whose good will he especially prizes, whose good opinion may be helpful to his own advancement. If the reader doubts the effectiveness of such a hold, he need only reflect how sore a blow would be the loss of the good will of those in the group with which he most closely identifies his career.

In the case of the union, there is likewise the threat of loss of organized support in future struggles, a threat which may be doubly effective if, because of the vital nature of the service involved, the strike ceases to be a reliable weapon. In that case, political pressures may become the most feasible means of securing improvements in working conditions, and in winning political support a solitary union might well regret that it had alienated the affections of a federation whose influence in political circles could be helpful.

Intervention by Other Third Parties

In addition to those intervenors already mentioned, there are sometimes other third parties who respond to public pressure and in turn

8 *The International Teamster*, May, 1946.

apply pressure to the strike participants. Although in specific instances their influence may be persuasive, their intervention occurs less frequently and can be noted here without elaboration.

Ministers, priests, and other religious representatives sometimes seek a settlement of a strike out of sympathy with the distress of the strikers. In numerous instances this is intervention in response to an appeal from the unionists themselves. In other situations, however, the appeal comes not from the union or its members but from the wives of strikers, who beseech assistance to end the strike—favorably or not— to protect their families from privation. Since we consider the families of strikers part of the affected public, a ministerial response to such a plea must be viewed as a response to the public. In some few instances there appears to have been church intervention out of regard for the distress of a consuming public, as in a utility strike.

In these instances, what sanctions does the public hold over the churchmen, and what influence do the latter wield with the striking parties? We can only say that failure of the minister to intervene may place him in the position of—to borrow familiar religious analogies— the shepherd who deserts his sheep or the father who forsakes his children. The extent to which he is subject to this feeling depends on the frequency of contact with those in distress. If there are many of the affected public in his own congregation or parish, the pressure on him to perform the role of caring for his flock and ministering to the needs of his people will be great. If he is pastor of a "downtown" church whose members are widely scattered in well-to-do suburban areas and supplemented on Sundays by transient visitors, there is likely to be no pressure at all. The degree of pressure on him depends on the kind of conduct expected of him by those who are important to him. If they expect his aid in ending the strike and he fails them, the respect and esteem in which he is held will suffer. For a church official to feel his congregation cool toward him or fall away from him would constitute a severe punishment indeed.

The influence which he holds over the strike parties is more nebulous. It is likely to be ineffective unless the parties are themselves of the same religious persuasion, so that refusal to heed the appeal of the church intervenor seems almost a rebuff of their own church, possibly involving a loss of standing in their religious community. We have information on the intervention in two threatened utility strikes of the same Catholic priest, who sought to avoid the public suffering which seemed imminent. In one situation he used his influence with the management, which was Catholic. In the other situation, his influence was directed to a Catholic union leadership. In both cases the only pressure exercised was that of an influential Catholic leader in two communities where the Catholic population predominated, where refusal to have heeded the plea might have subjected the strike participant to a feeling of estrangement from a faith that in turn tied him into his community.

Service organizations and at times even respected individuals acting alone may intervene to seek the end of a strike. Here the pressures on the intervenors are likely to be similar though perhaps not as intense as those operating on churchmen, and their influence over the parties to the strike derives only from how significant to the union or management is the support and esteem of the organization or individual. At times the influence is likely to be negligible, at other times significant.

None of those mentioned in this miscellaneous category, however, is likely to achieve unaided the objective of terminating the strike.

The canvass of this and the preceding chapters should make this clear in any event: There are a few highly effective sanctions of a social, political, and economic nature which can be applied directly by an affected public or be invoked to secure the intervention of an influential intermediary in a critical strike situation. There is a considerable variety of sanctions available to intervenors to influence the parties to end the strike. We may make our generalizations somewhat more pointed. The public pressure on any individual to intervene in a strike situation comes from the role which that individual plays in the community. The positions of certain individuals—political leaders, editors of newspapers, officials of other organizations, churchmen—by their very nature tend to *compel* action in certain circumstances. Individuals occupying such roles are expected to perform certain functions, and failure to measure up to these expectations tends to deprive them of reputation, influence, and perhaps office as well. The influence which is theirs must generally be used in the appropriate circumstances in order to be retained. In a strike which vitally affects a public, if the individual or individuals from whom that public *expects* to find protection and support fails to provide what is expected of him, he endangers his position with that public. Those who have been disappointed will no longer entertain the same expectations of him. A leader gambles on losing his following by failing to exercise a leadership which has voluntarily been accorded him. If he fails to play the role which his position assigns him, others may be sought who will meet the expectations held of them. The sanction which a public holds over a public figure, then, is the loss of a position and a standing which it and other publics have granted to him. The individual can afford to frustrate the expectations of a given public only if he is convinced it is a small enough segment of his general public to do no substantial harm to his position.

The basis for whatever power the intervenor exercises over the strike participants has been summarized by one of our respondents, the executive director of a mediation agency. "When there have been third-party intermediaries such as public officials or prominent local citizens who have made suggestions for the settlement of disputes, it has been the recognition of their potential power, influence and leadership in the community which has caused their suggestions to be given weight, rather than any [explicit] promise of benefit or threat of reprisal by them." This statement agrees reasonably well with our evidence. It appears to be seldom a direct threat which is made to influence the strike parties. There is, however, a recognition by the parties of the general power of position and influence possessed by the intermediary, a general power which can be referred back to the specific sanctions catalogued in this chapter. If the general power of the intervenor is challenged by continuation of the strike, then the intervenor may meet the challenge by bringing specific sanctions into play.

A classificatory description of sanctions, such as has been given here, does not by itself adequately convey an impression of their use and effectiveness. We turn now to case studies of two strike situations, to observe the sanctions at work.

The Sanctions at Work: Strike of a
Public Utility

IF WE are interested in the sanctions which a public may impose to
secure the end of a strike which adversely affects it, it will be instructive to turn to case studies of the sanctions actually employed in
specific strike situations. In doing so we shall pay less attention to the
actions of the parties than to the actions directed against the parties,
stimulated by public opinion, either actual or anticipated.

In Chapter 8 we discovered that there were two types of situations
in which management and union officials, as well as neutral observers,
believe public opinion to be most effective on the strike parties: (1)
where the product or service is especially vital to consumers, as notably
in the case of public utilities, and (2) where the struck firm employs a
substantial proportion of the community's labor force, as notably in
the case of a dominant firm in a small town. Both cases we can trace
back to the high urgency rating of the strike. In the first instance, the
high urgency rating comes from the impact on consumers. In the
second instance, it is derived from the effect on producers and suppliers
and their associated families. We shall, therefore, undertake two case
studies, one for each type of situation. The utility strike we shall
examine here and in somewhat greater detail than the dominant-firm
case (Chapter 13).

The longest utility strike of record appears to be that conducted by
the Independent Association of Employees of the Duquesne Light
Company in the fall of 1946. This strike lasted for 27 days and was
directed against a company which supplies electricity to the greater
Pittsburgh community.[1]

[1] The data on which this account is based have been obtained in direct interviews with
a number of individuals actively concerned with the strike and with three labor reporters
who covered the strike, as well as from newspaper accounts and court records.

The Independent Association began its life as a company union, whose purpose was to counter the organizational efforts of a national union. A change of leadership brought to its presidency George Mueller, an employee with personal ambitions who used the union as a vehicle for achieving them. Under Mueller, who sought to improve his talents by taking numerous courses at evening colleges, the IA achieved genuine independence and became a force to which the company had to attend. Nevertheless, the company appears to have been slow in modifying its ways. The complacency which characterized it in the days when the union was company-dominated held over to the days in which the union was self-determining. The company's attitude thus provided an excellent foil for Mueller's efforts to build a fighting organization. It provided unusual opportunities for him to demonstrate the quality of his leadership. One who was close to Mueller during this time[2] says that by the beginning of 1946 the union president had concluded that only a strike would "bring the company around."

Following a breakdown in negotiations, a strike was indeed called, suddenly, at 4 A.M., February 12, 1946. It lasted for 12½ hours and was then called off, at the insistence of the city administration, to allow for further negotiations. A new strike deadline of midnight February 26 was set. Twenty-six minutes before that deadline the union agreed to a further postponement of one week. On March 1 the strike call was canceled when the union agreed to submit its case to a board of arbitration, which on April 12 awarded a wage increase of 18 cents an hour. Although this amount was subsequently found by the Wage Stabilization Board to exceed the still-existing wage ceilings, the full award could be and was lawfully paid, the company simply being unable to use the amount in excess of wage ceilings as a basis for price relief or as an element of recoverable cost in any contracts with the federal government. On July 28 the union announced more than fifty new demands, including a further wage increase of 20 percent, a master contract to replace nine separate contracts, and a union shop. The next day it filed its notice of intention to strike at any time after the expiration of thirty days.

The city administration did not delay long in intervening. Following the "off-again, on-again" strike threat of the spring, it was in no mood to dally with a new threat. In this resolve it was bolstered by a con-

[2] Mueller himself was unavailable for interviewing at the time this study was made, in 1952.

siderable receipt of letters from angry and worried citizens, asking assurances of "complete and absolute protection" (a phrase taken from one of such letters) during the spring difficulty. Consequently, on August 7 Mayor David Lawrence released a public statement to both parties:

This city is in no mood to be victimized in another war of nerves such as we endured in February. . . .

If—and this should be clear in a few days' time—negotiations across the table offer you no hope of settlement, there is only one thing for you to do. I have already stated it: refer the dispute to arbitration and keep the lights on while you try your case.

This is where you will end, in all events, if you cannot otherwise agree.

You have great power. Do not abuse it.

You have great obligations. Live up to them.

Or, and this is as sure as the rising of the sun each morning, your powers will be stripped from you and new and more burdensome obligations will be imposed.

The American people, our own people of Pittsburgh, are long-suffering and very patient. But they will not permit the abuse of power which they have conferred. They will not live under the threat of irresponsible action that cuts off their economy, suspends their work, puts their way of living back one hundred years.

Public utilities live by sufferance of the public. They are created by franchise of the state.

What has been given can be withdrawn.

Both management and labor in a public utility must realize that what they have is a grant from the people.

Inevitably, if the terms of that grant are violated, if service is not continuous, the people, through their government, will act.

Negotiations and arbitration are now voluntary. They will remain voluntary only if they are used to prevent stoppages. Otherwise, the people will impose compulsory arbitration.

Failing agreement between the parties, the mayor stepped in as mediator on August 30. There is considerable evidence that his public statement that he would "put the pressure" on both company and union was borne out in fact. He flayed the parties for their disregard of community welfare and sought the intervention of other unions and managements. Department store owners and industrialists, large consumers of electric power, were urged to try to persuade the company to make an offer that the union might entertain. Two of the nation's most eminent industrial leaders, residents of Pittsburgh, were among those who responded to his request to use their powers of persuasion on the management.

Events began to move rapidly. On August 31 the union threatened to break off negotiations that night unless agreement had been reached, but Mayor Lawrence gained the promise of both parties to continue their bargaining. Finally, on September 3, in response to the pressures on it, the company made its first and long-awaited offer to the union. The effect was stunning. The company's proposal was so meager and trivial that the *Pittsburgh Press* editorially condemned it as insulting. At a membership meeting, which was broadcast by radio, Mueller presented the company's offer with sarcastic comment. Only four of the more than 1,500 assembled voted for acceptance. Then they approved a motion "that a strike be called," 1,008 to 568, and empowered their general policy committee to set the date of the strike. When asked whether the union would give special consideration to vital facilities, Mueller replied, "The union does not furnish power." The mayor was reported now ready to put some "real" pressure on the company.

The result of Mayor Lawrence's efforts was the company's consent to arbitrate all issues in dispute, but subject to Wage Stabilization Board policy. This concession represented a substantial achievement for the mayor and marked one of the several turning points of the dispute. While the city administration's pressure had been largely concentrated on the company, up to this point, from the time that the company consented to arbitration the pressures became almost exclusively concentrated on the union.

The union's strike committee rejected the company's arbitration offer. The basis for rejection was not made entirely clear. It was said that the objection was to the limitation that arbitration must conform to Stabilization policies, that arbitration was too expensive, and—by Mueller—that "we are refusing to arbitrate because we know the company has something up its sleeve." According to one newspaper, "Mayor Lawrence was reported to have handled the union rather roughly because of their refusal to arbitrate."

The next move was the union's. In a radio address the night of September 7, Mueller set the strike for 12:01 A.M. September 10.

The following day the mayor asked that the union membership be allowed to vote on the arbitration offer. Mueller refused but consented to poll the general policy committee, which had been given full strike authority by the membership. In an effort to make his influence more effective, Lawrence requested that the 51 members of the policy committee meet with him in his office at noon, September 9, assuming personal responsibility for any loss of earnings they might suffer. Only four appeared. To them the mayor said, "Last week after your meeting, the strike was declared, and then and only then did they [the management] come in with an offer of arbitration, and I want to say to you and I want you to carry back to the other members that the plan of arbitration was my plan." Subsequently the full committee voted, 42 to 9, to reject the company's offer of arbitration. The objection given was that Stabilization policy would prevent arbitration on the merits of the dispute.

As if anticipating this result, the mayor had given a fighting speech on the radio the previous evening. Asserting that the community was the victim of a "psychologically incompetent management[3] and a poorly led, ill-advised union," he added, with respect to the latter, "It belongs neither to the CIO nor the AFL. It has no international officers, no men like William Green or Philip Murray to give it wise and competent counsel." (Lawrence's intent here became apparent. The independent union was to be isolated from the Pittsburgh labor movement and deprived of its support, if possible. Its actions were to be branded as irresponsible, in consequence of its lack of that maturity which the national organizations would have supplied. Mayor Lawrence's position as a liberal Democrat, who in the state legislature had supported bills amenable to the unions, favored the success of this maneuver. It had already been reported that, unofficially, the AFL Central Labor Union and the CIO Industrial Labor Council were opposed to the strike; and AFL President Green, although refusing "to interject myself in this problem," supported voluntary arbitration on principle and "particularly in public utility disputes.") Then addressing himself to the public at large, in this same radio address, the mayor said: "I am asking you to join me in applying every pressure to prevent the paralysis of Pittsburgh. No small group of men—union or employer—can withstand the full impact of 1,400,000 people. Use every means you know to reach out in your community to let the men of the Duquesne Light Company—workers and officials alike—to let them know that you will not allow them to strangle this city."

[3] So strong an impression did these harsh words make on the company's officials that six years later, when interviewed, one of them repeated almost this precise phrase in describing the mayor's efforts to achieve settlement.

The strike was now imminent. If it was to be averted, whatever action could be taken must be taken without delay.

The city had been faced with a similar threat in the spring, it will be recalled, and decisions had been made then which cancellation of the strike made unnecessary, but which now could be put into effect. At the time of the spring threat, the city administration had explored the possibility of federal seizure of the company, presumably under the government's remaining war powers, but federal authorities had preferred not to intervene in a situation which they believed could be handled locally. Municipal seizure had been considered, but the city solicitor, Miss Anne X. Alpern, advised against it on the ground of doubtful legality. Instead, despite the fact that she was of the same liberal Democratic faith as the mayor, she advocated that the city seek an injunction. No final decision had been reached, but the papers had been fully prepared, requiring only the insertion of the proper date and time, and the court had been asked to be ready to sit on short notice if they were served. The strike was called off, however, and the papers were relegated to the files.

The city was now confronted with a similar situation, and similar steps were taken to meet it. A fresh bill of complaint was prepared. Conversations were held between the mayor and his advisors. Miss Alpern, although warning the mayor that his request for an injunction would endanger his political standing with the unions, urged this as the only remaining course to avert what promised to be a disaster to the community. Without committing himself, the mayor consented to an arrangement whereby, on word from his office, papers would be immediately served upon both union and management, with the court notified in advance so that it would be prepared to sit. Multiple copies of the bill of complaint and notice to defendants were drafted, needing only insertion of the hour of day at which the court would entertain the motion. The stage was set for trigger action as the day of September 9 wore on. The strike had been set for that midnight.

Hoping to avoid the stigma of asking for an injunction, which had become a symbol of antiunion activity, Lawrence sought to have the company itself enter the petition. The company was indeed then considering such an action, but preferred to avoid it if possible. It had information, or at least suspicion, of the city's tentative plans to seek a writ. The situation developed into a kind of cat-and-mouse game, in which the city delayed action, hoping that the company would move, while the company marked time, anticipating that the city would act if it did not. By personal connections the company had arranged to be notified the moment the city solicitor applied to the court.

The hours passed. The suspense increased. Finally, at 11 P.M., word was flashed from the mayor's office to the city solicitor to proceed with service of the papers. The waiting deputies were on their way within the minute. It has been suggested that subsequently the mayor sought to create the impression among influential political and labor leaders that overzealous subordinates had forced this action without his full approval. There is a story current that he even attempted to recall the injunction papers within minutes after the original instruction to proceed with service, but too late to halt proceedings. Whatever the validity of these accounts, there is no doubt that the action placed the mayor in a difficult position. The union group, among his most militant political supporters, was firmly set against use of the injunction. County Commissioner John J. Kane, himself an AFL man, had warned the mayor against resorting to such an instrument. The die was now cast, however.

The scene of action now shifted to the courtroom. The director of the Department of Public Health entered the bill of complaint on behalf of the City of Pittsburgh. He was represented by Miss Alpern, the city solicitor. The hour was fast approaching midnight. The situation was electric. One observer remembers the drama of the occasion even after a lapse of six years. "There was Miss Alpern pleading before the court, with one hand pointing to the clock as she told the judges, her voice tinged with indignation, of the hardships which would befall the city in a matter of minutes should the strike be permitted." The bill of complaint elaborated these expected consequences:

Petitioner avers that the impending power strike will have disastrous consequences to the million and a half people who live and work in Pittsburgh and the vicinity affected by the strike.

The strike will endanger the lives, health, safety and well-being of our citizens.

It will paralyze the governmental, industrial, commercial and civic life of this entire area.

It will result in tremendous and irremediable hardship.

It will cut off the supply of water. Six of the nine water pumping stations of the City of Pittsburgh will be rendered useless and there will be no reliable supply of water within twenty-four to forty-eight hours after the strike takes effect.

It will cause the spread of disease through lack of water for sanitation purposes.

It will cause grave danger through lack of water for fire-fighting purposes.

It will cut off the supply and distribution of food because of the necessary closing of stores and interference with transportation facilities.

It will cause the spoilage of large quantities of foodstuffs in homes and storage buildings through lack of refrigeration, at a time of serious food shortages.

It will prevent the pasteurization and storage of milk, drastically reducing supplies in this area with untold danger to infants and young children.

It will imperil the health of residents in their homes, the sick in their beds, the inmates in hospitals, nursing homes and hundreds of institutions. It will interfere with hospital care and medical treatment and endanger those requiring special and uninterrupted treatment.

It will create a health menace due to interference with the collection of garbage and operation of garbage disposal plants.

It will darken the homes, streets and public thoroughfares.

It will expose the populace to acts of criminals and vandals and prevent adequate police protection.

It will cripple the transportation system throughout the area. It will prevent the operation of ambulances, fire-fighting equipment and radio cars.

It will prevent access to buildings where access is had by means of elevators.

It will cut off the communication system.

It will close the courts and schools.

It will deprive people of their property and destroy property of incalculable value.

It will result in staggering economic losses and will deprive hundreds of thousands of men and women of work and subsistence.

Available auxiliary power from other sources of supply, for which the City authorities have made tentative provision, is inadequate to meet the staggering needs on all sides and is only sufficient for a minor fraction of the pressing uses for power which will inevitably arise.

The estimate of the impending calamities was supported by affidavits from the director of the Department of Public Health, the president and secretary of the Allegheny County Medical Society, the director of the Department of Public Works, and the director of the Department of Public Safety.

The city's complaint was directed against both company and union.

Arguing that the "negotiating meetings have been unattended by any of the officers or directors of the Standard Gas and Electric Company or the Standard Power and Light Company, the real owners, who are non-residents of the City of Pittsburgh and direct the operations of the Duquesne Light Company and associated companies from their offices and residences in New York, Chicago and other cities," the bill went on to state:

The absentee owners are seemingly indifferent to the peril with which the citizens of the City of Pittsburgh are confronted and are content to continue to collect substantial revenues from their investments while suffering none of the hardships incident to the recurrent power strikes resulting from the poor labor relations between management and workers.

With respect to the union, the bill read:

A strike called by the Independent Association, ostensibly against the Duquesne Light Company and its associated companies, is in fact a strike against the life and safety of every man, woman and child in the City of Pittsburgh and the entire populace of the area served, and is illegal and should be enjoined. Failure to successfully negotiate modifications and amendments to existing contracts with the defendant companies affords no legal basis for striking against the people served by the companies.

The relief asked was an order restraining the officers and members of the Independent Association from calling any strike against the Duquesne Light Company and enjoining the officers and directors of the parent companies to come to Pittsburgh to participate in bona fide negotiations to reach an agreement with the union. Those who had sworn to affidavits were available as witnesses, but the defendant attorneys, called into court on such short notice, waived any examination. The court forthwith granted the order substantially as requested, and set a hearing for September 13 on whether the order should be made permanent. The strike was now off.

The injunction proceedings marked a second turning point in the long-drawn-out dispute. Sentiment which had begun to firm against the union because of its intransigence in refusing arbitration now became divided. Unionists and some liberal elements in the community rallied to the support of the Independent Association out of opposition to that hated legal instrument, the injunction. For something more than two weeks George Mueller, IA president, enjoyed a burst in popularity as he became a symbol of union martyrdom. The CIO and AFL, previously

tending strongly toward condemnation of the strike, now became de-
fenders of the union faith by attacking the city's action, while still not
approving the union's. Officials of the AFL Central Labor Union dis-
patched telegrams to all Democratic candidates for the state legislature,
then campaigning for the fall election, asking their stand on the injunction. All but one stood by Mayor Lawrence, reminding the unionists of his prolabor record and arguing that "this is no ordinary labor
dispute." Central Labor Union officials were reported to be alarmed
that this use of the injunction might become a precedent which would
be extended to other strike situations.

If the injunction aroused labor's opposition, there were many members of the general public in whose eyes the mayor had increased in
stature by his actions. Some who had suspiciously regarded him as a
"labor mayor" now conceded that in a time of crisis he was the people's
representative, who could disregard political ties to special-interest
groups. If there were those who regarded the injunction as a great
mistake, there were probably many more who applauded the mayor for
his courageous use of it.

Meanwhile, the injunction appeared to be having its effect. Leo T.
Crowley, president of the Standard Gas and Electric Company, parent
of Duquesne Light, arrived in Pittsburgh. Here was a man high in
Democratic party circles, whose language Lawrence, himself a Democratic national committeeman, could speak. The union had presumably resisted the company's arbitration offer because of the attached
condition that Stabilization policies should be controlling on the arbitration board. From the Federal Conciliation Service assurance was now
obtained, in writing, that stabilization policy need not apply where
both parties voluntarily entered into unconditional arbitration. (This
policy was indeed already known to the union, since it was on such a
basis that it had received the above-ceiling wage increase of April 12.)
The mayor prevailed upon Crowley to make such an unconditional
offer. He then called in the union negotiating committee and its attorney, asking them to consent to arbitration under the new offer.
Mueller and Crowley met and discussed terms. The result was an agreement between the two, signed September 12, submitting to arbitration
all issues in dispute, with no conditions attached. A second paragraph
provided for the establishment of a top-level committee composed of
union and management officials, whose personnel would have full authority to settle any dispute brought before it. This arrangement was

designed to meet a union charge that it had been unable to negotiate grievances with company representatives having the authority to settle.

Mueller hailed the arbitration agreement as a "victory" for the union. To allow time for membership ratification of the agreement, the hearing on the injunction was postponed until September 24. The great crisis appeared to be over. In fact, however, it had hardly begun.

The evening of September 20 the union membership met to consider the arbitration offer. Mueller was in charge of the meeting. Instead of speaking on behalf of the agreement which he had himself signed, however, an agreement which he had publicly declared to be a union victory, Mueller charged that the company had "reneged" on the manner in which the arbitration was to be conducted. He entertained a motion that the membership reject arbitration, explaining, "If you vote yes you mean you don't want arbitration. If you vote no your body and your soul belongs to the Duquesne Light Company." The vote was 1,035 to 329 for rejection. Mueller then advised the membership that hearings on the injunction had been set for 9:30 A.M., September 24, and that since the entire membership had been named in the initial restraining order, they should all appear at the courtroom. This would, of course, result in the company's being shut down.[4]

From the membership meeting Mueller went to a radio station. In a fighting speech he attacked the city administration for seeking an injunction and asserted that the union would resist: "Now, can the City Solicitor, under the Mayor of the City of Pittsburgh, direct that the company shall have a monopoly on our bodies? It cannot . . . and we will not in any way uphold the injunction because it is not a legal document that is backed up in any shape nor form of law in existence on the books today. . . . Even if we are unjustified in our strike, there is still no law that says we cannot strike and as long as we are American citizens, we demand the protection of the laws of the United States and not that little handful of politicians down in City Hall in Grant Street."

The next morning Mueller was confronted by reporters with the company's denial that it had gone back on its arbitration agreement. He admitted that the articles of arbitration, drafted by the company's attorney, had been approved by him. "But the members are just fed up on arbitration," he said. "They don't want any more of it." To a

---

[4] Union handbills confirmed this announcement, instructing all members "to attend the injunction hearings. . . . It is your duty as a law-abiding American citizen to attend these hearings. The injunction has been issued against YOU. It is your duty to appear and defend YOUR civil rights. All members of the independent union are named as defendants."

reporter, too, he declared that the strike had been set for 9:30 A.M., September 24—not simply as a repetition of the previous instructions to the members to appear at the court hearings, but as a definite strike call. "As far as we know, it is a direct violation of the injunction; it is a direct challenge. We are challenging it not only as to its validity but as to its legality and enforcement."

What led to Mueller's repudiation of the Crowley agreement? There is no ready answer. Father Charles Owen Rice, then head of the Duquesne University Labor-Management Institute and a close friend of Mueller, in a broadcast said that Mueller had in effect gone back on his word, but that he had done so "only because he felt that way lay the desires of his people." Others, less charitable and perhaps more numerous, believed that Mueller had been enjoying his notoriety. The picture of himself as controlling the fate of a metropolis, with which he had been repeatedly confronted, had given him a sense of power; some said that he was becoming intoxicated with that heady feeling. He was frequently compared with John L. Lewis. That ambition which had been remarked by others, and was said to have been admitted by himself when he assumed the presidency of the IA, fed on this diet of publicity. To surrender to an arbitration agreement, under pressure of an injunction, might sweep away the prospects for a brilliant future in the labor movement. To fight the injunction meant the chance for a hero's role. Whichever of these interpretations one chooses, the fact remains that Mueller repudiated the agreement of September 12 and issued a new strike call for September 24.

On the 22nd Crowley returned to the city and announced that he was willing to meet anyone at any time to avert the strike. He met with Mueller, but the latter was adamant in refusing to discuss terms until the injunction had been withdrawn. Scores of telegrams and hundreds of phone calls poured in on City Hall, virtually all condemning the union. It was urged that Mueller be jailed; some suggested picketing the homes of the strikers themselves if the strike was called. On September 23, Mayor Lawrence in a radio address urged the powerhouse and distribution men to stay on their jobs, saying they would thereby obtain public support for the demands they were making on the company. County Commissioner Kane told Mueller and three other members of the strike committee that the Duquesne employees had little to gain and much to lose by going on strike. "I don't think you can gain anything substantial during this wave of hysteria," he said. "Everyone is emotional and excited."

The court hearing on whether the injunction should be continued began the morning of September 24, with an estimated 800 persons seeking admittance, among them many of the Duquesne employees. The Central Labor Union and the District Council of the Brotherhood of Teamsters asked leave of the court to intervene. The labor movement, as a whole, felt it had much at stake in the outcome of this proceeding. City Solicitor Alpern tried to calm their fears with her opening statement to the court: "It was only after weeks of attempted negotiation day and night . . . that this injunction was asked from this Court. We know only too well how often the injunction process has been used to oppress labor, and because we realize that we attempted every means within our power, within the Administration's power, to bring to bear upon these parties the conscience of the people of Pittsburgh so that we would not have a strike and so that it would not be necessary to come to this Court for relief." The Pittsburgh situation was an unusual one and constituted no general precedent for the use of the injunction. "We are anxious to have labor in these proceedings so that they too can watch this litigation and make certain that the Order that is issued here will be confined to the facts that prompted it and will not be enlarged by the foes of labor to situations where it has no applicability whatsoever."

The city solicitor then provided the legal grounds for the injunction which was sought:

I am not going to cite to this Court from case after case based on entirely different fact situations. I rest the case of the people of Pittsburgh and of the surrounding area upon the basic law of this Commonwealth and upon our Constitution, too, which protects the people of our city. . . . This is a Court of Equity before whom I am submitting my case, and under the powers of a Court of Equity in Pennsylvania, and in every other common law state, there are broad powers to protect the public welfare by exercising the police power of the state. In the Equity Act of 1836, which has been in existence for one hundred years, in Section 13 it states that this Court may prevent as a Court in Chancery the commission of any act prejudicial of public welfare or the continuance of any act prejudicial to public welfare.

Witnesses were presented and cross-examined. The Court's decision was to continue the preliminary injunction in full force and effect.

Then came a sequence of events which the city administration had not anticipated. The court pressed Mueller for an explicit answer as to whether he had called a strike in violation of the court's order and as to whether he intended to obey the injunction. The union president's evasive answers were swept aside as the court prodded him for an unequivocal reply. The union attorney, now sensing the court's purpose, sought to intervene on behalf of his client but was told to let Mueller speak for himself. It was apparent that the three judges on the bench had been more than irritated by what observers described as the arrogant manner in which Mueller had conducted himself throughout the proceeding. When Mueller finally answered that he had ordered the strike and would not abide by the injunction, the court summarily found him guilty of contempt and sentenced him to one year in jail. Trial by jury and bail were both refused, because "it is contempt in open court." The remaining members of the strike committee were ordered to appear the following morning to determine what action should be taken with respect to them.

It was the city administration, not the union, which was most stunned by this action. The mayor was reported as "sick" over the court's decision. His presentiment of adverse consequences was fully borne out. Quickly the word spread throughout the city that "Mueller has been jailed for a year for striking." Nearly 300 CIO steelworkers staged a sympathy walkout at Jones and Laughlin in protest. Three Westinghouse plants were closed when 3,000 workers refused to operate with current from the struck Duquesne Light Company. Other sympathy strikes began simultaneously. Local unions throughout the area quickly issued statements condemning the jailing of Mueller. Telephone calls protesting the action poured into City Hall from other labor unions. By the next day it was estimated that up to 20,000 workers in the area had left their jobs in protest. Crowds of angry unionists milled around the City-County Building. Communist agitators moved in to whip up the growing sentiment. Even representatives of the Duquesne management admitted that the threat of a citywide general strike was becoming real.

Meanwhile, the nine remaining members of the strike committee appeared in court for judgment. There it was revealed that two of their number had met with Crowley the previous evening and had worked out an agreement that would end the strike. One by one they affirmed to the court that they would call a membership meeting for that same night (September 25) and promised "in good faith to this Court" that they would recommend and urge the members as a whole to accept the offer and call off the strike. On the strength of this promise they were released, with instructions to report to the Court the results of the membership meeting.

The meeting was called. Mueller, however, was still in jail and the threat of a general union uprising had not been dissipated. At this stage the tangle of efforts to remedy the situation is difficult to unravel. It appears, however, that it was a labor reporter for one of the Pittsburgh newspapers who urged two of the three judges, whom he personally knew, to release Mueller to attend the union meeting. His intervention was prompted by a desire to quiet the widespread union uprising which promised to develop into a general strike. There seems to be little doubt that the mayor acquiesced in this action. At 8:50 that evening, while the membership meeting was already in session, Mueller was again called before the court. There he made apology for his statements to the court and gave assurance that if released that evening (though not freed of the contempt sentence) he would urge acceptance of the agreement which had been negotiated by two of his committeemen.

With police escort, sirens screaming, Mueller was whisked out to the meeting hall. He entered through a side door. His appearance on stage was the signal for general pandemonium. What followed thereafter is in dispute. Impartial observers maintain that despite his promise to the court Mueller, without openly denouncing the agreement, managed to sway the feelings of the members against the settlement by reminding them of the injunction. The members tore up the ballots which were to have been cast on the agreement. By a vote of 1,771 to 402 they determined to remain on strike until the injunction was lifted. In a subsequent radio statement Mueller admitted that the agreement which he had promised to support was never put to a vote, saying that the motion had not even received a "second" due to the uproar which attended his appearance.

If Mueller was inspired by public attention, as has been maintained by many who knew him, he was now in his element. A crowd of 400 to 500 sympathizers milled around the auditorium while the vote was being taken. A report in the *Pittsburgh Press* (which had been flailing Mueller since the first rejection of the company's arbitration offer) described the scene as Mueller left by the same side door which he had entered: "A group of bobby-soxers, not employes, threw their arms around him, kissed him, pulled his necktie and mussed the little hair he has. George loved it. Flashlight bulbs exploded." Mueller was indeed the man of the hour.

The secretary of the union reported back to the court: "We refuse to consider the offer as it was made until the injunction is dissolved—at which time a vote will be taken to determine the acceptance of the company's offer."

The morning of September 26 Mueller and the mayor met together. The issue before the city administration was whether to request dissolution of the injunction. The decision was not an easy one. Some within the mayor's cabinet opposed such a move. They argued that Mueller was untrustworthy, as shown by his previous actions: twice he had promised to support an agreement and twice he had repudiated that pledge. They contended that a distinction should be drawn between a leader of such irresponsible character and "legitimate" labor leaders, and that that distinction should be sold to the unions and to the public. It was argued that to back down now would be a weak surrender to a man whom they accused of betraying signs of megalomania. On the other side, there were those who believed that if the primary objective was to restore electricity to the city, then the injunction stood in the way of accomplishing that objective. It would be difficult enough to defend the injunction, at least to labor leaders (whose support was considered necessary), but it would be impossible to defend the contempt conviction which rested on the injunction. If the injunction were dissolved, simultaneously dissolving all judicial actions taken under it, pressure to settle the strike could once again be concentrated on the union. As long as the injunction and the jail sentences stood, the city itself became a center of attack.

Mayor Lawrence decided on the latter course. In doing so he obtained from AFL and CIO leaders their promise that on dissolution of the injunction they would again support him against the Duquesne union on the strike issue. The city solicitor entered a motion in court to dissolve the order, on the ground that an agreement had been reached between union and management which the strike committee had advised the city was acceptable to the membership. The agreement referred to was that negotiated with Crowley the night of September 24, on which the members had said they would not vote until the injunction had been withdrawn. The court acceded to the city's request.

This was Mueller's "finest hour." At this point he had defied the city administration and brought it to his own terms. He stood as the unchallenged leader within his own union, whose membership had followed him loyally through his legal vicissitudes. The strike which had been outlawed was now in full swung, with pickets patrolling all Duquesne installations, free of any censure of the courts. He showed no haste to put to membership vote an agreement which had been made not by him but by his subordinates, while he had been in jail.

Nevertheless, despite Mueller's achievements, dissolution of the injunction marked a new turning point in the prolonged dispute. The issue of the strike had been muddied by the issue of the injunction. Public pressure which had previously been focusing on the union had been split by the court action, with important groups in the community deflecting their pressure from the union, on the matter of the strike, to the city administration, on the matter of the injunction. With the latter out of the way, pressures were again concentrated on the striking union.

The day after dissolution, September 27, other labor leaders made good their promise of support for the mayor. Anthony J. Federoff, top CIO official in Allegheny County, asserted that the strike of the Duquesne employees would "embarrass the entire labor movement." He continued:

We want to make it clear to the public that our support of the independent union stopped when the injunction to which all labor objected was vacated. The withdrawal of the injunction was a victory for the entire labor movement, and not for Mueller's union alone. That should be made clear. We are looking out for the interests of all legitimate labor organizations. We do not want to be embarrassed when we help any people who will not keep their word or assume courageous leadership. Had this been one of our unions involved in this dispute we would have had a settlement long ago. We would have kept our word.

County Commissioner Kane, an AFL leader, told a reporter:

Now Mr. Mueller has refused to put the settlement to the membership to put it over. I told him in a meeting last night that he should quit posing as a leader if he can't be one. He is getting the credit for what happened but claims he can't bring about a settlement. If he can't make good then he should step aside and let somebody who can settle the strike do so. I do not feel that he is making a sincere effort to end this strike.

If these statements were effective on the union's rank and file, there was no evidence that they had an influence on Mueller. Indeed, there were some who maintained that the more that other union leaders besought him to end the strike, the greater his feeling of importance. One participant in the dispute remarked in subsequent interview, "The AFL, the CIO, and District 50 of the Mine Workers were all pleading with him to call off the strike—and at the same time they were all licking their chops at the thought of taking over the independent union. Mueller was like the girl whom all the boys want for the junior prom, and he loved it."

Other pressures on the striking union were called into play. Local radio stations, which had made their facilities readily available to Mueller, were reported to be unavailable to him until he was ready to announce the end of the strike. The mayor urged that clergymen ask their congregations and associates to use their influence as they best could. Some spoke out against the strike from their pulpits, as the mayor had hoped, thus influencing directly any members of the union who were also members of these church congregations and perhaps evoking moral pressure, or at least the feeling of moral censorship, from fellow church members on strikers, whether expressed or not.

On September 29 Mueller brought the Crowley agreement before the membership for vote. It was rejected, 1,170 to 553.[5]

The mayor now went before the people with a radio address that was designed to organize public sentiment against the union and to make clear his own role in the strike:

I cannot, in honesty, announce to you this afternoon that our situation has improved. Nothing that has happened in the last 24 hours has brought us closer to normal living. We are continuing for the time to get enough power for our absolute necessities. We still have a limited supply of water. We have lighted streets and we are able to operate our hospitals and institutions. Beyond that we are a stricken city.

Each day since this strike was called has brought us closer to paralysis. Thus far, no life has been lost for lack of power. But the work we live by has come grinding to a halt. The loss of wages is almost beyond calculation.

[5] There was repeated a pattern of voting which by now had become familiar. A motion was made from the floor that the agreement be rejected. The membership was then instructed that all those opposed to the agreement vote "yes," while a "no" vote was for the agreement. On previous ballots it had been pointed out to Mueller that such a manner of wording the proposition was bound to be confusing, but he purported to have no control over the way the motion came from the floor. Reporters remarked on the peculiarity that every motion accepted by the chairman appeared to be worded in such a fashion that a "yes" vote in fact meant "no" on the issue. Suspicion had also been cast on the manner in which ballots were distributed and votes were counted, but on this there was no conclusive evidence.

I have said repeatedly that although this was a strike against a company, it results by its very nature, in a strike against a people. The real suffering tonight is in the home of the steel worker, the coal miner, the store clerk, the street railway man. The loss is his and his family's. In these times of high prices, no family budget can stand indefinite and unlimited loss of wages.

Beyond that we face the prospect of total black-out. To this hour we have staved off that black-out. We have maintained our right to live in health and safety. No one can truthfully say that we can do so in the future. The facts are these. We do not owe one kilowatt-hour of electric current to the independent union. The power we are getting comes from two sources. Some of it is produced in far points of the country. The quantity of this power is not limited by capacity to produce. It is limited by capacity to transport. There are no transmission lines in this area which permit the importation of more electric power than we are getting.

The rest of our power supply is that provided by the supervisory force of the company, not eligible for union membership, who have lived in the plants since the independent union pulled its men off the jobs. Our present power supply depends therefore upon the thin threads of very delicate mechanisms and very limited human endurance. As the mayor of Pittsburgh, it is my duty to see to it that we use every strength we have to support our power supply. Every county and state official is under the same obligation.

I do not have to tell you, I believe, that your city government did everything within its power to prevent this shutdown. We have been concerned with it constantly since August 24th, every day and almost every night. I am sure everyone understands today the crisis which we foresaw and which we tried to stop—tried to stop by negotiation, by mediators, by arbitration, by the pressure of public opinion and finally by law. We have not been pro-company. We have not been pro-union. We have been pro-people. That is why you have a mayor; that is why you have a government. We worked with the tools we have upon the forces which confronted us.

The independent union had poor and ill advised leadership. To that I must now add the word "dishonest." It has broken its word to me three times in the present crisis. I have criticized the company for incompetent labor relations. That still goes. In the earlier days of this dispute they were invariably coming forward too late with too little. But in the end they offered to arbitrate. And once it had been given, they kept their word. The union president has not done so.

I have in my pocket the signed agreement which the union president made to accept arbitration. He turned that agreement into a scrap of paper the very day that I was in Washington to see the Secretary of Labor to assure the union a fair arbitration. That was bad faith. Last Wednesday the union attorney was in my office to tell me that the strike committee had agreed to call off the strike on the basis of a negotiated agreement. Two minutes after he came into the room, he was followed by a union emissary who told him that the agreement was off. The strike committee had changed its mind while it rode up the elevator in the City-County Building.[6] Last night the union rejected an agreement with the company which its own negotiating committee and the union president had worked out with the highest company representatives. Those are two more instances of bad faith.

The unions in this country that stand up, that endure, that are powerful, are the ones that keep their word. The whole labor movement is blackened by the untrustworthy, irresponsible, public-be-damned leadership in this independent union. No organization in the CIO or the AFL would have called this wanton strike. They would have kept their word and they would have told their membership the truth.

It was to protect the city against such bad faith that we went to court for aid—for an order which was to be binding against both the company and the union, so that the power would stay on while they negotiated an agreement. As the mayor of Pittsburgh I know that my first duty lies in the protection of its people. If I did not know that, and so act, I would be less than a mayor and less than a man. It was to serve that purpose that we exhausted every remedy. The court order halted one strike that had been called and provided time to negotiate the two agreements which the leadership of the independent union has since repudiated. Then it outlived its usefulness. It was made to appear as a barrier to settlement, so the City withdrew it.

But no settlement has followed. I fully understood the fear that labor has for injunction law, I know how it has been abused. I wrote and helped to pass the state law which forbids the issuance of injunctions in private labor disputes. I would do it again. The order was obtained by the public, the city government, and not by the company. And it bore with equal force on both sides. But all of labor feared the precedent and opposed its use. We cleared the air by taking it away.

Now labor shares with us the responsibility of dealing with this unnecessary strike of an uncontrolled union. The whole community is suffering, working people worst of all. We must unite this area to achieve a lasting peace—to establish a labor relationship in our power service that will not bring this blow upon us again every six months. This settlement must be final. It must establish a pattern that will last. It must protect the future of this city.

[6] This must have been preliminary to the appearance of the strike committee (except for Mueller, who was then in jail) before the court, at which time it again agreed to speak for the agreement.

In one district of the steel workers' union alone there are 9,000 men out of work. In a second district there are 16,000 idle. There are 3,400 street railway and bus men not working. Additional thousands are losing wages in the stores, the office buildings, the laundries—in every business and industry we have. It can't go on much longer. The full pressure of the whole community must be massed. We must clear away the untruths and appeal to the individual members of the union.

The offer to arbitrate still stands. Under it, every union demand will be weighed by an impartial unbiased expert, interested only in a just award. It is absolutely untrue that an arbiter cannot award wages in excess of the wage stabilization formula, and the union leadership knows this is untrue. The union president has a telegram from Edgar L. Warren, chief of the conciliation service of the Department of Labor, which tells him that the wage stabilization formula does not apply. But the telegram has been buried, and the old misstatement repeated and repeated, on the Hitler principle that people will believe any lie as long as it is big enough.

This strike can be settled if there is a will to settle it. The whole community must bring about that will. All of us have an abiding interest—labor most of all. Our present security and our future prosperity are at stake. We must all help.

In our homes, we must help by conserving power and by conserving water. Remember, if the power goes, water goes next in most sections of the city. Begin conserving it now. Don't sprinkle lawns. Don't wash down walks. Don't let a tap run a second more than is necessary. Save the water. Keep your use of power to an absolute minimum. Your cooperation has been wonderful. Make it even better. Save the current. Turn down the lights. Together, we will see this through.

If one man, the union president, had kept his word, we would be a normal city today. One million and a half people must prove that a pledge given must be kept, and that we, all of us, this great city, will against all obstacles exercise our right to live.

One man who was working closely with Mueller at the time says that this speech of the mayor, however much it may have aroused the public, served only to antagonize Mueller and to make him less inclined than ever to come to terms. He refused any cooperation with the city's efforts to soften the impact of the strike on the city. The trolley and bus lines had ceased running, as the operators respected the picket lines of the Duquesne union, thrown around the car barns because the lines obtained current from the Duquesne Light Company. Leaders of the trolley and bus operators' union asked the mayor whether he could have the pickets removed, so that the lines could resume operation. The mayor asked Mueller and his strike committee to come to City Hall to discuss the matter. Mueller refused.

It was in this attitude of mutual recrimination and hostility that the city and union squared off for a showdown fight. The lines were clearly drawn. The union insisted on continuing negotiations, with the strike providing continuing pressure on the company to make concessions greater than it had. The company held out for arbitration of all issues. The city administration sought settlement, however obtained, but was convinced that a negotiated settlement was less likely and in any event more time-consuming than arbitration. It therefore supported the company's demand that the union call off the strike and submit all issues in dispute to an impartial board. The company was thus in a position where it could let the city serve as its protagonist—and this despite the known record of Mayor Lawrence as a champion of labor.

What pressures could now be brought to bear on the Independent Association? The city administration had played its ace—the injunction. Because of the opposition which this had aroused in a strongly unionized community, it had largely failed. It could not be tried again. The administration was now seeking to focus public opinion more effectively on the striking union, but time would be required for the results of this to materialize. There were, however, a few weapons still available.

1. The mayor sought to encourage any back-to-work movement within the union membership and any opposition to Mueller's leadership. Early in the strike it became apparent that there was not unanimity on policy within either the 10-man strike committee or the 51-man general policy committee. A telephone survey by one of the newspapers was said to have revealed that in the larger group a number were demanding an opportunity to sit in on future negotiations to "find out what was going on." Such disaffection as there may have been in the strike committee, however, was kept in check by Mueller, whose authority was sufficiently great to permit him to replace those who did not respond to his leadership. More formidable were the several rank-and-file movements which developed and the raiding efforts of several other unions.

On October 3, with the strike in its tenth day, an eight-man delegation of former members of the IA petitioned the Pennsylvania State Labor Relations Board for recognition of a new independent union to be called the Utility Workers Union of the Duquesne Light Company. The business agent of the group was a former member of the strike

committee who had resigned in protest against the policy being followed. The new group claimed to represent 700 shop workers, whose
purpose was said to be "to eliminate Dictator Mueller and have an
American democratic union." This petition brought in three other interested unions, all filing notice of intent to intervene in the election.
These were the AFL International Brotherhood of Electrical Workers,
the CIO Utility Workers, and District 50 of the United Mine Workers.
After consultations, the new independent group cast its lot with District 50, withdrawing its petition for an election in favor of the latter.
The election petition was subsequently transferred to the National
Labor Relations Board, which authorized an election within 24 hours
after the hearing in Pittsburgh. Originally set for October 22, the election was moved up to October 15. The petitioners had little hope of
victory, however, conceding that the rivalry among the three new unions
placed the IA in a strong position. Their pessimism proved justified. In
the vote, conducted for hourly employees only, the IA received more
than twice as many votes as the three other unions combined.

Concomitantly with these efforts to unseat the IA as bargaining representative, a group of insurgents sought to secure greater influence
within the IA, if not to change its leadership. These efforts were supported by Mayor Lawrence. First overt indications of dissatisfaction
within the rank-and-file came on October 7 when a group of rebel IA
members of unknown number offered to return to work if pickets were
withdrawn, an offer of little value. However, on October 10 one hundred members of the Western Division of the union signed a petition
asking Mueller to submit the company's arbitration plan to another
membership vote. The next day a group of 119 members, presumably
including many of the original 100 signers, met in St. Mary's Church
Hall in an announced effort to secure 325 signatures on a petition demanding that the union president convene the union membership for
a vote on whether to arbitrate the dispute. The number of signatures
sought was determined by union bylaws requiring that 10 percent of
the membership must sign a petition to call such a mass meeting. There
was some doubt as to whether the goal was reached, but the petition
was nonetheless presented to Mueller, who said that union bylaws required a five-day notice of such a meeting.

Without waiting, the group secured the support of Mayor Lawrence
in calling a membership meeting in Carnegie Music Hall the evening
of October 14. About 1,100 persons showed up, but it appeared that

considerably more than half were there as "Mueller's men" to pack the meeting. Mayor Lawrence and County Commissioner Kane addressed the group, urging acceptance of arbitration. A Mueller supporter asked the mayor why the company did not sign an agreement to waive Stabilization policies in event of arbitration. The mayor pointed out that the union had already received the assurance of the Federal Conciliation Service that such policies need not apply.[7] He added, "I will stake my reputation as a gentleman that you will get a fair deal." The vote was taken. With more than half of those present abstaining, the result was 430 to 128 in favor of arbitration. The vote was without legal force, but it seems likely that it made some impression on Mueller. The insurgents did not rest with this outcome, but hired an attorney and on October 18 sought a writ of mandamus requiring Mueller to release to them the names and addresses of all paid-up members, so that a mass meeting might legally be called. The end of the strike made this action unnecessary, however.

2. Other pressures on the IA came from AFL and CIO unions in the area. The IA, it is true, was not wholly isolated from union support. Its picket lines were respected by the streetcar and bus operators, and the consequent disruption of the city's transit system was said by some to have created at least as much hardship as the power strike itself. Coal drivers refused to cross picket lines to deliver coal to downtown office buildings, with the result that they were without heat. Both these groups ceased to recognize IA pickets during the last week of the strike. The collapse of their support, in part attributable to the mayor's intercession, was probably a decisive factor in bringing an end to the strike. Top AFL and CIO leaders supported the mayor against the union throughout the strike, however. It is doubtful if their continuing opposition had much influence on Mueller. (Indeed, it was his gratuitous insult to the union representing the streetcar and bus operators—an implication that they were weak and would do better to throw in their lot with his union—that was the proximate cause of their return to work, despite IA pickets.) It seems probable, however, that the opposition of the combined labor movement had some influence with the IA rank and file. The criticism of their own leadership by much more

[7] This question was repeatedly raised. Confusion seems to have stemmed from the fact that although the Crowley arbitration agreement of September 12 had waived the condition that an arbitration board be bound by Stabilization policies, the company had insisted on retaining the right to introduce Stabilization policies in argument before such a board.

widely recognized labor leaders could not be without some persuasive effect.

3. Pressures of business groups on the union were relatively slight. Going over Mueller's head, the Smaller Manufacturers Council, representing 400 manufacturers most of whose plants were closed due to the strike, publicly appealed to the general policy committee to call off the strike. Such an appeal had no force behind it other than a reminder to union leaders of their possible loss of community standing if they continued to work hardship on others. Other than this, business's primary contribution was to undercut one argument which the union had raised against arbitration—its cost. On October 4 the executive vice-president of the Chamber of Commerce told conciliators that if this was a legitimate barrier he was "sure that the money could be found." The following day the Chamber's president guaranteed to assume the union's share of arbitration expenses. Mueller had other arguments against arbitration which he could readily substitute, however.

4. Aside from any general community antipathy which may have caused the striking unionists some fear of loss of respect and good will, the primary remaining expression of public opinion was that attempted through a movement to "mass public opinion." On October 2 it was announced that representatives of civic, community, business, and labor organizations having total memberships of 300,000 would hold a public mass meeting at Carnegie Music Hall the evening of October 6. Ministers were asked to announce the convocation from their pulpits; forty did. Children brought notes home from school advertising it; veterans' organizations urged members to attend; firms that had been affected by the power shortage were asked to spread word of it by any means at their disposal. Some 1,500 people showed up at the meeting. A resolution was passed asking for a new union vote "under supervision" on the question of arbitration. Citizens were urged to phone or visit both union and management members to ask for a prompt settlement of the strike. Another resolution advocated new legislation if present laws were incapable of protecting the public in such an emergency. The Civic-Community Group's request to the union for a reconsideration of arbitration was met with a refusal from Mueller. On October 9 the same group, meeting at the Congress of Women's Clubs, voted to use its influence to force a new meeting of IA members so that the arbitration question might be resubmitted to them. A four-point resolution called for (a) a statement from Duquesne Light management declaring

the company's willingness to submit all strike demands to arbitration and to abide by the decision; (b) publicity concerning such a statement, via newspaper and radio, so that union members would have knowledge of it; (c) aid to IA members to arrange for a meeting in a hall large enough to accommodate the entire membership; (d) impartial observers at such a meeting. It is not clear to what extent this group may have supported the insurgent movement which has previously been described. The relative success of its program, however, was measured by the relative success of the rebel faction. As we have seen, that group, while succeeding in arranging for a meeting, had no legal standing and could not bind the membership, but it probably impressed Mueller with the fact that his hold on the membership was slipping in some degree.

The end of the strike came not dramatically but almost as a drab anticlimax to the more colorful events which had preceded the strike. During the early stages of the walkout Mueller had continued in negotiation with the company; state and federal conciliators were present. He had even presented on October 8 what he described as a new proposal, though the company called it "a mere re-shuffling of proposals made in the last offer." As the strike wore on, however, Mueller became less and less accessible. Previously he had irritated the mayor and company negotiators by being two or three hours late for scheduled conferences; now it was difficult even for his attorney to locate him at all. Other members of the strike committee were out of touch with him. The strike drifted along more from its own momentum than from any active leadership. Then, in a surprise move, Mueller met Secretary of Labor Schwellenbach in Washington on October 19. The ostensible purpose of the meeting was to secure from Schwellenbach an assurance that Stabilization policy would not bind an arbitration board. It seems highly speculative whether Mueller was genuinely concerned about this matter or whether he was seeking a face-saving way out of the strike impasse. He had already received written assurances of a similar nature from other federal officials responsible to Schwellenbach, and had himself been party to an earlier arbitration in which the amount of the increase had not been limited by wage ceilings, even though such ceilings limited the company in how much of the additional cost it would recover through price relief or under government contracts. In any event, the move indicated that Mueller was at last entertaining the notion of submitting to arbitration.

The union's attorney succeeded in locating Mueller upon his return to Pittsburgh, not without difficulty. In a three-hour session he told the union president that a membership meeting could no longer be put off and that a new vote on arbitration could not be avoided. Mueller, who apparently had been coming to the same conclusion independently, finally agreed to issue a call for that same night. As the two men emerged from the attorney's office they found waiting in the anteroom a committee of the union membership that had come to request legal assistance in calling a new meeting. It was evident that the rank and file's limit of tolerance was rapidly being reached.

At this final membership meeting, all was in order. Suspicion had previously been cast on the form in which the motion had been presented and the manner in which votes had been counted. Now it was arranged for Sheriff Walter Monaghan to supervise the balloting and count the votes. This time Mueller argued in favor of accepting the arbitration offer, saying that he had been given to understand that the Wage Stabilization Board would no longer be in existence by the time arbitration hearings had been completed, so that its policies need not affect the outcome. The men would thus benefit more from arbitration now than if it had been agreed to earlier. It is hard for an outside observer to view this argument as anything more than casuistry designed to cast in a different light something whose complexion had not changed. The union obtained nothing it could not have secured from the Crowley agreement of September 12, which had been rejected in the membership meeting of September 20, four days before the strike began.

The 27-day strike ended when the membership voted 1,197 to 797 to accept arbitration.

Why did the strike end when it did? No sure answer can be given, but there appear to have been several factors operating.

1. Mueller could no longer count on the solid support of his membership. One outsider who was close to him says that Mueller's contacts within his union had never been very strong, as he played a lone wolf's game. He had gained his following because he seemed able to produce results. During the prolonged dispute, as long as the pressure on Mueller to capitulate was great, the membership stood loyally behind him. His support was probably never stronger than at the time he was sentenced to a year in jail for contempt of court. From the moment of his release, however, the solidarity of the organization began to crumble.

Throughout the subsequent period of the strike there developed a general reaction among the membership away from his leadership—not marked but still significant. The members remained loyal to the strike call, but there were increasing signs of discontent. The strike proved to be less disastrous to the city than had been contemplated (as we shall shortly see), and as a result the intensity of the pressures on Mueller relaxed. Indeed, the pressure on Mueller was far more intense to avoid the strike than to call it off once it had started. As the pressure on Mueller relaxed, the pressure on the members to provide him solid support likewise diminished. The time came when it appeared that if the strike were not brought to a quick ending the membership might take the lead away from their leader. To what extent this increasing disaffection was an effect of adverse public opinion, to what extent a straight dissatisfaction with the way the strike was being run, no answer can be given. One member of the city administration believes both elements were present. "The utility workers (probably security-conscious, as most utility people are) had been almost a month without pay on their first real strike, community sentiment was mobilized against them, their leader had been repeatedly branded as irresponsible. They began to believe that there was little or nothing to gain by prolonging the strike."

2. Despite the general opposition of the labor movement, from the time his pickets appeared Mueller had been given the sympathetic support of the streetcar and bus drivers and the coal drivers. The former adherence was particularly valuable. Lack of local transportation was said to have concerned the city administration as much as the shortage of electricity, and its efforts for two weeks were directed to meeting this strike within a strike. When the transit men returned to work on October 14 (with the coal drivers abandoning their sympathetic support a few days later), the IA was left completely isolated. Only the various factions of the Communist party continued their support. The realization of this isolation in the community, extending even to the labor movement itself, probably influenced both union president and rank and file, perhaps implanting a feeling of hopelessness.

3. The course of the strike had been such that pressures on the company to make further concessions had not materialized. It had played a relatively minor role in the lengthy controversy. From the moment the company consented to arbitration, the city administration took over its battle. The injunction and the contempt sentence focused attention

upon this conflict relationship between mayor and Mueller. Mayor Lawrence's address of September 29 had publicly branded Mueller as irresponsible and the sole cause of the city's difficulty: ". . . this unnecessary strike of an uncontrolled union. . . . If one man, the union president, had kept his word, we would be a normal city today." It therefore became difficult for him to press the company for further concessions to palliate the irresponsibility which he had charged. With the pressures thus concentrated on the union, likelihood that the union could win meaningful concessions beyond the arbitration offered appeared to be slim. This was true, however, only because the city discovered, somewhat to the surprise of everyone, that the strike was not as crippling as had been anticipated. The city could thus afford to wait out the union, and the company was relieved of any needling to modify its stand.

4. If the views of a number of those involved in the strike, including some who were friendly to Mueller, are to be accepted, Mueller responded to public attention like an actor to an audience. As a confidante of his remarked, "His character seemed to change or develop in consequence of the strike. The attacks on him by the newspapers both angered and inflated him. He became a public figure." The same person said that if it had not been for Mueller's stubborn and ambitious character, the strike would not have continued as long as it did, and then added, "But if it had not been for that same stubborn and ambitious character he would never have attained the position that he did nor achieved an independent union bringing benefits to its membership, as he had." If this estimate of Mueller's character is accepted, then it is arguable that as the strike developed and the city weathered the crisis unexpectedly well, less attention was centered on Mueller. The city worried less about the consequences and hence tended to go about its business, ignoring the union president. As he became less of a public figure, the value of the strike to him diminished. It became a matter of extricating himself and the union from a difficult situation by a face-saving maneuver. This was the function served by the trip to Washington and the conference with Secretary of Labor Schwellenbach.

There may have been other reasons why the strike ended on October 20, after 27 days, and perhaps the reasons given above were not genuinely operative. Nevertheless, as nearly as discernible, these were the primary causes underlying the decision of Mueller to put the matter of arbitration to the membership once more, as well as the favorable vote by the membership.

Effects of the Strike

X We have now examined the course of the strike and the sanctions which were brought to bear on the parties. Since it has been our assumption that the strength of sanctions is directly correlated with the real costs of a strike, let us consider briefly the effects of the power strike on its public. In doing so we shall be in a better position to evaluate the effectiveness of the sanctions employed. In its application for an injunction the city administration had listed some of the anticipated consequences of the shutdown. How did the actual effects compare with those expected?

In the first place, the city was never completely without power. The Duquesne Light Company was integrated with other suppliers of electricity in a grid system, which enabled it to obtain some current from other facilities than its own. In addition, its own operations were substantially maintained by supervisors who worked on four-hour shifts— four hours on, four hours off. Auxiliary equipment for vital operations was hastily obtained, chiefly from the Army.

Response to the strike, which was called at 9:30 A.M. September 24, was spotty at first. Although all four power stations in Allegheny and Beaver counties had continued to operate, the ouput dropped to 50 percent of normal. In the next few days, as picket lines were set up at all installations, power output fell substantially below this figure. At the same time, however, the company was improving its own emergency organization. By September 28 power supply was back to 38 percent of normal, and by October 1 it had inched up to 40 percent of normal supply. It remained at about this figure throughout the remaining weeks of the strike.

Consumer Effects

1. Water supply and garbage disposal. One of the gravest dangers feared was loss of water supply. The director of public works had reported a three-day water supply at the start of the strike. After that was exhausted there would be limited service to downtown Pittsburgh and certain adjoining areas, but to other areas no water could be furnished without electric pumps to fill the reservoirs from which the supply must be drawn. It was said that it would be difficult to fight fires, for lack of water, at distances greater than a half mile from river water. Actually, although water conservation was urged upon consumers, no shortage

developed. On October 6 it was reported that water in the city reservoirs was almost to the rim, the greatest supply in fifteen years.

The fear of a health hazard from inability to dispose of garbage was similarly dissipated. Basis for concern had been the fact that the electrically operated incinerator had only two days' storage capacity. No difficulty developed in securing adequate power to maintain incineration throughout the strike, however.

2. Hospitals. At Municipal Hospital the auxiliary power equipment would be inadequate for X-ray work or for other electrically operated instruments, the director of health reported prior to the strike. Other hospitals would be no better and some much worse off. Hospitals were in fact adversely affected, but not critically. By September 26, some were restricting new admissions to serious cases. The failure of a power line on October 3 blacked out nine hospitals for a period of seven minutes, an interruption probably directly attributable to the strike. A break in power supply of even so brief a duration is fatal where certain equipment such as the iron lung is in use. In one hospital an iron-lung patient was saved by the prompt action of nurses, assisted by an elderly custodian, who provided temporary power by hand generation until auxiliary equipment was brought into use.

3. Food storage and preparation. It was feared that a strike would threaten the partial spoilage of some 44 million pounds of perishable foods in the city's storehouses and endanger the milk supply, through lack of refrigeration. No real danger emerged, however. The milk industry did operate on a restricted basis for a time. A five-day power failure in the Mt. Washington area did lead to considerable food spoilage. Aside from these effects, and an increase in housewives' demand for nonperishable foods by way of precaution, there were no untoward results.

4. Street lighting. Greater Pittsburgh at the time had some 1,300 miles of city streets, whose lights, it was feared, would be darkened by a strike. There is inadequate information on how outlying areas were affected, but the fears were justified with respect to the downtown section. On October 3 it was reported that half of the downtown street lights were out, due to the lack of carbon replacements and repairs. A newspaper survey of October 14 discovered that every downtown street light except those on Water Street had been out since the 12th. Lights on all the bridges were failing, too, from lack of service. The darkened effect was heightened by restricted use of illuminated advertising dis-

plays. The day after the strike ended, thousands flocked to the down-town area to see the lights come on again.

5. Households. When the strike began households were supplied with only 55 percent of normal energy hours. As the strike progressed, however, all household needs were met providing consumers practiced reasonable conservation measures. Use of household electrical appliances, such as irons and washing machines, was restricted to the daytime. The spotty power failures which developed throughout the Pittsburgh area during the strike led to a run on candles, as housewives prepared themselves against emergencies.

6. Stores, hotels, etc. On the first day of the strike fifty downtown buildings were closed. Most major downtown restaurants ceased operation due to insufficient power for ventilation and dishwashing. All department stores were closed, although they maintained "firefly batteries" of clerks who met customers at the employees' entrance to fill emergency orders, escorting the customer through the store by flashlight. Phone orders were filled. By October 7 most department stores had installed auxiliary generators. On their reopening October 8, after two weeks of closing, they were jammed with shoppers. By October 4, five scheduled conventions, involving 3,000 visitors, had been canceled. All buildings in the Triangle area had heat and hot water cut off, as coal drivers refused to cross picket lines to deliver coal to the Allegheny County Steam Heating Company, a Duquesne affiliate which serviced 384 downtown buildings. By October 13 the larger office buildings had set up complete heating plants of their own, and on the 16th the coal drivers agreed to cross picket lines, restoring heat and hot water to all in that area.

7. Schools. All public and parochial schools remained open. The University of Pittsburgh, Duquesne University, and some private schools closed till further notice. The University of Pittsburgh resumed classes October 10, and all colleges were back in session by the 14th.

8. Local transit. To conserve power, service was cut in half on the first day of the strike. On the second day nine routes were canceled, and operation was further cut to 25 percent of normal during rush hours. On September 26, streetcar and bus operators began a sympathy strike which the Pittsburgh Railway Company said stranded a million riders. A by-product of this action was to bring more private cars into the streets, creating traffic jams. Taxi facilities were used to the limit. The telephone company booked over 1,000 rides daily to get operators and

essential employees to work. Western Union and Pennsylvania Railroad followed a similar practice. Wartime defense organizations and members of the general motoring public were enlisted in transporting employees of Allegheny County's 26 hospitals to and from work. The sympathy strike ended October 14, and local transit service was restored to 25 percent of normal during peak hours and 50 percent of normal in off hours. Late the same day, however, a rifle shot substantially cut off the flow of power from the large and vital Colfax power station, necessitating a further drastic curtailment of transit service. Thirty-eight out of ninety routes were canceled. On October 15 "normal" reduced service was restored until 5 P.M., when it had to be cut again due to an excessive drain of current for home consumption. Full service was not provided until the end of the strike.

Producer Effects

Producer effects in the form of unemployment were probably more marked than the consumer effects just enumerated. Estimates placed the number of unemployed at 25,000 on September 25, and 70,000 by the following day. (An additional 20,000 were out on sympathy strike, but most of these returned to work shortly.) The United States Employment Service added thirty clerks to handle applications for unemployment compensation. Up to October 8, 50,000 claims had been processed, and within a single week 75,000 unemployed were interviewed. A USES estimate of October 4 placed the total number of unemployed between 100,000 and 125,000. A newspaper estimate that 125,000 workers were unemployed at some time during the strike thus appears to be conservative. The dollar loss was set at $300,000,000 but unquestionably some portion of this amount might have been recovered through subsequent "make-up" operations.

Effects of the strike were felt beyond the Pittsburgh area. A Chicago firm wired Mayor Lawrence on October 1 that it had shut down because it could not get parts from a Pittsburgh supplier. Railroads were affected by loss of traffic. No estimate has been made of the magnitude of such out-of-town repercussions, however.

Nevertheless, steel operations were said to be back to normal by the third week of the strike, and approximately 350 small manufacturing plants, chiefly steel fabricators, had arranged for a midnight-to-7-A.M. shift, during which their power needs could be met by Duquesne.

These, then, were the principal strike effects. The evidence supports a finding that the consequences of the strike were considerably less severe than had been anticipated. Bearing out this conclusion is a confidential public opinion poll of a selected sample of 322 Pittsburgh residents, made shortly after the strike had ended. Only 30 percent reported that they had been seriously inconvenienced by the shutdown, another 26 percent said they had experienced "some inconvenience," while 44 percent reported "not much" or no inconvenience. The effects of the strike were real and should not be minimized, but it appears evident that they did not add up to the calamity which had been foreseen. In view of this, we perhaps have some explanation of why the pressures on the parties were not greater, enough greater to have brought an end to the strike before it had gone for 27 days. Again, the pressures were real and should not be minimized, but they were insufficient to prevent the strike from dragging on like a bad cold for almost four weeks. If the effects had been more drastic, the pressures would unquestionably have been more telling, and the strike would have come to an earlier end.

The above finding does not, however, support a generalization that all power strikes do not importantly affect the public. It is clear that the Pittsburgh city administration anticipated a more serious situation than actually developed. In doing so, it likewise anticipated strong public pressures on it to do something to end the strike, and in consequence brought to bear its most potent sanctions to head off the strike before it got started. There is no basis for charging an error in judgment to the city government in so acting. The fact is that Pittsburgh was lucky during the period of the strike. The Duquesne Light Company was in a poor position to maintain service in the face of repeated breakdowns, but fortunately only five major interruptions to service were reported during the 27 days: on September 30 a group of 300 families in the Mt. Washington area were deprived of electricity when a power line went down, and they remained without electricity for more than five days; on October 2 a rope was thrown over a high-voltage wire, blacking out two suburban communities for half an hour; on October 3 a power line failure left the downtown district without current for a few minutes; on October 9 sabotage at a Duquesne plant cut off power to two residential areas for four hours; on October 14 came the damage to the Colfax power station, reportedly creating more hardship than at any time since the start of the strike. Yet the number of such interruptions—either planned or accidental—could have been much greater, and the hardship on the public much more intense. The fact that threatened difficulties did not materialize did not remove the threat. And it was of the threat that the city administration had to take cognizance.

Other special circumstances served to lessen the emergency in this instance. The power company was integrated with other suppliers of electricity, from whom it could obtain some supplementary current. The protraction of the dispute prior to the strike permitted the city to prepare for the event and in particular to secure auxiliary generators, enabling it to keep vital services in operation. The supervisory staff was adequate to stand the strain of an onerous schedule. The unemployment effects were more tolerable, coming as they did after a period of high employment and substantial savings.

We conclude, then, that the *anticipated* consequences of the strike were great, leading to the employment against the parties of the strongest sanctions available. The *actual* costs of the strike proved to be much less than expected, so that pressures on the parties were relaxed, permitting the prolongation of the strike.

The Sanctions

Finally, let us summarize the nature of the sanctions employed and assess their effectiveness.

It is difficult to judge the strength of direct sanctions. Unquestionably there was some community antipathy directed at both parties to the dispute, and in the later stages particularly at the union. There is no basis for concluding how effective these sanctions may have been upon the parties—how the fear of loss of reputation and standing may have influenced their conduct. It seems fairly certain that the company was mindful that a strike, particularly if it should be attributed to obduracy on its part, might damage its good will. Even six years after the strike there were high officials who still wondered whether its standing was impaired by the 1946 conflict. There were some who discussed the desirability of a public opinion poll among Pittsburghers to ascertain how the company's reputation was affected by the events described in this chapter, but such a course has been rejected on the ground that it might only stir up old memories which had best be kept submerged. To what extent this concern for community good will affected conduct during the dispute, we cannot say. It was probably responsible in part for the company's consent to arbitrate. As for the union, there is no evidence that Mueller was much swayed by fear of public disaffection.

He had no hesitancy in returning a direct refusal to the pleas of the Civic-Community Group (perhaps the most formal vehicle of direct public expression) to recanvass his membership on the question of arbitration. It seems likely, however, that individual members might have been more responsive to such direct sanctions. While there is no proof, it appears probable that the disaffection within the IA, indicated by insurgent movements and pressures on Mueller to reconvene the membership, was in part attributable to a dislike of being marked for community opprobrium.

Indirect sanctions played a more important part, however. Although it is possible to identify others, there were three major intermediaries whose influence was brought to bear on the parties in response to public sentiment. These were the mayor, the press, and other unions and managements. The actions of all these have already been described and we shall do no more here than summarize.

The mayor, responding to both anticipated and actual expressions of public opinion, first exercised the arts of persuasion and condemnation on both parties. These were effective with respect to the company but had no influence on the conduct of the union. At this point the mayor resorted to two other principal weapons. The first was mobilization and organization of public sentiment, intended to augment the direct sanction of possible loss of community good will, which as we have seen had little effect on the union president but perhaps some eventual effect on the union membership. The second was use of the injunction, which was rendered relatively ineffective by the opposition it aroused among other unions, whose support was essential both to the mayor's strike plans and to his long-run political career.

The press, likewise responding to its role of "tribune of the people" which it could ignore only on pain of losing its position of influence, employed all the sanctions at its disposal. Its condemnatory editorials in the early stages of the dispute were directed at both parties. Their potency lay in the desire of the parties to avert, if possible, the antagonism of such powerful organs of public conscience and opinion. After the company's arbitration offer had been made, newspaper fire was centered on the union, in a campaign that largely involved vilification of one individual, Mueller. The press served, too, as an organizer of a more effective public opinion.

In the period in which the company was still sparring with the union, other managements had pointed out to the company the importance of electric supply to them, urging it to effect some settlement with the union. Here the only sanction involved was possible loss of customer good will. After the arbitration offer, attention centered more exclusively on the IA, and here the influence of other labor organizations was brought to bear. In part, their pressure was exerted in support of the mayor (indeed, as part of a bargain with him, leading to dissolution of the injunction which they so bitterly opposed), but in part their opposition to the IA stemmed from a fear that its blameworthy conduct might be made the basis for condemnation of unions generally.

The fact that the strike ran a course of 27 days suggests that these pressures were not particularly effective. This was true only with respect to the union, however. The company responded to these sanctions by making the arbitration offer which was sought from it. We are thus left with the question of why the union was so largely unaffected by the sanctions described.

The answer suggested is that the relative inefficacy of the sanctions was due to the character of the union president, Mueller. If the estimates of those who knew and worked with him are to be trusted, supported, it is true, by inferences that may be drawn from the events themselves, it would appear that here was an individual who welcomed the strike role in which he was cast, since it created an opportunity to preempt the stage and command an audience such as he had never before enjoyed. As the dispute progressed, the very condemnations made of him—the analogies to John L. Lewis, for example—may have only served to fire an ambition already possessing him. There were many who regarded him as a rising star in the labor movement, and some still remain who believe that expectation was then justified. For him to have called off the strike or to have surrendered to arbitration at an early stage would have been to drop the curtain before the star's reputation had been made. Against such an antagonist, even the mayor's injunctive weapon fell harmless; the injunction in a sense gave Mueller his greatest chance; from being the representative of a striking independent union, he became the representative, the symbol, of an aroused labor movement. After such an hour, quick capitulation could not be contemplated.

There are two respects, however, in which the sanctions might be considered to have been more effective than appears evident on the face of the facts. It will be recalled that, to be effective, sanctions must *either* induce termination of the strike *or* punish the offending party in such a manner as to deter other disputants from following the same course. It appears that the sanctions were relatively ineffective in bringing an early end to the strike. If one considers the IA—or Mueller—to have been the offending party, however, then it is possible to argue that the strike brought penalties upon them which might discourage other union leaders from imitating their lead. In 1947, in part as a direct consequence of the Pittsburgh strike, General Assembly Act No. 485 was passed, restricting the right to strike in public utilities. If we accept union professions at their face value, and in this respect we are entitled to do so, there are few calamities greater than limitation of the strike privilege. It therefore appears that the IA's intransigence led to a penalty of a nature which might cause other unions similarly positioned to hesitate before following the Duquesne IA's lead.

In the case of Mueller, the strike was probably an instrument in his decline. In 1948 he sought to lead the IA into the CIO Utility Workers Union. The opposition which greeted this move was no doubt attributable in part to continuing resentment of his strike leadership, to a questioning of whether the affiliation was intended primarily for union welfare or for personal aggrandizement (as, some believed, the strike had been prolonged to promote his personal reputation). The rebellious group joined forces with the AFL Electrical Workers, and in a representation election which followed eight of the nine bargaining units repudiated Mueller and accepted the AFL union. Mueller remained with the ninth unit for a time, but it was the tail of the dog. He was taken in as a CIO organizer and became involved in a strike fiasco at the Pittsburgh zoo, which subjected him to ridicule. The brilliant prospects in the labor movement which some had foreseen for him became faded. Are we entitled to say that this was a penalty—the disaffection of his membership and its eventual repudiation of his leadership—which might deter others?[8]

[8] In this post-morten of the strike, mention might be made of two other participants. Mayor Lawrence came out of the fray undamaged. He gained a reputation for putting public interest above personal political interest by going after the injunction in the first place. Although in so doing he endangered his labor support, he substantially recaptured it by consenting to dissolution of the injunction. There are those who say the mayor never fully recovered the confidence of his labor following—but that he is too strong a candidate for them to disavow, if they would, and his record *is* a liberal one. Another participant fared less well. To purify the mayor's sin of seeking relief in the injunctive process, a sacrificial offering was made of the city solicitor. It was said that it was she who had persuaded the mayor against his will or had precipitated action without his full consent. Recognized as an able attorney, she had had reasonable prospects of a judgeship. When a federal judgeship subsequently fell vacant, however, and her name was mentioned for the appointment, her claim fell—it is said—before the opposition of the unions, who were unwilling to forgive her for her part in obtaining the injunction.

CHAPTER THIRTEEN

The Sanctions at Work: Strike of a
Dominant Firm

ASIDE from strikes affecting so-called vital goods and services (such as supplied by public utilities), strikes at firms supplying a high proportion of a community's employment can be expected to arouse public opposition, according to union and management officials. We shall therefore examine a strike at such a firm to observe the impact on the public, the sanctions employed, and their effectiveness.[1]

The Blank Company manufactures products for use both by households and producers. It or its subsidiaries operate five manufacturing plants in the United States, one in Canada, and one in Europe, besides several establishments which provide raw materials and a large number of retail outlets for the marketing of its household products.

Two of its manufacturing plants were shut down by a strike which occurred several years after the end of World War II. Both plants are located in highly industrialized areas along the Eastern seaboard, the larger plant (employing altogether about 9,200 persons at the time of the strike) in a city known here as Westville, the smaller plant (with about 2,100 employees) in a city known here as Eastopolis, located in a different state. This study is concerned almost exclusively with the strike at the Westville plant.

The Blank plant is the largest manufacturing establishment in the city of Westville (population about 100,000), in Westville's heavily industrialized county, and indeed it is one of the largest in the state.

---

[1] Information was obtained in interviews with representatives of the company and the union, state and city officials, and newspaper reporters, who were involved in the strike, and by examination of newspaper files and a master's thesis written by Kenneth L. Biro. Most of the information was given only on condition that the identity of its participants not be revealed. Accordingly, in the following account all names of organizations and places have been disguised and the name of the master's thesis has not been cited.

The 6,000 Blank employees who live in Westville comprise about 20 percent of the city's total labor force.

At the time of the strike the Blank Company's plant had been located in Westville for 75 years, having originally arrived there as a "runaway" from a strike in another area. In Westville the company had acquired the reputation of being a firm which "looks after its people." During the depression the company had carried share-the-work policies to the extreme rather than resort to layoffs; even after the substantial turnover of the war, average length of service was high: over one half of the labor force had been employed for more than five years and over one sixth for more than 25 years. The company's wage rates were somewhat higher than those paid for comparable work in the area. Prior to the stoppage considered here there had never been a plant-wide strike in the Westville establishment.

During the war and after a rather hard-fought organizing campaign, the IBPW, a large international union which organizes "industrially," was certified by the National Labor Relations Board as bargaining agent for the Westville plant's production employees (of whom there were almost 7,000 at the time of the strike).[2] The IBPW became bargaining agent for the Eastopolis plant about a year later. Each local had its own, separate contract with the company.

Factional disputes had been going on in both locals for more than a year prior to the strike. The principal offices in the Westville local were held by men who supported the leadership, policies, and actions of the national and district officials of the IBPW. The contending faction, whose members held no important local offices, opposed the national and district leadership, mainly on the ground that the leadership was "left-wing." In Eastopolis the situation was reversed: the "right-wing" faction had control of the local. In Westville, at least, this factionalism did not impair a united support of the strike by both right and left wings, however.

Almost a month before the contracts of the two plants were due to expire the parties opened negotiations for new agreements. The issues in dispute were similar at both plants, involving a general wage increase, a shortening of the work week, a change in seniority provisions, and a question regarding the "yardstick" to be used in the wage incen-

[2] It may be helpful to distinguish the three employment figures which have been cited for the Westville plant of the Blank Company. At the time of the strike the total number of employees was 9,200. *Production* employees numbered 7,000. About 6,000 employees *lived* in Westville.

tive system. The so-called yardstick question concerned the production norms to be applied, chiefly whether there should be joint determination (later arbitration) of the pace of work which would be made the standard. In Westville this latter issue overshadowed all others. In Eastopolis the yardstick question was considered less significant than that of seniority.

Six days before the Westville contract was due to expire, state and federal conciliators, on the request of union officials, began sitting in on negotiations. On this same date the union officials asked the mayor of Westville to intercede. Two days later the members of the bargaining unit voted by 10 to 1 to strike. Shortly thereafter the parties and state and federal conciliators met with the mayor in a seven-hour session in his office, and in another long session the following day. No agreement was reached; the contract expired, and the strike at the Westville plant began. Three days later, upon the expiration of its contract, the Eastopolis local struck.

Both sides settled down to the struggle. A joint strike strategy committee made up of district and local officials from Westville and Eastopolis was set up; representatives of each local agreed that they would not make a settlement except by agreement with the other local. The company made no attempt to operate either plant; executives did not even try to enter their offices in the plants.

On the eighth day of the strike the mayor of Westville met with state and federal conciliators to devise means for getting the parties together in negotiations, which had lapsed when the strike began. On the 18th day representatives of each party met separately with conciliators; on the 31st day they met face to face, only to break off meetings on the 37th day. Face-to-face sessions were not resumed until the 53rd day and continued then for five days before they once more broke down. Apparently, not until eleven weeks later did the parties again meet each other.

On the 62nd day, a group of employees quite distinct from the regular opposition in the Westville plant (who were supporting the strike) announced the formation of an independent union. Having obtained a mailing list, they circularized all Westville plant employees, urging them to leave the IBPW and join the Independent, promising that it could secure a settlement with the company. On the 64th day a letter to Blank employees from the Westville plant superintendent, suggesting that the strike was "planned by a small group to wreck the efficiency of production in this country," was published in a local paper; a subsequent letter stated that the IBPW was "as usual" following the Communist line, and that the strikers must decide whether they wished to continue to "back a losing Communist fight" on the yardstick question.

By this date (the beginning of the tenth week of the strike) several of the state officials involved were convinced that the strike in Westville could be settled if the parties would resume face-to-face negotiations. The union leadership was secretly prepared to be "very reasonable," reasonable, in fact, to the point of withdrawing its demands on the major issue. The reasons for the leadership's willingness to retreat appear to have been that (1) they felt the rank-and-file determination to continue the strike was weakening; (2) they expected the already considerable threat represented by the right-wing opposition would be soon increased through support given it by the labor federation of which the IBPW was currently a highly tenuous member. The incumbent leadership therefore wanted a contract (even a bad one) with the Blank Company, so that it would be ensured of control of the Westville local for at least one year before it might have to face a recertification election against a rival federation-chartered opposition union.

The top management of the Blank Company refused, however, at this point to have any of its officials enter into further negotiations with leadership of the Westville local as long as that leadership was "dominated by Communists."

After various efforts (described subsequently) to get the company to meet with union representatives had failed, the conciliation panel on the 73rd day issued a statement to the effect that a basis for settling all issues existed but that negotiations had broken down because the company was unwilling to meet with the union. On the day this statement was issued the Independent union sent a wire to the company claiming to represent a majority of the employees in the Westville bargaining unit and requesting the company to bargain with it. The result of this action was a consent election to determine the bargaining agent, which was held by the conciliation panel on the 87th day. Four days before the election the company announced that it would not bargain with the IBPW, even if it won, unless the incumbent leadership filed non-Communist affidavits according to the provisions of the Taft-Hartley Act. The leadership announced its intention to do so immediately. The election resulted in a victory for the IBPW by an 8 to 5 margin. This victory was interpreted by the union leadership as a mandate for continuing the strike. One reason for the defeat of the Independent, however, was that many employees considered it to be a creature of the company's making, a belief that was strengthened by the fact that foremen had visited strikers and urged them to vote for the Independent.

The day following the election the governor "ordered" the parties to resume negotiations, and the union made known its retreat on the yardstick issue. No negotiations occurred, however, as the company maintained its reluctance to deal with a union which it considered left wing, despite the announced signing of the affidavits. On the 102nd day the governor conferred separately with the parties in the state capitol and arranged for face-to-face sessions to be resumed some time in the future. A few weeks later the Westville City Council attempted to expedite face-to-face bargaining, which had not yet been resumed, but its efforts failed. The reason for this protracted delay in the resumption of negotiations, even after the governor's prodding, is not clear. The suggestion has been made by one informed observer, in close touch with the strike throughout its duration, that the company was stalling in the hope of concluding Eastopolis negotiations and making the settlement there the basis for a Westville agreement. It appears, moreover, that although the public statement of the company had been that it would not meet the union until its leaders had signed non-Communist affidavits, privately it had said that it would not meet with "those Reds," period. Eventually, however, it did.

On the 135th day the management and local union officers in Eastopolis met with members of a local Citizen's Committee and agreed to reopen negotiations there on the condition that union representatives from Westville, who theretofore had been participating, should be excluded. On the 136th day Westville negotiations were finally resumed, only to break down. On the 146th day Westville and Eastopolis local officers met and "jointly proclaimed unity to win the strike." Eight days later, however, the Eastopolis local officers reached a separate agreement with the company, ending the strike at the Eastopolis plant.

An observer who talked to pickets at the Westville plant two days afterward reported them to be "completely demoralized" and of the opinion that the Eastopolis settlement had destroyed their chances of holding out. On the 159th day all strikers received letters in which company officials urged them to accede to the company's position on the yardstick issue and "follow the [Eastopolis] workers back to their jobs." At a mass meeting held later that day, Westville leaders promised to find out "exactly what we can get," and negotiations between the parties began that same evening. On the 167th day a settlement was reached which represented almost a complete surrender to the company's position of the yardstick issue, but which was "overwhelmingly" approved by the membership of the local the following day. So ended the 24-week strike.

Effects of the Strike

The Blank Company strike at the Westville plant was said to have been the costliest strike in the state's history, due mainly to the effects of the loss of about $12 million in wage payments. The members of the public most strongly affected were the families of strikers and the local suppliers of these families.

The over-all impact of the strike on strikers' families is difficult to estimate. It was generally agreed that "nobody had starved" during the strike. A statement of a local banker, to the effect that during the first few weeks a considerable number of strikers cashed war bonds but that after this period bond redemptions ceased because the strikers "were getting enough from union and welfare sources," may indicate a relatively easy time for the strikers with little forced dissaving, but it may also indicate that their financial resources were quickly exhausted. In any case a loss of income which falls short of causing an actual deprivation of the "necessities" of life may nevertheless be highly "affecting" to strikers' families. The testimony of one *striker* (not a member of the public) indicated that the loss of income had affected him mainly by causing him to feel that he had lost status in his social group. "When you are on strike, you can't go to a bar; you can't buy what other people buy, and go along with people on things. You feel that people look down on you because you don't have money." Similar considerations might apply to strikers' *families*, who are members of the public.

The over-all impact of the stoppage on the 2,200 nonstriking employees at the Westville plant was much less. All of these were given eight weeks' pay; salaried employees with more than one year's seniority were given full pay during the strike.

The loss of a payroll amounting to around $600,000 weekly for 24 weeks could not help but affect Westville suppliers of goods and services to strikers. The first and worst affected were merchants in "the Flats," the area around the plant where a high proportion of its employees live. "Almost overnight" sales of retailers of clothing, furniture, and household equipment fell by 25 to 60 percent, and collections by one furniture store on installment-plan purchases dropped 50 percent within the first month. A Flats grocer, who derived most of his revenue from sales of meat, reported that his sales had decreased by 75 percent within a month after the start of the strike. In general, however, the *sales* of grocers' in the Flats did not fall off much, but their weekly *cash receipts* decreased substantially since they were obliged to carry their striker customers "on the book" longer than the customary week. Such extension put a heavy strain on the grocers' limited credit resources.

The rapidly multiplying effects of a loss of income to persons concentrated in a relatively small area are indicated by a statement of the president of the Flats Merchants' Association to the effect that "the worst effect of the strike was not the decline in purchases by the strikers but the psychological effect on other people who held back buying for fear their businesses would be affected," and the report of a paper-products salesman that orders from Flats retailers had decreased considerably.

Effects on downtown department, furniture, and household-equipment stores were less severe but perceptible; the head of the Westville Merchants Association estimated that the sales of these had fallen off by about 10 percent by the end of the first month, though decreases of 20 to 25 percent were reported by individual merchants. Altogether, it was estimated, the strike caused a loss in gross sales to Westville merchants (including the Flats) of $20,000,000. Both the circulation and advertising revenues of a local newspaper decreased.

It was said that many landlords had received no rent payments from striker tenants during the entire course of the strike.

The municipal treasury also felt the effects of the strike. By the end of the first month city relief costs had jumped from $6,000 to $11,000 monthly. A total of almost $23,000 in relief payments was distributed to the strikers. Since the state law prohibited use of state funds for relief payments to strikers, the city had to bear the full cost of these payments.

Because the Blank Company itself supplies much of the material which goes into its products, there were fewer members of the public in a position to be affected as suppliers. However, a representative of the firm which supplied the Westville plant with "all its paper products" reported that, "like all Blank suppliers," his firm was "hard hit by the drying up of the plant's orders."

Users of the Blank company's products were apparently little affected by the strike because (1) stock-consumption ratios for many of its own products were high; (2) the company supplied only a small proportion of the total industry output of other products in its line. The strike occurred during a period in which demand for its products in general was falling because of a business recession, and demand for the products taken by its most important user industry was low because it was that industry's slack season. The company had foreseen the likelihood of a strike and had taken the precaution of building up large stocks of most of its products; it was able to fill 75 percent of all orders received during the strike from these stocks. Supplies of those products for which the rate of consumption exceeded existing stocks were made available to customers by means of (1) imports from the company's European plant; (2) subcontracts undertaken by other firms, some of them Blank's erstwhile competitors. (A company official remarked: "Because they believed in our cause, our competitors were very cooperative and helpful; we had a good understanding with them.") As to whether the industry which constituted Blank's principal customer suffered from a shortage of one particular Blank product, the evidence is conflicting; the truth seems to be that firms in this industry experienced no actual shortages but were continually in fear that such a shortage might develop.

Thus members of the public who were most clearly affected by the strike included families of strikers and local suppliers of strikers' families, especially Flats merchants and retailers of durable consumers goods in the main business district. More remotely affected were some suppliers of the company and, because of relief expenditures, Westville taxpayers. Possibly affected were nonstriking employees and their families, other suppliers of the company, and some users of the company's products.

The Direct Sanctions

Efforts to terminate the Blank Company strike in Westville were largely directed to one of two proximate ends—persuading company officials to engage in face-to-face negotiations with union representatives, or fostering a revolt of the membership against the incumbent leadership—in the belief that achievement of these ends would lead to a termination of the stoppage.

Direct sanctions were invoked against each of three groups: the rank and file of the union membership, the union leadership, and company management. We shall examine each of these.

1. The union membership was apparently subject to several types of direct sanctions. Probably the most compelling were those at the command of one of the most affected publics—the members' families. The extent to which these were imposed is not certain, but it is certain that they were invoked. The nature of these penalties need no detailed description; most readers will be aware of the ability of the female members of a family to "make [a man's] life miserable by those unofficial methods with which all women are familiar."[3]

Those strikers who lived in Westville were also made aware of the disapproval of some members of the community regarding the strikers' participation in a dispute conducted by a union whose leadership was said to be Communist. Local suppliers were among those voicing this disapproval. One union member reported: "Businessmen and people you met—if they knew who you were—would say, 'Oh, you're one of the [Blank] strikers; you're backing Reds.' It got on our nerves."

2. Local suppliers were also able to utilize, as a penalty against the union leadership, the disapproval by unaffected members of the community of Communist penetration of unions. Newspapers devoted much space to accusations that the national and district leaders of the IBPW were Communists and that the actions of the incumbent officers of the Westville local were entirely controlled by these leaders, and local merchants discussed these charges with associates and customers. Whether the expressions of disapproval made any local or district official feel that he was losing the esteem of persons whose good opinion he valued is not known. Nevertheless, the significance of this public-expressed disapproval on one union leader can be documented. Sometime after a newspaper had produced a document purporting to demonstrate conclusively the Communist alignment of the IBPW district official most active in conduct of the strike, the official's small son began coming home from schools in tears because other children had been taunting him with remarks to the effect that "Your old man's one of those strikers, and he's a dirty Red!" The official is reported by two reliable observers to have said, "My God, I've got to settle this strike and get off the hook; it's too hard on my family."

Public disapproval of the strike also threatened the union leadership with possible loss of control in the local. We have already seen how rank-and-file uneasiness at being identified with a "Red" strike was stimulated. To the extent such identification weakened the members'

[3] Ralph Linton, *The Study of Man* (New York: D. Appleton-Century Co., Student's Edition, 1936), p. 187.

resolve to continue the strike, the position of the leaders was endangered. But an even more positive threat materialized. Among the affected public there were some who encouraged the rise of a rival union, the Independent.

Throughout the last 18 weeks of the stoppage the Westville leadership was thus under strong pressure to accede to a settlement or risk losing not only their own position but the local itself. Support of the Independent's attempts to gain control of the membership, oust the incumbent leadership, and negotiate a settlement with the company became advantageous action for those adversely affected by the shutdown. Whether the Independent would succeed in gaining control of the local and negotiating a settlement, or whether the threat of so severe a penalty as loss of control to the Independent would force the incumbent leadership to end the strike and thus eliminate the conditions on which the Independent was thriving, scarcely mattered to the affected public. The affected public, however, possessed no sanctions by means of which to compel the formation and development of an Independent; its role was merely that of donors of aid and backing to an instrumentality which was motivated by drives of its own, but whose objectives served the public's purposes.

There is no question but that merchants gave considerable aid to the Independent. An owner of a large furniture store contributed money and office space in his store and permitted Independent members to pass out literature and solicit contributions from shoppers at the front door of the store. When asked by an IBPW leader why he was thus supporting the Independent, the owner replied, "My business is completely knocked out. They said if they got control they'd take the people back to work." One union leader asserted that, altogether, merchants had contributed "thousands" of dollars to the Independent.

3. If these were the direct sanctions invoked against the union membership and leadership, what direct pressures, if any, were felt by the company? The Blank Company had or was believed to have the reputation in Westville of being a "grand old firm" whose officials were known for a sense of responsibility toward the company's employees, customers, and "the community." Did this make the incumbent officials vulnerable to the penalty of possible loss of company good will and personal standing in the community?

Several "important" Westville merchants went to see company officials, and one member of management appeared, on request, before the members of Westville's principal merchants' association. According to a company official, however, these merchants merely offered to act as go-betweens and described the financial hardship they were undergoing. Any feeling of pressure which management may have experienced from such visitations appears to have been too slight to have affected its conduct.

Several observers said that at the time they had been of the opinion that at least one of the company officials who lived in Westville felt his status in the community was suffering as a result of the company's attitude toward negotiations. This official, however, insisted (whether or not accurately, there is no way of telling) that at no time had he experienced or feared any coldness from friends or business associates or community organizations. "The people whose good opinion I value most highly are the members of the chamber of commerce," he said, "and I always felt that they supported the company's position in the matter. Everybody I talked to, once they had the issues explained to them, agreed with the company's position."

The Indirect Sanctions

Three groups of intermediaries were important in the Blank strike: public officials, the press, and the Catholic Church. We shall consider each briefly.

1. As we have seen, public officials are likely to intervene in a strike situation only if it so affects a *voting* public as to endanger their political careers by failing to act. While the term "responsibility to the public" is usually used to cover the situation, there is a sufficient understanding that those to whom that responsibility is owed can punish the public official who fails to live up to it. There is no question that government officials involved in this strike were aware of the nature of the sanction; and when affected persons appealed to an official to "do something" to end the strike, it was the realization that the affected persons had some control over the political fate of the official which gave force to the petition.

Such appeals were made by various groups to various officials. A local reporter stated that during the first few weeks of the strike Flats merchants, especially grocers whose credit facilities were overextended, put "considerable pressure" on their councilmen to "do something to end the strike." Westville's form of government, under which each councilman's job depends on his standing with a geographically concentrated group of voters who may be also his main social contacts and certainly are his neighbors—with all that term implies—facilitated the application of this pressure. Somewhat later the spread of effects to the "downtown" section brought complaints to non-Flats councilmen, but since the residences of these merchants were distributed over the city the "pressure" on any one councilman was less concentrated.

Moreover, the downtown merchants were apparently more inclined to make their desires known to the mayor himself. Several observers said that these merchants (and Flats suppliers) put "terrific pressure" on the mayor to "force" a termination of the strike. The mayor's own account suggests that the pressure was more often of an implicit rather than explicit nature. He said that he had never been approached formally by any merchant or any merchants' committee or members of a merchants' association.

They didn't need to; they knew what moves I was making and knew I knew about the effects of the strike on them. Look, it was all very obvious. A payroll of half a million was being lost and 75 percent of it went to residents of [Westville]. I didn't have to be told formally how bad it was.

"Individual businessmen who were my friends" did phone him—"informally"—from time to time, but only to tell him how far their sales had slumped and to ask "if any progress was being made and if there was anything they could do."

Letters from strikers' wives asking him to "end the strike and get the men back to work" constituted, if not a pressure themselves, a supplement to other pressures being exerted on the mayor. Finally, with respect to the mayor, he was acutely aware (according to observers) of the importance of respecting the views of taxpaying voters who were disinclined to have city funds used freely for relief to strikers. Whether such views were the product of simple tax-consciousness or of a desire to put further pressure on the strikers, to induce settlement, we have no way of knowing. The result, however, was to influence the mayor to see that relief funds were doled out to strikers very cautiously ("meagerly," the union leadership said), thereby increasing for union members the cost of continuing the strike.

The strike in Westville occurred during a year in which the governor was campaigning for re-election. On the 103rd day of the strike the governor had secured the company's agreement to resume face-to-face negotiations at some time in the future. On the 131st day, when sessions had still not been resumed and the breakdown in negotiations had persisted for eleven weeks, the rival gubernatorial candidate, speaking in Westville, charged the incumbent with "disregard for the plight of the people of [Westville]" and said that the governor should "have sat down personally with the representatives of both sides" and used the "prestige and power" of his office to have settled the strike, devoting "days, even weeks if necessary," to the effort. The strike did not develop into an important campaign issue, but it seems evident that the political implications could not be entirely neglected by officeholders.

According to a state official the governor intervened in the strike to secure a renewal of negotiations because "it was his job, his duty, his responsibility," to make an effort to end a strike that was affecting so many persons in the state. A reliable observer stated, however, that a principal instigator of intervention by the governor was the publisher of a Westville newspaper who was a close friend and political supporter of the governor. The penalty of losing the backing of a person who exercises considerable influence in party councils or over particular types of voter is a sanction of a different, and in some cases perhaps more compelling, nature than the penalty of losing the support of individual voters.

There is some indication that the mayor, too, was subject to sanctions of this "influential supporter" variety. He was visited by political leaders (themselves impelled by sanctions at the disposal of Flats merchants belonging to their political party) and by Catholic priests from the Flats whose opinions regarding the desirability of candidates for office might carry weight with some (especially "old country") parishioners. There is no reason to doubt the veracity of assurances that these visitors "made no threats" or "exerted no pressure," but the "great concern" over continuation of the strike which they displayed undoubtedly reinforced the mayor's feeling about his "responsibilities."

These were the pressures on the relevant public officials. What sanctions did they in turn invoke against the parties to the strike?

The answer appears to be that these authorities—councilmen, mayor, and governor—limited themselves to the pressures of public persuasion and mild condemnation. The parties were charged to recognize their responsibilities. The company was asked to resume face-to-face negotiations, not simply in statements released to the press but by personal visitation to the president of the company. Possible loss of good will was the sanction which lay behind the public statement of the governor's conciliators that the company's refusal to negotiate with the union was blocking termination of the strike. The closest approach to the imposition of any more substantial penalty came from the governor, who after three times meeting with a company official announced that something "had to be done" about the strike—a statement which, in context, was interpreted as a veiled threat that some unfavorable action would be taken against the company if it continued to hold out against resumption of negotiations. Apparently, however, no stronger actions than these were attempted.

2. The press did not quite limit itself to editorial injunction to the parties to settle their dispute. It helped to organize public opinion, notably by publicity concerning alleged Communist domination of the union, publicity which as we have seen stimulated some members of the public to apply the direct sanctions of contempt and castigation. The local newspaper also gave publicity and editorial support (and, acording to two observers, money) to the Independent union, which was seeking to end the strike by replacing the IBPW.

3. There remains for consideration the intermediary role of the Catholic clergy. Several priests having parishes in the Flats sought to induce members of the union to forsake their leadership and, under the aegis of the Independent or any other "proper" leadership, negotiate a settlement which would end the strike. One priest addressed mass meetings of strikers, others preached sermons on the subject, and all frequently discussed the matter informally with striker-parishioners. In a typical sermon preached late in the strike a priest commented that it was well known that the Westville local was "tainted with Reds" and urged the strikers to "get rid of the Reds," clear out members dissenting to such action, and "under proper leadership" reach agreement with the company. He added that since members disagreed as to the importance of the yardstick issue it could hardly be worth a strike, and asked, "Why then have these people been kept in misery so long?" A union member reported that priests had advised strikers that with a change in leadership the strike could be settled in a day.

This intervention of the Catholic clergy may not have been in response to public sentiment. There is, indeed, a widely held view that the priests' activities can best be explained as a by-product of the general position of the Catholic Church against communism in the labor movement. If so, they performed no intermediary role—that is, a role assumed on behalf and at the instigation of the affected public. The

reason suggested appears to be no more than partial explanation, however. There is evidence that some of the priests were responding to the
role expected of them by certain of their parishioners and were seeking
settlement of the strike as a means of assuaging hardship and distress
which afflicted the families of strikers, one important segment of the
affected public. The mayor of Westville, himself a Catholic, reported
that several priests who visited him were "much concerned about
family problems in their parishes. Where was the rent money coming
from? Would the family have to be broken up, with the wife going
home to her mother in [another state]?"

Another observer suggested, more positively, that the priests perhaps
stood in the relationship of intermediaries to that important affected
public consisting of women relatives of strikers. Among the strikers
were many immigrant and first-generation families who had not been
fully assimilated, who retained many "old country" ways. The women
in such Westville families (especially if they are Catholic) tend to be
dependent on the clergy for assistance in practical, economic matters
as well as in spiritual problems. It appears likely that such women had
appealed to their priests to use their influence to "get the men to go
back to work."

The exhortations of priests to throw out the church-condemned
Communist leadership and thus end the strike were believed by several
observers to have had a compelling influence on many "old country"
wives for whom the cost of disregarding the church's advice was heavier
than for their striking husbands. Public—and particularly church—
criticism of the strikers' loyalty to allegedly Communist leaders apparently caused some wives to feel that their own status in the community
had fallen, an understandable reaction since in most social groups a
wife largely derives her status from that of her husband.[4]

Effectiveness of the Sanctions

In view of the fact that the strike at the Westville plant lasted for
more than twenty weeks after the point at which its effects on local
suppliers, city finances, and strikers' families had become pronounced,

[4] The priest here appears in the same kind of intermediary role as the mayor who
"organizes" an already existing public sentiment. In this case wives of strikers appeal to
the priest to help end the strike, and the priest organizes the opinion of these same wives,
as well as the wives of other strikers who may not have voiced their sentiments openly.
The priest provides an opinionative authority on which these members of the affected
public can draw for support in their efforts to influence the conduct of the strikers.

one must conclude that none of the sanctions present was very effective as a strike terminator. Some of the participants and observers interviewed held that sanctions had played no part at all in ending the strike; that the cumulative effects of absence of income on the strikers and the defection of the Eastopolis local were solely responsible for the reaching of an agreement at the Westville plant.

The union leaders and members interviewed, however, were inclined to attribute a significant role to some of the sanctions directed against the union membership. They believed that some members felt that continued participation in a strike led by persons characterized by many in the community as Communist was causing them (the members) to lose the approval of community groups or to run the risk of violating religious obligations. The utilization by affected publics of these social and religious sanctions was successful in that it weakened members' determination to continue the strike, but unsuccessful in that the penalties were not sufficiently strong to make the membership *demand* that the leadership accept any terms it could get from the company until the operation of external factors (the accumulation of economic hardship and the Eastopolis settlement) made further resistance appear too costly.

The relative success of the religious sanction can be at least partially explained by the facts that (1) a large proportion of the Blank strikers were Catholic; (2) a large proportion of the Catholic strikers and their families had retained the "old country" dependence on guidance by the clergy in all spheres of living; and (3) the issue of continuation of the strike was for many strikers transformed into the issue of continuation of support of leaders said to be dominated by views which had been strongly condemned by the Church. Such success as the social sanction achieved was probably largely attributable to the fact that, as one union leader put it, the Blank strikers were accustomed to regard themselves and be regarded as "very solid citizens—working class, of course—but very solid and respected." Before one can be in fear of losing something, he must believe that he has something to lose.

It also seems fairly certain that these sanctions were to some extent effective—indirectly—on the union leaders. Their awareness that members had begun to feel themselves penalized for support of an allegedly Communist leadership, with consequent possibility of a revolt, was one of the factors which by the tenth week had made the leaders eager for a settlement.

In any case these achievements cannot be considered to have been very far-reaching. Why were the sanctions invoked or threatened so relatively ineffective?

A partial answer is to be found, perhaps, in the attitude of the Blank Company officials. It seems safe to conclude, on the basis of all the evidence gathered, that they visualized the strike as furnishing an opportunity to secure the ousting of the incumbent leadership of the Westville local—an objective so desirable to them that it would compensate for a considerable amount of whatever financial loss or loss of community good will might be generated by a continuation of the strike which had been publicly attributed to the company's refusal to have any contact with the union leadership. Moreover, it was the opinion of one informed observer that the top company officials believed that in firmly rejecting any compromise on the "Communist-espoused" issue of union participation in what was conceived as a management prerogative, determination of the production yardstick, and in refusing to bargain with a Communist-dominated union leadership, they were rendering service to and increasing their standing in the eyes of the top leaders of American industry. There is no doubt that the company officials were determined to resist most strongly whatever pressures might be exerted on them by the union or the public. The president of the Blank Company was quoted in a newspaper as having said that the strike could last for a year or more before he "would consent to any demands of the strikers" (a statement subsequently denied) and by a public official as having said "I won't have anything to do with those Reds." Another company official told a Westville merchant that "the company will shut down before it will give in to the union on the [yardstick] issue."

Moreover, the power to settle or not to settle was vested in company officials who did not live in Westville or even in Westville's state, and who consequently were somewhat isolated socially and physically from contact with the struck region's public and its public officials. Even those officials who lived in Westville seem not to have been much affected by the "social" penalties at the command of affected publics, however. Their standing depended to a considerable degree on the esteem of their business associates, and since (except possibly for the smaller merchants) the latter were "sympathetic" to the company's position, no loss of status was felt. The members of the chamber of commerce included merchants strongly affected by the strike, but as an observer put it, "the merchants were not inclined to condemn the company because they, after all, were management people themselves." It may be that the Blank Company's eminent position as the owner of the largest manufacturing plant in the area had something to do with their attitude. A participant stated that businessmen were sympathetic to the company's position because its officials were opposing (1) a demand that, if granted, would have destroyed management's ability to run the plant; (2) a Communist-dominated union. But one must also take account of the statement of a union member: "Nobody would ever buck [Blank]; they're king-all in this town."

This partisan support of the company by merchant-members of the public who were relatively hard hit by the strike thus appears to be explainable on grounds of ideological affinity. Nevertheless, one might question whether such an ideological attachment would hold, where business fortunes were being so adversely affected, unless there accompanied it an expectancy that pressures on the *other* party to settle the strike would be effective. Here there was such hope—springing from the belief that the Communist issue could be sufficiently exploited to cause a division in the ranks leading to settlement.

The union leadership felt that it, too, had a lot at stake in the strike. Several participants and observers believed that the national office of the IBPW, worried about the tenuousness of its position in the labor federation to which it belonged, had selected the Blank Company (for lack of a larger company with a contract up for renewal that season) as the adversary in an "all-out" struggle, the termination of which in a union triumph would demonstrate to the leaders of the federation and to workers within the IBPW's jurisdiction its vigor and ability to protect and advance American labor's interests. But after the company had demonstrated a greater resistance to the pressures exerted against it than that possessed by the union membership, the leadership decided that it stood to lose more by a continuation of the strike than by a surrender to the company's terms. At that point the leaders became willing to do almost anything to settle the strike as long as they remained in command of the union, but they now found the company obdurate in its unwillingness to discuss settlement terms with them. Thus sanctions were ineffective against the union leadership in the early days of the strike, since the pattern of union conduct was controlled by forces outside the community. And when it was seen that the strike could not be won (perhaps in part because of sanctions operating on the membership), the company's intransigence prevented for a time agreement on terms which substantially met the company's original demands. The only additional concession which could have won agreement was abdication by the left-wing leadership of its authority in the local, a price too great to be compelled by any except the most extreme sanctions.

A further explanation of the relative ineffectiveness of pressures to end the Blank strike is to be found in the power of the parties to counteract or nullify some of the sanctions which others sought to impose on them. One example may be cited. The merchant who gave especial support to the Independent in the hope of overthrowing IBPW leadership happened to be a leader in the Jewish community in Westville. Some of the Independent's literature had anti-Semitic overtones. A union leader reported that when he learned of the merchant's actions, "I dropped in to see him and asked if he wanted to start a pogrom here in Westville; then I had a bunch of other leading Jewish businessmen call him on the phone and tell him to stop it." The merchant discontinued at least open support of the Independent.

If the sanctions brought into play were ineffective in causing an early settlement of a strike which was adversely affecting so many strikers' families and local suppliers, why were not other, stronger penalties invoked?

In the first place, the absence of sanctions which might have been imposed by users of the company's products can be explained by the fact that the users—household, private producers, and government—experienced no serious deprivations.

Second, the circumstances of the situation inclined public officials to move cautiously. It is very difficult for a public official to utilize sanctions against both parties equally and impartially; so many of the penalties invoked or threatened apply only to one of the parties or, if to both, with uneven force. The officials involved in this dispute were much concerned not to appear to be "taking sides." As one observer explained, the balance of political forces in Westville was evenly divided between the company and the union. The union membership represented many more votes than did the company officials, but the company was a better source of public revenue and the dominant source of local employment. About one twelfth of Westville's revenues are derived from property taxes paid by the Blank Company, and much of the value of residential and commercial property depends on the presence of the Blank plant in the area. Fear that the company might move the plant away was apparently widespread; it was given credence by the previously cited statement of a company official to a merchant that "the company will shut the plant down before it will give in to the union on the [yardstick] issue," and by the fact that the plant had originally come to Westville as a "runaway" from a strike in another area. An observer pointed out that even if the mayor thought the probability slight, the repercussions would have been so immense if the plant had been moved away that his political career would have been seriously jeopardized. If the loss of the plant could be attributed to any action of his, he would be "finished" politically; even if he could escape the blame, the removal of the biggest single taxpayer and employer would have enormously complicated his task of balancing the city's budget and even of maintaining the functions of the community.

The governor was also apparently confronted by the problem of an even "balance of political forces." A close associate of the governor, when asked why the governor had not taken a more forceful position with the parties, replied:

If [the governor] had put pressure on either side to settle the dispute—aside from just insisting that they keep negotiating—he would have offended more people than he pleased. He would have pleased the union or the company and the merchants in [Westville] but he would have offended the other side and all the people on that side throughout the state, besides a lot of citizens who would have objected to what they believed was a violation of law or ethics. Why worry about the voters in just one community? He has to think all the time about all the voters in the whole state.

Attempts to apply sanctions against company officials were further impeded by the fact that such actions could be considered to give support to a union whose leadership had been branded as Communist. As one participant said, "Public officials are very careful about doing anything which would be construed as backing a Red union."

The force of all these points is summed up in the statement of an observer: "None of the public officials involved wanted to be a hero in this strike; they wanted, rather, to stay out of trouble politically."

Finally the actual circumstances of the strike itself prevented the application or threat of some varieties of sanctions. There were no outbreaks of disorder or violence, hence no pretext for using police or militia; consumers in the city or state were scarcely if at all affected and thus there was no reason to seek or use emergency powers to break the strike and operate the plant.

In these two case studies we have observed the sanctions at work and analyzed their effectiveness. In both instances the effects on the public were great (though not as great as expected), but the sanctions invoked were too weak to force a prompt termination of the strike. In both cases there were circumstances limiting the effectiveness of the sanctions. We have here a suggestion as to why we found unreliable our hypothesis that at some identifiable level of strike effects the force of public opinion, expressed through sanctions, would secure an end of the strike before frustration of public rights of expectancy became "intolerable." It may be the uncertain operation of the sanctions supporting public opinion which is the explanation. In the next chapter we shall examine this possibility.

The Reliability of the Social Sanctions

SOCIAL responsibility is the obligation to seek a compatibility between the rights of expectancy enjoyed by one individual or group and the important rights of expectancy entertained by other individuals and groups—an obligation which is enforceable by sanctions. With respect to industrial relations, we have found the strike to be the only significant union-management relationship which large numbers of the general public have identified as inconsistent with their own expectations—expectations of a continued supply of goods or services or of continued productive employment. We have assumed, though with limitations, that people's opposition to a particular strike is a function of the real costs imposed on them. We set up the hypothesis that there is some identifiable level of real costs at which, in any strike, sanctions will be forthcoming sufficient to end the strike before (or at the point when) it imposes what the public believes to be unreasonable hardship. This hypothesis, however, appeared to be faulty. In seeking an explanation as to why it was not borne out, our path of inquiry has led us to suspect that the sanctions imposed against the offending parties in particular strike situations may be unreliable.

Our examination of the types of sanctions which may be applied in particular strike situations should caution us against the suggestion that they are generally ineffective. Numerous examples are available—some have been cited—of how pressures generated by public opinion were successful in terminating a strike. Nevertheless, our case studies of a dispute in a public utility company and another in a manufacturing plant constituting the chief source of employment in a community provide adequate grounds for believing that at least in some situations the sanctions are ineffective. We can therefore conclude that, if not generally ineffective, they are at least uncertain and unreliable. They cannot be counted on. In this chapter we shall explore why this is so.

We shall find that the reasons may be grouped under three principal headings: (1) limitations on the effectiveness of the direct sanctions due to their nature, (2) limitations on the effectiveness of the indirect sanctions due to their nature, and (3) limitations on the effectiveness of both direct and indirect sanctions due to the characteristics of the parties against whom they are invoked.

Limitations of the Direct Sanctions

Direct sanctions are those which the affected public can itself impose on the parties to the strike. Some members of an affected public—business suppliers or customers, for example—are in positions where their resentment can be expressed directly and forcibly to the union or management. Other affected individuals, however, a somewhat more general public such as household consumers or workers in companies which have had to suspend operations due to the strike, have no avenues of communicating their sentiments directly to the parties. They become a privately grumbling but publicly inarticulate group. Their very identities are usually unknown to the parties. They have little consciousness of a power to initiate pressures on the parties. In the words of one of our management correspondents, "Before public opinion, if it is sufficiently aroused, can have an influence, there must be a channel for expression. It is not enough to suggest that someone write to his Congressman. It is my observation when obvious self-interest is involved, as, for example, when an oil strike deprives an individual of the use of his automobile because of a gasoline shortage, or the babies' milk is not delivered because of a milk drivers' strike, a situation is created where the public is stimulated to act because of their direct involvement but they do not act effectively because they are not told how they might act effectively."

As is true with respect to all the limitations on the effectiveness of sanctions which we shall consider, this one is not always applicable. There are times when the amorphous mass secures effective direct representation, as in the case of the Pittsburgh milk strike when women's organizations directly represented their affected members or in instances when a union whose members have become unemployed in consequence of a strike brings direct pressure to bear on the striking union. This difficulty of channeling public sentiment to the parties explains the ineffectiveness of the direct sanction on some occasions, however, and thus provides one reason for the uncertainty of its result.

To avoid repetition we shall emphasize now that none of the limitations on the effectiveness of sanctions discussed in this chapter is pertinent to *every* strike situation. The limitations are sometimes present, and because of their possible occurrence we are faced with the uncertainty whether in any given situation public pressures will achieve their objective.

Wherever members of the affected public are incapable of communicating their resentment directly to the parties, the effectiveness of the most important of the direct sanctions—damage to the parties' good will or community standing—depends on the estimates of the parties themselves. These estimates may be little more than "feelings" or "presentiments," at best, guesses. Says a union official, "There is seldom a way to gauge public opinion accurately." Says a staff representative of a large insurance company, "It is unfortunate that both the union and the company do not have a better sounding board or measurement of the public feeling during such an issue." In this respect the effectiveness of this direct sanction lies with the optimism or pessimism, the perceptiveness or blindness, of the parties. There is no certain way of alerting them to the prevalent sentiment of their affected public, even should they be anxious to know.

In some instances, however, there may be little anxiety as to the state of their public's opinions once a strike has been determined on. The parties have assessed the likely costs of an adverse public sentiment and have decided to incur them rather than accept, as the only prospective alternative, the costs of conceding to the other's demands. With the decision once made, they face even a hostile public attitude if not with equanimity at least with resolution. The sanction is ineffective because it has already been anticipated in the party's calculations. In the words of a Boston labor reporter, "Once a union has determined to take extreme measures to back up its demands, and once a company has decided to allow its functions to be suspended rather than to accede to these demands, neither of them, I feel, will be materially influenced by external pressures until one or the other, or both, has become economically exhausted." Only in the event that unforeseen sanctions are encountered, imposing costs of unexpected magnitude, will the resolute parties be shaken from their predetermined positions.

Once a strike has begun, the nature of the contest may induce a spirit of belligerency, a stubborn determination to "see this through" regardless of the cost. Such an attitude is not conducive to a careful calculation of the cost of an adverse public opinion. The contest may become a cause, and an organization-centered antagonist may conceive that the public owes a duty to it to support its just cause, to accept sacrifices if necessary in defense of justice. Comments of two members of management suggest this possibility.

1. A strike situation is usually a highly emotional drama in which both Union and Management cast themselves in the role of Hero. They both imagine (usually) that they are Fighting for Principle and Right and either that intelligent public opinion is solidly behind them or that the irresponsible and selfish public has yielded to wicked influence.

2. Once a strike situation has developed, both parties are in a sense fighting a holy war and each side can usually find plenty of support for its position. In this situation while the parties are tremendously conscious of public opinion and try to enlist support for their cause, unfavorable public opinion is usually ignored as being heretical.

Moreover, neither of the parties is likely to accept public opinion as "given," but is more likely to regard it as something which can be molded. However dim the hope of influencing others' opinions, seldom does either party to a strike fail to publicize the justification for its position. Even those union officials who bitterly complain that the public is only concerned with its own comfort and convenience and cannot be induced to think in terms of issues do not hesitate to release statements designed to influence opinion. Parties who believe that an uninformed public can be persuaded to play a neutral if not a supporting role may respond to a hostile public simply by redoubling their propaganda efforts. Union and management may become engaged in a battle to weaken the effects of each other's propaganda campaign. A representative for an employers' group reports of one strike, "Our efforts and tactics throughout the three and a half months were designed to neutralize and counteract the union's efforts to win public favor, so that public pressure even at the end of the strike was extremely light."

We have been talking here about the most general of direct sanctions, the threat to an individual's standing in the community or to the good will of his organization. There are sometimes limitations on the more specific direct sanctions as well. Business suppliers or customers of the struck company or of the striking workers may hesitate to apply pressure to the parties whom they are in a position to influence. A supplier may fear that through pressuring tactics he will arouse the resentment of the struck firm, raising the threat of loss of a customer when customers are most needed (as at a time of business recession), while a customer of the struck firm may hesitate to apply pressure for fear that he will lose a vital source of supply at a time when it is most needed (as during a boom period when materials are in short supply). Merchants may hesitate to restrict credit to strikers, as a means of inducing an early end to the strike, when their own prosperity depends on their retaining the trade of those same individuals after the strike is over.

Limitations of the Indirect Sanctions

The same difficulty which the parties face in appraising public sentiment faces a third-party intermediary in equal degree. How many letters complaining of a strike's effects must a mayor receive before he concludes that enough members of the general public are aroused that he runs a political risk in remaining on the sidelines? To what extent should he accept newspaper judgment as to the likely effects of a strike, so that he may anticipate the public pressure which such a strike would evoke?

These questions are acutely important to an elected public official, dependent on political support for retaining office. He must weigh the danger of offending a strike-affected public, if he fails to intervene, against the danger of offending the parties and their sympathizers, if he does intervene. Faced with such a dilemma, his inclination is to remain free of the dispute as long as possible. A mediator of some years' experience summed up the position of the public official in this manner: "Whenever a politician intervenes in a strike situation, you can be sure that some kind of pressure has been put on him, whether by the public or by the parties. His first thought is to avoid getting into the picture. A strike situation is too hot to take on voluntarily. He is bound to offend someone. If he tries to force a settlement, he's likely to lose friends among either management or the union or both, so he'd rather stay out of the matter. If he can't stay out, he tries to steer a middle or a neutral course. It may be perfectly true that a mayor, for example, feels that the public at large expects him to do something about a strike, or that a particular portion of the public expects action from him, but he is also made aware by the parties themselves that they control votes."

Other informants express the same opinion. A labor lawyer, long familiar with the ways of public officials from dealings with them, remarks, "All public officials have 'clubs,' but they won't necessarily want to use them. A public official must weigh several considerations. He's worried about the letter-writers, but he also doesn't want to antagonize the union or the company. So he doesn't rush in to use his 'club' every time." A labor relations consultant, writing from a populous Illinois area, says with respect to local governmental officials: "Most of them won't go near a labor dispute if they can at all avoid it. Some time ago all the restaurants in this area were closed for a period of over six weeks as the result of a labor dispute. While the impact on the public, and even the health and welfare of a segment of the public, was affected, local officials felt the case was too 'hot' to touch even though they were invited to participate and help mediate the dispute."

The international representative of a CIO union speaks of a six months' strike in which he was involved, at a plant which employed a sufficiently large proportion of the town's labor force to make the affair "a major concern to the community." The situation described bears a close resemblance to the case of the dominant firm given in the preceding chapter.

The mayor had an interest of his own. On the one hand, he could not speak out against the strikers. These men and women constituted a large block of votes. It wouldn't do him much political good to alienate them. On the other hand, the company was one of the town's chief sources of income. He couldn't afford to alienate the management either. He offended neither, and he aided neither. Instead, he put on an exhibition of impartiality which, while it had no positive effect upon the public, or upon the parties, must have been painful to the extreme so far as the mayor was concerned, for clearly it is impossible to sit on a fence for as long as six months without some fundamental repercussions.

The lesser public officials played the same role as the mayor. Not one of them took a decided position on one side or the other. All of these officials bent over backward attempting to be all things to all men. The results very clearly left the public with no notion concerning the real issues of the dispute, other than the one which had been created by the original arguments of the parties. Consequently, third party intervention had no effect on the final settlement of the strike. Certainly, the public reacted and some of this reaction was certainly tempestuous. The total effect, however, merely produced a modern tempest in a teapot.

We have seen the considerable arsenal of sanctions which a public official is likely to have at his disposal. The efficacy of these weapons, when exposed, may be blunted, however, by the counterattacks of the parties. The mediator previously quoted remarks, "What can a mayor do if the company or the union warns him that if he tries to intervene or break the strike they will see to it that he regrets it at the next election?"

Among a local official's weapons, as we have seen, may be the threat of an adverse health or fire inspection or the reassessment of property values or some other penalizing use of regulatory or administrative authority. It is perhaps not surprising that our respondents report little knowledge of the use of such sanctions. A company vice-president writes, "I am sure that we would not take such a threat lying down." A union staff officer says, "There are few politicians or government officials who would dare tamper with reassessment of property values because of labor disputes. It would lead to far more trouble for the government officials involved than would the labor dispute itself."

The public press, another powerful intermediary, may be made to feel the weight of counterpressures if it seeks to intervene. Partisan pressure may remain implicit no less than public pressure, but it may be no less effective. A strike affecting numbers of employers in a community, as would be true of an association-wide strike, may raise the specter of loss of advertising revenue if editorial opinion should be brought to bear on the employers, however intransigent. The safest course might be, as for the public official, a neutral or nonintervention-ist one. An attorney for a group of employers writes, "We had a committee visit the editors and publishers at the inception of the strike, explaining the issues, pointing out that it was due to be a long strike, and asking for an open-minded attitude. I do think that these meetings with the press at the outset did assist us greatly in enjoying an unbiased, even favorable, press. Also, toward the end, when two of the local editors ran editorials, we again approached them and explained that they were prolonging rather than shortening the strike,[1] and they willingly backed off and stepped out of the picture." No explicit threat need be made to an editor in such a conference to lead him to weigh carefully the cost of involving his paper "needlessly" in the dispute. News coverage will suffice; editorial comment may, after all, be gratuit-

---

[1] How an attempt to apply "even-handed" pressure on both parties to reach a settlement may strengthen the weaker party, on whose collapse strike termination depends, is suggested elsewhere by this same attorney. "We were in off-the-record negotiations when these editorials came out and were making substantial progress. The effect of the editorials was to prolong rather than to shorten the strike because it gave the union the impression that they were getting public support, causing the union leaders to immediately toughen up. As a result negotiations broke off, and I would say we probably lost a week or two as a result of this public pressure."

ous, dispensable. A newspaper cannot enlist in every cause; why weaken its strength for future and perhaps more important causes by offending one's supporters now?

The effectiveness of third-party intervention is likely to depend on the vigor of the intervenor. A timid intermediary may not be taken seriously; one who can bluster it out with the parties and who is unafraid to use the power he possesses can expect to be more influential on the parties' conduct. Writes one employers' representative, who had been engaged in a prolonged strike which ended without intervention despite considerable public inconvenience if not actual hardship, "Probably if the mayor, the newspapers, and other employers in town rose up in indignation and demanded that we yield to the union, the results would have been much different." The effectiveness of Mayor La Guardia's intervention in New York City disputes was undoubtedly attributable to his own fiery temperament, his willingness to bulldoze others when he believed it necessary. Other officials possessing the same power to impose sanctions but without his vigorous personality would have achieved more meager results.

Finally, the effectiveness of third-party intervention is sometimes limited by the fact that the public itself or some influential portion of it, on whose behalf intervention is undertaken, may limit the sanctions which can be employed. The efforts of the mayor to employ the injunction in the strike at the Duquesne Light Company, recounted in preceding Chapter 12, were stultified by the widespread resentment which that weapon aroused among unionized workers throughout the area, despite the fact that it was intended to prevent that unemployment which subsequently affected many of their number. An attorney active in labor relations writes, more generally: "During fifteen years in public life, I have yet to see politicians or governmental officials bring pressure on either side through any threat of retaliation and indeed, I would think them very foolish if they did for the resentment which it would cause not only to the party involved, but to fair thinking citizens of the community." The anticipation of such an unfavorable reaction may be all that is necessary to inhibit an intervenor from using sanctions actually within his power.

Limitations Imposed by Characteristics of the Parties

In addition to characteristics of the direct and indirect sanctions themselves which sometimes limit their effectiveness, the influence which they exert is sometimes limited by characteristics of the parties.

The consequence is to render less reliable the sanctions which a public may impose on the parties to secure the end of a strike which frustrates their expectations of continuing to receive some good or service considered vital in their way of life. Just as, in broader social intercourse, the thick-skulled individual blunts the effectiveness of sarcasm, or the thick-skinned individual refuses to be perturbed by the mutterings of others against him, or the stout-hearted individual resolves to continue a course of action despite ostracism or even physical danger, so in the course of strikes sanctions which may have proved their efficacy in one situation may, in another situation, fail completely because directed against parties whose characteristics render them impervious to the threat invoked.

The leaders and rank and file in the union or management structure differ in the degree of their concern over community good will. Management leaders are frequently characterized as "individualists," a personality trait which would remove some of the sting that otherwise might come with isolation from certain groups in the society. Their orientation may be directed more exclusively toward the society of their own class, and loss of a general good will might be compensated for by an increase in one's prestige in his "own" circle. The employer who, despite the pleas of government officials, holds firm against union demands may gain considerable satisfaction from the respect accorded him by fellow employers. "We know that the many commendatory letters received from shippers and others expressing gratification at the fact that a large industry was willing to stand up and fight out an important issue on a toe-to-toe basis had an extremely stimulating and encouraging effect on railroad management." Similarly, the union leader who is castigated by the local press may be, for that reason, more loyally supported by his own followers, and the latter gain may for him be sufficient compensation for the former loss.

The responses of strike leaders to public opinion sometimes differ depending on "the sensitivity of labor and management leaders to their longer run as opposed to their immediate interests," writes one impartial observer who has been involved in many disputes as mediator and arbitrator. Their perceptiveness of the consequences of defying hostile sentiment partially determines their conduct. This observer continues, "I am thinking of secondary reactions through legislation or other indirect effects. Management has become somewhat more sensitive to longer-run consequences, partly as a consequence of bitter experience. The labor leaders have something to learn in this regard."

How differing personality characteristics may respond differently to public pressures, whether direct or indirect, is suggested in the comment of the director of industrial relations for a large corporation operating a number of plants in scattered communities.

I am certain that in plant locations in which our plant offers all, or a large part, of the available employment, our local, operating management takes into consideration the public effect of community sentiment which might result from a threatened strike or a failure of either party to measure up to its social responsibilities. Naturally, the degree of consideration will vary to a large extent with the personality of the responsible local official. In some locations a plant superintendent may be so public relations minded as to go to the extent of sacrificing either financial or managerial judgment at the altar of his community relations. I have no doubt that on the other hand we have certain plant managements who look only at the financial or managerial effect of strike issues and adopt a more or less "public be damned" attitude.[2]

It is possible that a strike itself serves to stiffen the attitude of the participants toward the affected public and to tighten the bonds knitting together the organization. If the public desires surrender, then the public—no less than the other party—must be viewed as an opponent. Union or management may respond to public pressure by steeling themselves to resist it. Indeed, some union leaders develop attitudes of hostility toward the public which outlast particular strike situations. The public is considered self-interested. Why then should workers, similarly self-interested, sacrifice their interests to those of others? Why should not others be called upon—with equal reason—to sacrifice their interests to those of the workers? Is one self-interest more inviolate than another? A lawyer influential in labor circles in a highly unionized area remarks that the union leaders he knows are not swayed by disgruntled consumers. "The great majority and probably all" feel strongly that they have no obligation to settle a strike in order that consumers can be furnished goods, "even in the case of absolute necessities."

The case of the Duquesne Light Company strike (Chapter 12) is instructive of how the personality of an individual participant can dull the effectiveness of sanctions. If a strike serves personal interests of

[2] The writer adds: "The latter approach is, of course, not in accordance with the company's general policy, and great pains are taken at the General Office level in threatened strike situations to see to it that appropriate consideration is given to public reaction."

dramatizing individual power or leadership ability or only capturing the public spotlight, the penalties for refusing to end the strike may be less than the penalties for failing to continue it.

This last consideration may be substantially broadened. Not only personality characteristics of the party may serve to make the sanctions less to be feared than a pressured settlement of the strike. In weighing the costs of the sanctions, when imposed, against the costs of settling the strike on terms more favorable to the other party than are believed wise, the economic characteristics of the company and the political characteristics of the union may dictate resistance to public pressures. One management representative writes: "What you can afford to do and stay in business; what you can afford to pay and still effectively meet your competition; whether union demands would so impair the efficiency of your business that you could not operate profitably; whether the length of the strike will lose you markets; whether, as a supplier company, the parent company would seek other suppliers—these to me are far more important considerations than whether the public wants a strike settled or not." In the account of the strike at the "Westville" plant, in the preceding chapter, the union leadership was fighting to retain control of the union, which would have been imperiled by settlement of the strike on the only terms on which a bellicose management was willing to settle. In such instances, the costs which sanctions might impose on either of the parties to the strike may be less than the costs of strike settlement, on pressured compromise terms more favorable to the other party than otherwise would have been granted.

Sanctions sometimes prove ineffective because control of the parties' policies lies outside the community where sanctions can only be applied. At times local union policy may be dictated by the national office; local union officials and rank and file may face the costs of public opinion because powerless to modify the policy prolonging the strike. Their only recourse would be withdrawal from the national body, an action which is not consummated without risk to local treasury and even loss of bargaining rights if a loyal faction carries on the name and organization of the original union which is signatory to an existing collective agreement. The absentee ownership of plants makes difficult the application of pressures to a distant management which may alone have the authority to determine whether a compromise settlement will be made in deference to public interest. In the account of the shoe workers' strike in Yankee City, Warner and Low write: "The three companies that threatened to move rather than submit to unionization were the ones that made shoes for the ABC chain. Their refusal to accept the union was dictated by the president of the chain; neither the local managers nor the community had any control over this individual."[3] Absentee ownership, likewise, makes more hazardous the application of sanctions, since a nonresident management, without roots in the community, will have fewer qualms about removing its plant to another location rather than succumb to insistent public pressures. In the dominant-firm case of the foregoing chapter, the fear of driving the company—with headquarters in another state—to move its plant from town was one factor limiting the application of sanctions.

There remains, as a final consideration concerning the manner in which the characteristics of the parties limit the effectiveness of sanctions, one which is less easy to identify since it has mixed with it other characteristics which have already been discussed, such as personality traits and the economic or political position of the parties. There is no question, however, that it deserves heavy independent consideration. It will be recalled that in our earlier analysis of the nature of social responsibility, mention was made of the fact that it operates as a conservative influence since it rests on a conception of rights of expectancy which have been built up out of past relationships. Modification of expectations comes with the impact of a destruction of existing rights. The change may come gradually, evoking only mild opposition. But in other circumstances the changes sought may appear destructive of the basic distribution of power and accompanying structure of rights and privileges within the society. They are likely to be expressive of ideological cleavages.

It is sometimes only through a contest of power, in which some present rights are disregarded, that social change occurs. Some strikes contain within them issues which involve a redistribution of union-management rights which the union considers vital to obtain and the management imperative to resist. If the only means of settling the issue is through strike, then both parties may accept the threat of sanctions rather than compromise on matters of such fundamental concern to them. If the public is subjected to hardship, that is only an incidental effect of a conflict which concerns—it appears to the parties—far more serious issues than the satisfaction of consumer or producer expectations

[3] W. Lloyd Warner and J. O. Low, *The Social System of the Modern Factory* (New Haven: Yale University Press, 1947), p. 49.

of continuity of service. If the structure of rights and obligations in the society is involved in the strike, it is involved more critically in the rights and obligations in dispute between the parties than in those in dispute between the parties and their public.

The major strikes over union "encroachment on management prerogatives" have been disputes of this nature. The protracted strikes of the International Typographical Union to secure some provision that would fulfill the functions of the closed shop which had been outlawed by the Taft-Hartley Act, and which the union conceived to be fundamental to its very survival, provide other instances. The politically conservative John L. Lewis has consistently precipitated strikes expanding the power of his union at the expense of the power of the operators, shifting the structure of authority within that industry by the only means at his disposal, the strike, without regard to the consequent effects on the public. An individual close to the mine workers' leadership and identified with their philosophy explains this disregard for public hardship:

It is only strong unions that seem to be able to stand up to adverse public opinion in the active stage. The weaker the union and its leadership the more apt it is to be influenced by public opinion, even in the verbal stage of unfavorable editorials, radio commentary, etc.

The UMWA, as an example of a strong union that is not influenced by adverse public opinion, either of the verbal or active variety, is used to public attacks. Ever since the UMWA was founded in 1890—and even in the case of the regional mine workers' organizations that existed as far back as 1840—coal miners in America have been berated by the organs of public opinion. To some extent it has strengthened the backbone of the union.

Consider the much-disputed welfare and retirement fund (says this UMW sympathizer), originally negotiated with the Secretary of the Interior after a breakdown in private negotiations and subsequent governmental seizure of the mines.

It's not too hard to sell people on the value of the UMWA Welfare and Retirement Fund—now. But it was a hell of a job trying to sell them on the idea of the fund when Lewis first proposed it and when it took a couple of bitter strikes and a few million dollars in fines before the UMWA got the fund and got it in working order. Then they would say that certainly the mine workers ought to have some sort of protection but Lewis was going about it in the wrong way. But Lewis got the fund and it's paying out now, and hundreds of thousands of coal miners and members of their families are benefitting. So what does a labor union do in such a situation? Does it bow to public opinion and say O.K., we'll not press too hard for our fund? Or does it lay its cards on the table and say in effect: "This is it. Either we get a fund or we don't mine any coal." That's what the coal miners "know." That's the thing that makes them militant trade unionists. They see results. . . . And Lewis knows that that's how the miners feel and he knows that his first responsibility is to them. And he's aware of the fact that the general public doesn't care very much whether the miners rot away in their mountain cabins as long as the general public gets its coal on time. . . .

So the leadership of the UMWA has come to the conclusion down through the years of bitter experience with the coal industry and the general public and hostile administrations that they have to stand up and fight. And as long as those 480,000 coal miners know what the fight is all about and back up the leaders, no public opinion . . . is going to have much effect on the course of action taken by the union.[4]

To the extent that a union is characterized by a militant intent to restructure the rights and responsibilities of industrial relations, as has been true of the United Mine Workers at least since 1932, the sanctions designed to terminate a strike are likely to prove relatively weak. Conscious that it is only by defying the sanctions invoked in support of an existing structure of rights that rights can sometimes be changed, the union risks the penalties which a hostile public can impose. Conscious that it is only by defying public opinion that rights deemed important can be retained, management chooses to rely on a public relations program to change opinion rather than to conform to existing opinion.

These, then, are the principal characteristics of the parties that explain why sanctions sometimes are ineffective: the personality charac-

[4] It is perhaps worth an aside to point out that the coal industry presents a situation which is not duplicated except in other mining operations. The coal workers, for the most part, live in relatively isolated communities, where the whole town revolves around the mining operations and the miners constitute the town's population. In these circumstances the rank and file of the union are largely freed from the threat of direct sanctions. They are not exposed to the hard feelings of neighbors whom they are depriving of coal or employment—the consumers of their products live in other communities and hence are in a poor position to bring direct sanctions to bear, while other affected producers likewise live in communities apart. Merchants who supply them are vitally affected, but because their own income is dependent almost entirely on miners' trade they are disinclined to be anything but sympathetic. Public pressures are thus likely to be directed primarily against the union's national leaders, who are resident in, and who presumably should be responsive to the social pressures of, nonmining communities like Washington, D.C. Insofar as the national leadership is union-oriented rather than Washington-oriented, however, deriving its standing and prestige from the organization rather than the community, social sanctions may at least in some degree be ignored as long as the membership supports them. Thus the coal union is in a peculiarly favorable position to withstand the influence of public opinion.

teristics of leaders, the economic and political circumstances of the organization, the locus of control, the strength of an intent to shift the balance of power between union and management. But if, for any of these reasons, the parties defy public opinion, are they not likely to be penalized severely enough to deter others who would follow their example?

Retribution is not certain. For a variety of reasons the threat may never be made good. The penalty may never be imposed because of public relief at the end of the strike, which arrives sooner or later as an outcome of purely economic forces. Or the sanctions may not be invoked because of a certain dependence on the organization and a resultant fear that it may retaliate—the fear that the firm may leave town, for example. Many parties rely on short memories among the affected public—it is expected that the indignation so vehemently expressed today will be forgotten as time goes by. For these and other reasons the threat of sanctions is not always made good against the offender who ignores it. And as some union or employer proves through its own experience that the public can be successfully defied, with greater benefits to it than would have been secured had it acted responsibly, this very unreliability of the sanctions may induce others to gamble that they too may succeed. The idea circulates that if an organization is only "tough" enough it can get away with the pursuit of its own ends irrespective of the expectations of others.

Yet these limitations on the effectiveness of sanctions in specific strike situations do not permit a more general conclusion that public opinion is powerless to protect its expectations of a continued supply of goods and services against the interruptions occasioned by a strike. If there is a sufficiently intense public opposition to permitting strikes to interrupt the flow of goods and services vital to consumption and employment, as our analysis suggests there is, we may expect that that opposition will find its own effective sanctions to support it. If the sanctions brought to bear in *specific* disputes prove unreliable, there seems to be every likelihood that pressures will be forthcoming to achieve an effective *general* solution. There exists as a nonlegal sanction the threat of creating legal sanctions; and while admittedly passing a law does not always solve a problem, it may nonetheless make life more difficult for those against whom directed—and some laws do work. The power of the state to enforce legal enactments is not lightly ignored.

If strikes—or certain kinds of strikes—are in fact regarded as threatening important rights of expectancy held by significant numbers of individuals, that one form of sanction proves unreliable is likely simply to induce pressures for other forms of sanctions which give promise of greater reliability. If nonlegal sanctions are insufficiently effective against specific strikes, legal sanctions under established procedures may be sought in the hope that they will prove more effective against strikes generally (or against classes of strikes). If, as seems probable, it is the unreliability of sanctions in specific strike situations which explains why, at some identifiable, critical level of public-affectedness, at the limits of tolerance, strikes are not forced to an end, a general solution is almost certain to be sought, on the premise that it will provide greater reliability in this respect.

The movement in some states toward compulsory arbitration in selected vital industries may perhaps reflect a general public dissatisfaction with the threat to rights of expectancy which are considered important and a recognition that the sanctions invoked in specific disputes have not been reliable enough to provide the assurances wanted. The constitutional question raised by the 1951 invalidation of the compulsory arbitration sections of the Wisconsin act involved only the conflict between state and federal legislation, and thus need not be viewed as a long-run hurdle difficult to surmount. Whether a more fundamental question of constitutionality will act as a more serious barrier remains for the future to reveal. In any event, there is no doubt that if the public pressure for general legislative solution of the problem of "emergency" strikes is great, we shall see experimentation with methods of achieving the objective sought. It appears likely that public sentiment is indeed so inclined; it will be surprising if experimentation does not develop. *The New York Times* editorially remarked following the 1945 elevator strike in that city, "Spasmodic personal intervention by individual officials, however well meant, firm or timely, will not be enough. A more fundamental solution will be necessary."[5]

[5] *The New York Times,* October 1, 1945.

Legal Sanctions in Support of Public Rights

WE HAVE now arrived at the following conclusions:
1. There are nonlegal rights of expectancy entertained by parties to various relationships as a result of established and generally accepted culture patterns. These have, as their correlative, obligations of performance on the part of the other parties to the given relationships. Private responsibility, then, is a performance which satisfies the rights of expectancy held by others in a particular relationship.

2. Relationships, when viewed as parts of a system of relationships helping to define a society, must be reasonably compatible with each other. The impact of the private rights and responsibilities of one relationship on those of other relationships becomes the crucial consideration. Social responsibility is the obligation to reconcile the exercise of one's private authority with the important rights of expectancy held by others who are not parties to the particular relationship but who are affected by it.

3. Social responsibility is not a matter of conscience but is enforceable by others through the medium of social sanctions. It is objective rather than subjective.

4. The acceptance or rejection of a relationship as compatible with the whole system of relationships is a matter of public opinion, with the public in this case defined as those not party to but affected by that relationship. Some relationships so significantly affect others that their acceptance or rejection has to be a matter of general opinion.

5. In the area of union-management relationships, the only relationship which we find condemned by public opinion as incompatible with important expected rights of others is the strike relationship. The strike may frustrate that expectation of a continued supply of goods and services which is the very basis for the specialized division of labor in our economic society.

6. Strikes are not condemned indiscriminately. Some are more injurious to the affected publics than are others. A rating scale may be devised by means of which strikes can be distinguished by their relative impact on the household, industrial, and commercial users of the struck product (and of products indirectly affected) and on suppliers of the struck firm (and of firms indirectly affected). The degree of public rejection of the strike relationship is proportionate to these "real" effects felt by the public. Management and union views generally confirm this assumption.

7. We set up the hypothesis that when the effects of specific strikes on their publics reached some level, social sanctions would operate on the parties to that strike relationship sufficient to terminate the strike. The nature of these sanctions we have examined. They involve direct pressures from the affected publics and indirect pressures applied by third-party intermediaries who themselves respond to public pressure. The point at which they would become effective we hypothesized to be some level (or range) of real costs, identifiable on the rating scale devised, beyond which the disregard for public rights of expectancy would be regarded as unreasonable. This hypothesis was not sustained.

8. Case studies of the two situations where the parties themselves most expect to feel the weight of sanctions suggest that it is the inadequacy of the sanctions supporting public opinion which explains why particular strikes can persist even in the face of an aroused public.

9. If social sanctions are an uncertain reliance for terminating particular strikes before they pass the bounds of tolerance, the affected public will presumably turn to legal sanctions of general applicability. The increasing resort to compulsory arbitration laws in the states is perhaps evidence of such a tendency.

We face, then, the problem of what to do about strikes which impose substantial hardship upon the public. This problem is raised by the apparent widespread opinion that such strikes are incompatible with important rights of expectancy enjoyed by others. To this problem there have been suggested a number of solutions—plans or programs or policies which are designed to meet so-called "emergency" strikes, usually by some legal sanction. In this final chapter we explore the nature and adequacy of some of the proposed solutions.

The first requirement which any solution must meet is that it respects the public's expectation of a continued flow of essential goods and services—not necessarily of the struck good itself but at least of a reasonably satisfactory substitute. This is the basic requirement which has raised the strike problem, and we must, at the outset, recognize the need for satisfying it. If this is the first requisite of a solution for strikes, however, it should not be the only one. As an ethical judgment, born of our culture, a second requirement is that any strike-control program should not threaten the basic voluntarism of our union-management relationships—that the decisions as to the terms of relationships should remain primarily with the parties themselves rather than be delegated to some state functionary. This second requirement is more difficult to meet than the first, for—as we shall see—most solutions to the strike problem depend upon a compulsive force, a sanction of imposed terms, an authoritative intervention.

These two requirements—that a flow of necessary goods and services to the public be maintained, that voluntarism in setting the terms of union-management relationships be preserved—appear to conflict. Whatever solution satisfies one of these conditions appears inadequate to solve the other. This dilemma has prevented a decisive legislative response to public pressures to "do something" about strikes. It is a dilemma the gravity of which should not be minimized. The development of the integrated economy, the large corporation, and the modern labor union have created an environment in which rights viewed as basic to the preservation of private liberties (in distinction to state control) seemingly conflict with other rights basic to economic life. It is as though the spiritual values of our society were at odds with the fleshly needs of existence.

The Particular Solutions

The principal solutions which have been suggested to the problem of public-affecting strikes are (1) mediation, (2) fact-finding, (3) injunction, (4) seizure, and (5) compulsory arbitration. We shall consider each of these briefly in the light of the two requirements for a satisfactory policy as just set forth.

Mediation

Mediation is the intervention in a labor dispute by a third party who seeks to find some common ground for agreement between the parties. It may come before or after a strike has begun. It depends for its effectiveness on the skill of the mediator in minimizing differences, suggesting compromises, impressing the parties with their responsibilities to others. Individuals who have stressed the importance of preserving voluntarism in labor relations, even at the expense of some hardship to the public, have been the strongest supporters of mediation as the chief reliance for settling strikes. They have argued that mediation is a powerful instrument, although it has often been undercut by public officials who have suggested and even imposed strike settlements over the heads of the mediators and although we have not adequately supported a mediation service. It is said that if our chief reliance were placed in a mediation service that was well staffed, well supported financially, and served by a competent research staff, and if unions and managements were made to understand that there would be no appeal over the heads of that mediating body, mediation would prove a sufficient solution for all except a minimum and tolerable number of strike situations.

Compulsory intervention is generally acceptable to advocates of the mediation process. In the event of a strike or strike threat, the public conciliator is empowered to enter into the negotiating sessions, with or without the invitation or consent of the parties. Here authoritative intervention ends, however. The mediator has no power to compel acceptance of settlement.

This complete reliance on voluntary settlement by the parties themselves, without legal compulsion, necessarily means that in the event of a strike the only sanctions supporting our first requirement—protection of the public—are those social sanctions which we have found to be uncertain in effectiveness. Mediation is admittedly a valuable assistance in reaching agreement, but it is no safeguard of a continuing flow of goods and services. The strengthening of the mediation service is eminently desirable, since it would eliminate many occasions on which the flow of goods to consumers and producers would otherwise be interrupted and thereby reduce the need for more compulsive intervention, but it contains no guarantees that strikes will not occur. Indeed, we have had numerous examples of the failure of mediation to effect settlement in important disputes. Mediation has been attempted in virtually every seriously public-affecting strike in recent years, yet the problem of what to do about such strikes remains with us. Even a strengthening of the mediation service is not likely to provide any solution. A former chief of the Federal Mediation and Conciliation Service, an active proponent of the mediation process, summarizes succinctly the role of mediation: "Where work stoppages cannot be tolerated, mediation has slight value. . . . Mediation is not a method of suppression of industrial conflict. It is, rather, a means for minimizing the conflict that is inherent in modern collective bargaining."[1]

The conclusion seems inevitable that mediation, while satisfying the second requirement of voluntarism in industrial relations, fails to meet the first requisite of protecting the rights of expectancy of the consuming and producing publics.

Fact-Finding

Fact-finding as a means of resolving strikes or strike threats relies on a public report of an impartial board as to the facts of a dispute and customarily includes a recommendation for settlement.[2] While no legal compulsion rests on union or management to accept the recommendation, the rationale behind the process is that public pressure will strongly motivate the parties to do so. Fact-finding boards are usually *ad hoc*, composed of men considered to be opinionative authorities, whose views can be expected to be acceptable to the public because of their reputations for impartiality and sagacity. It is expected that when they propound a "fair" settlement of the labor dispute, a rejection of that settlement by either party will bring it into public disfavor, subjecting it to the direct social sanctions which we have examined.

So understood, fact-finding relies for its effectiveness on the force of public opinion in specific strike situations. In this respect it is akin to mediation, and there are those who maintain that "fact-finding is actually only a strong form of mediation."[3] As such, it is subject to the weaknesses of mediation as a method of strike prevention, though presumably in lesser degree. The added strength which fact-finding is supposed to enjoy over mediation stems from two sources: (1) public opinion is more effectively focused on the parties, due to the recom-

[1] From the rough draft of a chapter, "Mediation and Fact-Finding," by Edgar L. Warren.

[2] Fact-finding boards appointed under the Taft-Hartley Act are precluded from making recommendations for settlement. This limitation on their authority fatally weakens their use as a strike-resolving medium, as will be evident from the discussion. Most proposals for fact-finding as a particular solution to the strike problem rightly enough make the recommended settlement the principal feature of the process.

Massachusetts has an unusual type of fact-finding, in which the appointed board enters no recommendation for settlement but, instead, makes a determination of which of the two parties is responsible for the deadlock, the underlying assumption being that public opinion will focus on the offending party and dissolve its intransigence. The process is sometimes referred to as "blame hearing."

[3] Warren, "Mediation and Fact-Finding."

mended settlement, and (2) the stature of the board in the public's eyes is greater than that of salaried mediators.

There is reason for questioning the supposedly greater strength of fact-finding over mediation, if based on these two reasons, however. As we have seen, public pressure to end a critical strike is likely to be undiscriminating with respect to the terms of settlement: it is simply settlement, on any terms, which is sought. The significance of the board's recommendations lies, then, in that if one of the parties rejects them, public opinion can be expected to focus on that party. The terms of settlement are thus intended not to rally public support as much as to provide a means of isolating one party—union or management— which can be said to stand in the way of settlement, so that public opprobrium can be fastened on it. Yet this function has often been fulfilled, without success, by public officials such as mayors, governors, and even presidents. The Duquesne Light Company strike of 1946, detailed in an earlier chapter, provides an example. The focusing of public opinion thus relies not on specific recommendations but on specific condemnation, which can be and has been achieved by less formal but probably equally effective alternative means.

As for the presumed value of the high esteem attaching to members of fact-finding boards, this, too, is of doubtful value. Actually, many members of such boards are relatively unknown. Their impartiality, sometimes under attack by one of the parties, is frequently not a matter of public knowledge. Nor is there any reason why, in difficult disputes, a mediator of similar stature could not be appointed. There is thus room for questioning whether fact-finding, viewed as a form of mediation, has enough added strength to warrant the hope that it would prove much more effective than mediation as a method of strike prevention.

The strength of fact-finding is sometimes presumed to rest on something other than public opinion concerning a particular dispute, however. The minority views of a Senate committee investigating the functioning of the Railway Labor Act, which provides for fact-finding boards, are instructive. "We think that the legislative history of this law would show most convincingly that labor, management, and the Congress felt at the time the act was framed and passed that the principal value of the emergency board procedure lay in the moral force of the Board's recommendations. In recent years this force seems to have lost much of its vigor, but while these recommendations clearly were intended to carry no legal obligation, we submit that they were intended to carry a significant moral force, if not a moral obligation."[4]

Emphasis on the moral obligation of the parties to accept the recommendations of a fact-finding board does not rely on public pressure in specific strike situations. If we search for a parallel to this form of dispute settlement, the closest approximation would appear to be the original jury of neighbors summoned by a public officer to answer questions under oath, whose conclusions might indeed be contested by others in the community but were accepted as definitive because of acceptance of this *procedure* of deciding controversial issues. It is thus not the settlement which must win acceptance but the process itself, and it is respect for the verdict resulting from such a process which imposes the moral obligation of acceptance.

If this approach to fact-finding is adopted, then the use of "juries"— not necessarily of men of outstanding reputation but simply of men of adequate competence—can be developed to deal with industrial disputes, with the pressure on the parties to accept the determination stemming not from public support for the settlement itself (a settlement concerning the terms of which the public may actually be disinterested) but from support of the process. While carrying no legal obligation, the board's decision may carry "a significant moral force," as the minority members of the Senate committee suggested. To achieve this result, however, the process would require greater formalization and a more widespread understanding of its purpose. There appear to be real possibilities of developing such a system of dispute settlement.

Nevertheless, to the extent such a system gained the acceptance that gave to its determinations the force of a moral obligation, to that extent it would lose the character of voluntarism. The findings of boards would become binding upon the parties to a dispute, morally if not legally, so that the terms of settlement would pass from the control of those obliged to live under them.

We conclude, then, that fact-finding considered as an extension of the mediation process is weak in satisfying the first requirement of protecting public expectations of a continuing flow of essential goods and services, while fact-finding considered as a system of representative community opinion imposing moral obligations on the parties is weak in meeting the second requirement of preserving voluntarism in union-management relations.

[4] *Dispute Between the Railway Carriers and Four Operating Brotherhoods*, Senate Report No. 496, 82nd Congress, 1st Session (1951), Minority Views, p. 26.

Injunction

The injunction as a device for dealing with public-affecting strikes relies on a court order which restrains both employees and employers from ceasing operations, and obligates each to maintain existing terms of relationship. By its nature it bears most heavily on employees when their union is seeking an improvement in terms, and on the employer when it is seeking an advantage such as a reduction in wages. By ordering a maintenance of the status quo, without shutdown, the expectations of the public to continued production are satisfied. By leaving resolution of the impasse to the parties, the voluntarism of collective bargaining is purportedly safeguarded. Nevertheless, it is clear that such an injunction cannot be continued indefinitely. If it were, it would obviously work to the disadvantage of the party pressing for a change in terms. If the union sought a wage increase, management would be more than willing to maintain the status quo under an injunction order indefinitely—but this would be to deprive the union of any bargaining strength. If management sought a wage reduction, the union would similarly be content to maintain operations under a court order obligating the company to continue wages at the existing level. The indefinite perpetuation of conditions advantaging one of the parties is infeasible. The prolongation of a status quo is not a remedy applicable to a world of economic change. It would, moreover, end voluntary agreement.

Since an indefinite injunction is unworkable, advocates of the injunctive procedure have usually limited it to a period of specified duration. Under the Taft-Hartley Act the period of effectiveness of an injunction invoked in national-emergency disputes is confined to eighty days, during which time the parties are directed to continue negotiations in good faith. It appears, however, that in the eighty-day period the parties "tend to lose a sense of urgency and to relax their efforts to reach a settlement. They wait for the next deadline date (the date of discharge of the injunction) to spur them to renewed efforts. In most instances efforts of the [Federal Mediation and Conciliation] Service to encourage the parties to bargain during the injunction period, with a view to early settlement, fall on deaf ears."[5]

At the expiration of the period of injunction, the union is free to strike. At this point the emergency re-emerges. In two of three disputes

[5] Federal Mediation and Conciliation Service, *First Annual Report* (for the year ended June 30, 1948), pp. 56-57.

exhausting the emergency procedures of the Taft-Hartley Act during the first year of its administration (that is, disputes in which the injunction was resorted to), the eighty-day period elapsed without a settlement having been reached, precipitating the strike that the procedure sought to avoid. It is apparent, then, that the injunction frequently does not solve but only postpones the strike problem.

Seizure

The seizure and operation of strikebound plants by the federal government was employed as a final expedient during World War II. It is part of the provisions of the so-called Slichter law of Massachusetts, and the heart of the Virginia strike-control legislation, both enacted in 1947. President Truman during the 1952 steel strike advocated the passage of legislation authorizing seizure of the steel plants. During the same period Senator Morse introduced a seizure bill of general applicability, a measure which in principle had been suggested by William H. Davis, a former chairman of the War Labor Board, three years previously.

The details of seizure legislation and proposals vary, but the basic idea is the same. The government assumes possession (not ownership) of the struck properties and operates them in its name, calling on management, employees, and "any other citizens of the United States having suitable qualifications" to continue production of the essential goods or services. In Davis's words, "it is the ancient common-law idea of the posse commitatus."[6] In this respect seizure provisions meet the requirement of public protection.

It is with respect to the conditions of employment during the period of government operation that important policy differences arise, however. All advocates of this procedure agree with President Truman's comment: "Seizure should not, of course, be regarded as a means of determining the issues in dispute between management and the union. Those issues will have to be settled by the parties through their own collective bargaining. Legislation providing for Government operation will not prevent collective bargaining."[7] This purpose of preserving the voluntarism of private collective bargaining, however, is in fact most difficult to achieve under seizure. It has been sought in two basically different ways.

[6] William H. Davis, "Government Action in Strikes," a letter to the editor of The New York Times, February 12, 1949.
[7] Address to Congress, June 10, 1952.

In the Virginia legislation, which is typical of one approach, the seizure operates as an injunction restraining any change in the existing terms of employment. Until the parties reach agreement, the state remains in possession of the properties and maintains the conditions which it found upon taking them over. After paying all expenses incidental to operation the state retains 15 percent of net income as compensation for its services in operating the utility. (In the event of loss, it assumes no liability, however.) The expectation is that the freezing of terms and the utility's loss of 15 percent of income will act as sufficient penalties on the parties to spur them to agreement. This expectation is likely to be borne out only in part. If in times of prosperity union demands exceed 15 percent of current income, from a purely economic viewpoint the management would prefer to leave control to the state, as a small price to pay for a freezing of wages, pension demands, and other fringe benefits. On the other hand, in a period of business slackness or recession a union would be content to operate under government orders maintaining a structure of wages which might be more than a private operation could economically sustain. A strike threat in time of depression would always forestall a wage reduction by introducing government operation and a freezing of existing terms. Without a time limit to government possession, the union might indefinitely refuse to conclude an agreement, and as long as it did so it would be indefinitely safeguarded against a decline in wages which less strategically placed employees might be forced to accept. Seizure procedures which provide for a maintenance of the status quo thus are subject to the same difficulties encountered in the use of the injunction. They are a possible deterrent to agreement, and the government might find itself a long-term proprietor of properties which it had possessed only as a "temporary" measure. Nevertheless, the innovation of the 15 percent fine on corporate net income while the strike continues appears to lessen this danger in some degree and must be viewed as a provision which, however desirable or undesirable on other grounds, logically moves in the direction of spurring a voluntary settlement and thus of meeting the second requirement which we have set for strike-control legislation.

A second type of legislation avoids the injunctive effect of seizure by providing for the appointment of special boards which are empowered to determine "just compensation" for employees and owners during the period of government operation. "Just compensation," uniquely determined in each case, may be more or less than current profits or wages. Here it is expected that the parties will be stimulated to reach agreement by the likelihood that governmental treatment would give them something less than they expect. "The companies will face the possibility of receiving something less than the normal profits as just compensation. And the workers will face the prospect of getting less than they think they are entitled to."[8]

This approach avoids the difficulties accompanying maintenance of the status quo. By specifically providing for an adjustment of terms of employment, it permits the granting of wage increases or decreases during the period of government operation. The assumption is that wage increases in times of prosperity would be smaller than the union would expect, while wage cuts in time of recession would be smaller than management would expect ultimately to obtain. There would thus, presumably, be an incentive to continue private negotiations for a new agreement. On further inspection, however, one wonders whether this result would be obtained. If a wage award was smaller than the union sought, so that it would be unwilling to conclude a collective bargaining agreement on the terms granted by the special board, management would have no incentive to press for an agreement unless the compensation to owners awarded by the board was less than could be expected under private management, even with a higher wage bill.

On the other hand, if the wage reduction was smaller than management sought, the union would prefer to continue under government operation rather than conclude an agreement with the company on terms less advantageous than the board had instituted. There is thus the likelihood that the terms of the board's award would become the minimum terms acceptable to that party which it most favored. The result would be a form of compulsory arbitration. Once again we are forced to conclude that the seizure process is incompatible with the preservation of voluntarism in union-management relations.

Compulsory Arbitration

Perhaps the most frequently mentioned method of controlling strikes seriously affecting the public is compulsory arbitration. An impartial board or court, generally appointed by the chief executive, is empowered to make a determination resolving the dispute and enforceable upon the parties. At least eight state acts passed since World War II

[8] *Ibid.*

have made use of this procedure. The question of their constitutionality need not detain us here, since this is a matter which is not likely to stand as any long-run barrier to such legislation.

Compulsory arbitration meets the first requirement of preserving a flow of essential goods and services to the public. It has often been argued that a decision unpopular with the union members cannot be enforced, since thousands of strikers cannot be jailed. Criminal penalties are not the only means of enforcement, however. To honor such an argument would be to admit that no legislation controlling unions but opposed by bodies of workers could ever be sustained, since by the simple act of striking they could make it a nullity or force its rescission. The same line of argument would make equally unworkable the fact-finding, injunction, and seizure approaches, since in all such cases refusal of the striking employees to return to their jobs would be equally possible. Any strike-control legislation must inescapably rely on compliance by the striking employees, a reliance which does not appear to be unrealistic. If any major groups in a society are above the law we have a more serious problem than strike control on our hands.

But if compulsory arbitration satisfies the public's economic needs, it inevitably destroys private discretion in union-management relationships. If either party forces decision by compulsory arbitration, because it believes it will do better before a board than in direct negotiation, determination of the terms of relationship comes by fiat rather than agreement. The collective bargaining process is incompatible with compulsory arbitration and is not likely long to survive it.[9] Admittedly no society can dispense with authoritarian determinations altogether— business managements and union administrations rely on it daily—but a society whose culture stresses the advantages of spontaneity, creativeness, and personal morality will rely on imposed decisions only where consent and voluntary agreement are ineffective. Compulsory arbitration fails completely to preserve voluntarism in industrial relations, the second condition which we require of any strike-control program.

We conclude that the particular solutions to the problem of public-affecting strikes which have been most frequently suggested are all unacceptable. Mediation, fact-finding, injunction, seizure, and compulsory arbitration are inadequate on one count or the other—to

[9] Although I advocated use of compulsory arbitration in an earlier book, *Collective Bargaining* (New York: McGraw-Hill Book Co., 1951), it was only as a temporary expedient until some preferable longer-run solution should be discovered.

safeguard the public's right of expectancy to continued flows of
essential goods or services, to preserve the governance of labor relations by agreement rather than dictation.

Reappraisal of the Problem: Fresh Solutions

The difficulty with most of the solutions which have been offered to
the problem of emergency strikes is that they by-pass the function
which the strike plays in collective bargaining. Collective bargaining
is a process of voluntary agreement, but agreement comes when the
terms proposed by one of the parties appear more advantageous to
the other than disagreement on those terms. Agreement thus depends
on making disagreement costly. It is here that the strike—whether
initiated by the union in support of demands which it makes on management or in rejection of demands which management makes on it
—plays its part.

A stoppage of work is the chief means which the parties have of
making disagreement costly to the other. The union threatens loss of
production if management does not grant the concessions sought, in
the belief that the consequent loss of employment to its members will
be less costly than agreement on the counterterms proffered by management. Or management threatens loss of employment if the union
does not consent to its conditions, in the belief that the consequent loss
of production will be less onerous than acceptance of the union's
position. It is only when for either union or management loss of employment or loss of production is less advantageous than acceptance of
the other's conditions that agreement is reached.

The strike thus emerges as the most effective method of bringing
pressure to bear on the other party in order to secure an agreement on
terms. Without it—or the threat of its use—the agreement process
would be unworkable. And without the collective bargaining process
we move toward an economy of regulated wages and conditions of
employment and, perhaps, beyond that to regulated prices.

It is worth repeating that the strike is so important an ingredient of
voluntarism in labor relations because it constitutes the primary means
by which each party can bring its power to bear upon the other to
make disagreement on its terms costly to the other. "Equality of power
around the bargaining table, which is the sine qua non of permanent
industrial peace, could only be achieved when each side tests out the
other's strength, particularly after the gage of battle has been flung. It

may be unfortunate, but it is true, that only through the strike can labor demonstrate the strength that is latent within it, at least to satisfy its adversaries in the arena of economic conflict."[10] If collective bargaining agreements rely ultimately on a contest of economic power, and if the strike or threat of strike is the fundamental means of contest, then any strike-control program which is in fact a strike-elimination program must destroy the bargaining process itself.

On this analysis, a strike-control program which is compatible with collective bargaining can succeed only if it provides an adequate substitute means by which the parties can display their strength against each other without simultaneously working hardship on those whom an integrated economy has made dependent on them. What is wanted is a solution that allows the power struggle to go on between the parties without frustrating the rights of expectancy of the affected public.

The solution required is one under which the strike substitute comes into play while production continues. We need a procedure which enables each party to "swing the ax" against the other in demonstration of its economic power in the institutional order, as a means of making disagreement on its terms costly to the other party, but which permits a continued flow of goods and services to consumers and other producers. The requirements may sound contradictory on first encounter, but only because of our present habits of thought; they are not logically inconsistent.

One tentative solution to the problem is suggested below.[11]

The Statutory or Nonstoppage Strike

If the function of the strike is to make disagreement on one party's terms costly to the other party, this objective can be achieved by alternative means. A strike is a contest of endurance, and it is possible to invoke such a contest without ceasing production.

---

[10] Henry Mayer, "Labor and Utilities," a letter to the editor of *The New York Times*, October 27, 1946.

[11] The proposal here made was arrived at independently, but subsequently I have encountered three other instances in which a remarkably similar plan has been outlined. The first of these is an article, "Strikes in Essential Industries: A Way Out," *Harvard Business Review*, May, 1949, where the authors, LeRoy Marceau and Richard A. Musgrave, designated the substitute as a "statutory strike." The second instance is "The Nonstoppage Strike," as proposed in *Labor Law Journal*, February, 1951, by George W. Goble. The third similar proposal was made by my colleague, Professor E. Wight Bakke, director of the Yale Labor and Management Center, who made public a like plan in a radio address over Station WTIC, Hartford, the evening of June 15, 1952.

The operation of such a substitute strike procedure can be simply outlined. At the time when negotiations between the parties have broken down and a stoppage of work would normally occur, in those cases in which a governmental authority determines that public hardship would result (perhaps as measured on some rating scale such as earlier elaborated) the private strike is converted into a statutory strike, or—to use other terminology—the work-stoppage strike is transformed into a nonstoppage strike. The governmental order which effects such a conversion directs the employees to remain on their jobs, unless as individuals they choose to resign their employment and all attaching rights. It directs management to continue production to fill all incoming orders, maintaining the schedule of prices then in effect. The interests of the public, both as consumers and producers, are thus protected.

In order to permit a subsequent voluntary agreement between the parties, each must have the power to impose penalties on the other by precipitating such a statutory strike, whether it is the union or management which initiates it by making or refusing demands. This means that although production continues each party must receive less during the period of the statutory strike than it would had no dispute arisen. By resorting to the statutory strike, the initiating party willingly subjects itself to some loss in order to impose a loss on the other party. It thereby invokes a contest of economic power, as it now does through the stoppage strike.

If workers and management are to continue production, *some* return must be earned by them. Continuing production must have some advantage over not producing. Each of the parties, then, must secure some advantage which it would not have in a stoppage strike, but at the same time each must incur some loss in consequence of the statutory strike. The gains to each party over the present strike method must be relatively equal, that is, the proportion of losses resulting from the statutory strike method to losses under the present method must be relatively equal, if the same relative bargaining powers are to be preserved. This result will probably be achieved if—while production continues during the nonstoppage strike period—the wages of workers are reduced by 50 percent and the returns of the company are reduced to actual out-of-pocket or variable expenses plus one half of fixed costs.

With operations continuing and with these losses bearing on the parties, the contest of endurance would be on. It would continue until one or the other or both of the parties agreed to concessions that made settlement possible. At this point the statutory strike would be ended, and the parties would revert to full payment for services under a new collective bargaining agreement. The plan thus appears to satisfy both of the requisites for a satisfactory system of controlling public-affecting strikes. Public rights of expectancy are honored. Voluntarism in union-management relations is preserved.

The acceptability of this suggested arrangement would seem to depend principally on whether it leaves the parties with approximately the same relative bargaining advantage that each now enjoys under a work stoppage.

A stoppage strike, as we now know it, imposes on the strikers a loss of all wage income. Under the proposed arrangement, workers would be subjected to a loss of half their wage income as long as they chose to resist management's offers or counteroffers. They would presumably be willing to entertain such a loss in order to impose on management a cost of disagreeing with them.

The present strike procedure now subjects the company to the loss of all income from current production, which is equivalent to a loss of return on fixed costs and of profits. We cannot allow to the company earnings equal to one half of lost income, however, as we did in the case of strikers, since this would be to overlook a further advantage which the statutory procedure would bring to it. In a shutdown the company is always subjected to the threat of permanent loss of markets to rivals, a threat which some management people have admitted to be one of the most telling effects of a strike. Under the statutory procedure, with production continuing, this threat would be removed. To allow for this additional benefit of the new procedure (a benefit to which the strikers have nothing comparable), the amount of return to the company of revenues which it would have lost during a stoppage must be reduced. Instead of being reimbursed to the extent of 50 percent of fixed costs and profits, it retains only 50 percent of fixed costs, sacrificing profits.

To be sure, the value to the struck unit of freedom from fear of losing markets to rivals is not the same in all cases. In some strikes, the possibility of such a loss is not great. Even if a local utility is closed down, there is relatively little opportunity for its customers to substitute another supplier. In the case of an industry-wide stoppage where most of the supply of some good is cut off, there is relatively little chance for users of that good to find another source. It might thus appear that in some of our most critical work stoppages, management is not now subject to any real threat of rivals raiding its markets. While recognizing that the force of the threat indeed varies with the circumstances, nevertheless we would be mistaken to assume that the threat is nonexistent even in the extreme cases cited above. We should not identify the possibility of losing markets with only the possibility of short-run substitution of other goods, nor should we consider that "rivals" must refer to other producers of the *same* product.

Markets can be lost through long-run substitution of other goods, and they can be lost to producers in other industries. Even the local utility has a measure of competition from other sources of power, a competition in which dependability of service is an important element. To some extent electric users may substitute gas; builders of new homes and new plants are in a particularly advantageous situation to make a choice among alternative sources of power and heat. To some extent industrial users may decide in favor of installing their own generators instead of purchasing power. Similarly, if the steel industry's supply is subject to interruption by strike action, users of steel may over time lessen their dependence on steel by substituting other materials, plastics or other metals being among the possibilities. Oil may substitute for coal when combustion units can be modified or when new facilities are installed. Trucks can replace rail transportation over some runs, and so on. Such substitutions frequently cannot occur in the immediate present, during a strike, but they may occur after, and in consequence of, a strike or a series of strikes. The danger of market loss can never be wholly eliminated, and it threatens the long-run capital value of the firm or industry. Moreover, in the case of industry-wide strikes, it is seldom that the entire industry is struck. To the extent that some members of the industry continue to operate, the possibility of rivals capturing markets which it will be difficult or costly to recapture always remains.

In the class of cases in which the strike is public-affecting through a company's position as dominant employer in a given community or region, the danger of loss of markets is of course inescapable. The strike is not critical in the community because adequate substitutes are unavailable, but only because of its impact on the suppliers of the firm and the firm's employers. Here the advantage of removing the threat of loss of markets is perhaps the greatest advantage which the statutory strike procedure would bring to management.

On balance, the company's loss of profits during the period of the statutory strike could be considered to offset the union's loss of the power to threaten market position. (Actually, of course, a loss of only half its profits is involved, since—in the absence of the market consideration—that is the amount to which it would be entitled if its relative advantage under the new procedure were to be made comparable to that of the union.)[12]

We conclude, then, that relative bargaining advantages between the parties would be substantially preserved if, while production continued, statutory strikers would receive one half of their wage income and the company would recover operating expenses plus one half of its fixed costs. In any given situation, the new procedure may confer relative advantage on one or the other of the parties, just as the present strike procedure now does. It would be manifestly impossible to devise a strike substitute in which the relative net increase in advantage would be precisely equal for both parties in all specific instances. What is important is to devise a system in which, while one or the other of the parties may gain differential advantage in one case or another, neither union nor management gains a differential advantage in all cases. It would appear that the statutory strike satisfies this important requirement.

Since output continues to be sold at the price level prevailing at the time the statutory strike is called, and since wage costs have been cut in half, and management receives in addition to its thus reduced variable costs only half of fixed costs, the receipts of the firm will exceed outlays, except in unusual circumstances. The amount of this excess is paid into the public treasury. Such payments should not be considered a penalty, in any sense. They constitute a simple forfeiture which is integral to the process of permitting the parties to the union-management relationship to impose costs on each other.[13]

---

[12] If it is believed that 50 percent of current profits is too high to be considered equivalent to the value of retaining markets and customer good will, an alternative would be to compensate management by some percent of "normal" profits but less than 50 percent. "Normal" profits mean the profits in some preceding period comparable to the present, of length equal to the strike's duration, probably a period either immediately preceding or in the year previous (in the case of seasonal operations). Such a base of "normal" profits, rather than current profits, would be necessary to prevent any slowdown during the non-stoppage strike from penalizing management.

[13] If lawyers worry about the rationale by which such payments can be justified, it may occur to some to tie this plan in with government seizure of the struck unit, so that technically the government is in possession of the plant and payments can be viewed as compensation for ultimate operating responsibility. Even for such legal purposes, how-

Several aspects of the suggested arrangement should be noted. First, in the present stoppage strike all losses which are incurred during the period of shutdown are not permanent losses; there is some possibility of making up for lost production. At least some of the orders which could not be filled during the stoppage can be held on the books and satisfied after the strike is over. On these make-up operations the firm receives (in most cases) its return on fixed costs and some profit, and workers receive full pay and in some instances even overtime rates. The statutory strike precludes such recovery of losses, however, since orders are not held on the books but are met from current output, on which workers receive half pay and the company half of fixed costs. The net advantage of the statutory strike over the stoppage strike, to the parties themselves, is to this extent reduced. It should be noted, however, that the effect on both parties is the same, so that relative bargaining powers are not disturbed by this element of nonrecoverability of losses. The equal impact of this consideration answers, too, any objection to the plan on the ground that management may try to stall off orders, in order to earn a higher return after the statutory strike is over. Aside from the fact that it will be limited in its ability to do so by the (presumed) pressure of public demand for critical production, any deferment of orders will advantage the workers no less than the company, so that relative bargaining positions are unaffected.

Second, the proposed arrangement renders relatively innocuous the danger that workers will not continue to apply themselves with equal assiduity to their jobs when their wage rates are cut by 50 percent. Slowdowns in statutory strikes are possible, but the procedure suggested discourages them. The chief function of a slowdown is to bring pressure on management. A slowdown during the course of a statutory strike fails to accomplish this purpose, however. It only adds to variable costs, for which management is fully compensated. It reduces total receipts to the firm, to be sure, but except in unusual circumstances the effect will be only to reduce the payments made into the governmental treasury. Under the circumstances, unions can add

---

ever, we would prefer that the plan operate without seizure, confessing to a repugnance to such means which, while in this case only technically applied, involve a remedy that is basically most drastic. Seizure is a process that should be reserved as a penalty, whereas in this case the statutory strike is not something which we should even try to discourage, since it constitutes an alternative method—on which as a society we place the stamp of approval—by which the parties can measure their relative economic strengths. The use of seizure under the circumstances appears unwarranted and paradoxical.

nothing to their bargaining power by slowing down but, on the contrary, are likely only to lose public good will. In addition, it can be argued that where the public's needs are urgent even a reduced output is preferable to no output.

Third, under present strike procedure the union has the tactical possibility of so choosing the time of its strike as to impose the greatest possible loss on management. If the expiration of agreements can be timed to coincide with the company's busiest production period, the pressure on management will be that much greater. In the statutory strike the possibility of such a tactical advantage is not excluded. If the union can select the time of the strike, it can set it for that period when the loss of profits will be the greatest.

It is to be expected, of course, that the statutory strike is not a perfect substitute for the work stoppage;[14] no perfect substitute is likely to be found. The question is not whether there are disadvantages in the plan, however, but whether the disadvantages which characterize it are greater than those accompanying our present system of uncontrolled strike actions or greater than those pertaining to other methods of strike control which have been proposed. The adequacy of the statutory

[14] The statutory strike is not suggested here as a feasible substitute for the stoppage strike in all situations, but only in those critically involving a public. Whether it could or should be extended to other situations should remain a question for the future, after there was some experience to go on. At the moment I see no reason, however, why the government should intervene in a strike that affects only a limited number of people and them only casually. This limitation on the use of the strike substitute should rule out the difficulty that some managements might object to having their corporate income reduced to variable costs when, within short order, through substitution of supervisory help or the introduction of new employees they would themselves be able to satisfy public need. Where managements can adequately protect public interest in a strike situation there would be no basis for government substitution of a statutory strike.

There are, however, some situations where public protection should be afforded and yet where the remedy here proposed is inappropriate. An illustrative case is a strike of elevator operators in apartment buildings. Where such buildings run to a height of many stories it is a matter of health and safety that residents should not be forced to climb steps to reach or leave their homes. It would appear that here is a case where the public is sufficiently affected to warrant intervention. Yet what substitute penalties would a statutory strike impose here? Could owner income be reduced to operating expenses only, when in fact a complete work stoppage would not deprive them of all current income? For owners would continue to receive rents from apartment dwellers even during the course of a complete strike of elevator operators, rents which cover more than variable costs, whereas under a statutory strike they would recover only the latter. The substitute is here more penalizing on owners than the present strike procedure, but less penalizing on striking employees, who would receive more than under present procedure.

The answer to such exceptions may become more apparent with experience and experiment, but it seems probable that they will be sufficiently few in number—involving only those operations where the public, while seriously inconvenienced, is able and continues to purchase the affected service—as not to invalidate the proposal on this ground alone.

strike depends in large measure on whether the effects on each of the parties are equiproportionate to the effects of the present stoppage strike on each of the parties. If the substitute method leaves the *relative* bargaining powers of the two parties substantially as they would be in most strike contests, then it can be argued that the plan submitted meets the test of superiority to the present arrangement and to alternative methods employing a dictation of terms. For the statutory strike technique preserves both public rights and private discretion.

Conclusion

If it seems to some that the analysis of this chapter rests excessively on legal approaches to the problem of strikes, ignoring its ethical aspects, the explanation lies solely in the conceptual restrictions of this study. There is no intent to deny that the strike relationship has a moral no less than a legal component, and that the perplexities posed by that relationship cannot be resolved by one without the other.

After all general "solutions" have been proposed there still remains the need for recognition of what one writer has called the moral mandate: "to accept a moral obligation to realize that narrow self-interests have to be transcended if our kind of society is to function." Morality must underlie industrial relations as all social relations. "Beneath all structural, procedural and operative methods, necessary as these are for revised and improved patterns of harmonization, there has to be a moral affirmation—a willingness to try to grasp the meaning of the public weal and to subordinate selfish interests to its realization."[15]

Within the framework of this study, however, we have defined social responsibility not as an ethical imperative, which relies on the conscience of the individual and may or may not achieve its response, but as an *inescapable* obligation imposed by his enmeshment with his society, enforceable against the individual whatever the state of his conscience. We have thus specifically delimited the concept to eliminate the moral component, not because of disregard for it, but to facilitate analysis more clearly directed to public rather than private policy. This kind of social responsibility leads to sanctions against the offending individuals, and where sanctions invoked in numerous individual instances prove weak and wanting, more general solutions, usually of a

[15] Ordway Tead, "Advancing the Public Interest in Labor Relations," *Industrial and Labor Relations Review*, Vol. 2, 1949, p. 398.

legal nature, are to be expected. It is to the problems connected with such a general solution that this analysis has been addressed.

The problem of what to do about public-affecting strikes so as to preserve voluntarism in labor relations and to safeguard the flow of essential goods and services is not insolvable, as a matter of public policy. No special claims are made for the statutory or nonstoppage strike procedure, outlined above, other than that it constitutes an example of what might be done to meet this problem. It appears to meet the test of logic. Yet it is not on the basis of logical adequacy that particular solutions are adopted.

In the wave of public-affecting strikes that swept the nation at the close of World War II, *The New York Times* editorially called attention to the need for fresh approaches to the problem of union-management relations in an integrated economy.

Mankind's desperate need is for new social inventions, new inventions in human relations, comparable in scope with the progress of physical science. A certain sort of human genius reached miraculous heights when it analyzed the final particles of matter, which no eye has seen or ever will see, and released, in the atomic bomb, the basic forces of the universe. The human mind has godlike possibilities. It will surely master external nature. Can it not also master its own nature?

The formulas cannot be jotted down offhand. Neither could the equations for splitting the atom. To win the battle for peace at home and abroad the best and most unselfish thought of which humanity is capable must be mobilized.[16]

While agreeing with this comment, we may note that the analogy between solutions to physical problems and human problems is deficient. The *discovery* of the secrets of the atom did not depend on opinion or authority. The *application* of methods of human relations does. However irresistible is the logic of any particular solution, its trial depends on an adoption by influential opinionative authorities. Less adequate solutions may find a readier trial because more promptly or ardently espoused by opinionative authorities commanding the necessary following. While meeting the needs of the situation less effectively, they may meet them sufficiently well to quiet an adverse public opinion. If we accept public-affecting strikes as being a problem area in which the demands of social responsibility will sooner or later force some solution, we need look, then, not only to the social inventions

16 *The New York Times*, September 30, 1945.

but to their sponsorship. Fresh solutions are not all that are needed. It is not only the idea but the proponent which is important.

If this analysis has validity, then these considerations should be of prime significance to the partisan authorities. These representatives of unions and managements have been virtually united in condemning strike controls (with the exception that management members are receptive to use of the injunction, presumably on the ground that it weighs more heavily on the union). This wall of resistance is based upon an understandable fear that limitation of the right to strike will act as a limitation on voluntarism in industrial relations, the freedom of private discretion. Yet, if our reading of the state of public opinion is accurate, such views are not likely to be accepted as discharging the burden of social responsibility. A public which is convinced that some restraint on the strike is needed, to preserve its right of expectancy to a continued flow of goods and services vital to its consuming and producing requirements, is not likely to accept inaction as a solution.

Partisan authorities are thus likely to be disregarded in the search for an acceptable solution; the contest will lie among the impartial authorities. And here the principal proposals, as we have seen, fail either to protect public rights of expectancy, in some cases, or to preserve freedom of action in union-management relations, in others. To the extent that public rights are not safeguarded by certain solutions, we may expect public opinion to remain dissatisfied should such solutions be tried. Under existing circumstances, then, the pressure would appear to drive us more and more toward compulsory resolution of industrial disputes.

That unions and managements dislike such an outcome is encouraging. Their attitude attests to the strength of the drive for self-determination; it is the same attitude which led to the development of collective bargaining. The principle involved is one that is vital in a democracy. Nevertheless, the parties had best realize that in the circumstances their attitude is negative only, relying on a principle—voluntarism—that is no answer to the specific problem—public rights. Their policy of inaction is a denial of the reality of social responsibility, considered not as a matter of conscience but as an enforceable obligation to attempt a reconciliation between rights which they enjoy and conflicting rights which are important to others.

To preserve the principle of voluntarism to which they laudably adhere, then, a positive answer to the problem is necessary. Refusal to face the problem appears likely to lead directly to the dictation of terms of union-management relations which they seek to avoid. It is the parties themselves, more than any other group, which should be searching for solutions which they, as opinionative authorities, can espouse—solutions which preserve their discretion but which, at the same time, satisfy public expectations. This is their social responsibility.

The rise of collective bargaining has brought with it a change in our industrial organization, the significance of which we have probably not yet fully comprehended. But one consequence of its development has been the creation of a private relationship which at times frustrates rights of expectancy upon which our industrial society is premised. Whether this frustration of rights is tolerable is a matter for judgment by the publics affected. There is evidence for believing that substantial-enough numbers are strongly enough inclined to a negative opinion, at least in certain types of situations, to justify an expectation of change of private relationships to restore a consistency among them. The *nature* of the change thus induced, if it is induced, lies outside the competence of public opinion, however, except in the matter of ultimate decision as to its compatibility with other major private relationships in the social system. The nature of the change rests largely with the opinionative authorities, who are limited only by the requirement of reasonable consistency in the social system.

None has a greater stake in preserving freedom of discretion in union-management relations—collective bargaining—than the parties themselves. Yet they have treated the matter as one of personal morality, denying their integration with a society and the enforceable demands which that integration imposes on them. They have adopted public relations programs designed to shift blame for violation of public expectations from each to the other, seemingly unconscious that both are parties to the relationship which has created the problem and both owe a social responsibility for modifying the nature of that relationship. That responsibility is nondiscretionary. It is upheld by a variety of sanctions which, over time, will make themselves effective, as long as our society remains a society.